Revolution
and the
Christian Faith

Evangelical Perspectives
John Warwick Montgomery, General Editor

How Black Is the Gospel?
by Tom Skinner

The Unequal Yoke
by Richard V. Pierard

God, Sex and You
by M. O. Vincent, M.D.

Revolution and the Christian Faith
by Vernon C. Grounds

VERNON C. GROUNDS

Revolution
and the
Christian Faith

J. B. Lippincott Company
Philadelphia and New York / A HOLMAN BOOK

For permission to quote from copyright material, thanks are due:

to The Macmillan Company for passages from *Containment and Change* by Carl Oglesby and Richard Shaull. Copyright©1967 by Carl Oglesby and Richard Shaull
to Charles Scribner's Sons for passages from *The Just War* by Paul Ramsey. Copyright©1968 Paul Ramsey
to The World Publishing Company for passages from *A Theology of Human Hope* by Rubem A. Alves. A Corpus Book. Copyright©1970 by Rubem A. Alves

Thanks are also due for permission to quote the following:

Bertolt Brecht verses from *The Revolutionary Imperative*, Ed. Alan D. Austin, National Methodist Student Movement, 1966. By permission of The Board of Education, The United Methodist Church
Passages from Paul Ramsey, *War and the Christian Conscience*. Reprinted by permission of the Publisher. Copyright 1961, Duke University Press, Durham, North Carolina
Passages from *Ethics in a Christian Context* by Paul Lehmann. Copyright©1963 by Paul L. Lehmann. Reprinted by permission of Harper & Row, Publishers, Inc.
Passages from *Movement and Revolution* by Richard J. Neuhaus and Peter L. Berger. Copyright©1970 by Richard J. Neuhaus and Peter L. Berger. Reprinted by permission of Doubleday & Company, Inc.
Passages reprinted from *The Presence of the Kingdom* by Jacques Ellul, published in the United States by The Seabury Press, New York, are used with permission of The Seabury Press and SCM Press Ltd.
Lines from *A Sleep of Prisoners* by Christopher Fry, reprinted by permission of Oxford University Press
Passages from *A Theology for Radical Politics* by Michael Novak, reprinted by permission of Herder and Herder
Passages from *Unyoung, Uncolored, Unpoor* by Colin Morris. Copyright©1969 by Colin Morris. Used by permission of Abingdon Press
Passages from *War and/or Survival* by William V. O'Brien. Copyright ©1969 by William V. O'Brien. Reprinted by permission of Doubleday & Company, Inc.
The Ballad of the Carpenter by Ewan MacColl.© 1960 by Stormking Music Inc. All rights reserved. Used by permission

Contents

Foreword

Evangelical Perspectives

Across the centuries the Christian church has faced two perennial challenges: the maintenance of a pure testimony and the application of revealed truth to the total life of man. Though these two tasks interlock (since application of the truth is impossible if the truth is lost, and truth without application stands self-condemned), theology has generally devoted itself now to the one, now to the other, and the cause of Christ has suffered from the imbalance. "These ought ye to have done, and not to leave the other undone" stands as a perpetual judgment over the church's history.

Today's theology and church life display such deleterious polarization in an especially gross manner. At the "liberal" end of the theological spectrum, efforts to become "relevant" have succeeded so well that the church has become indistinguishable from the ideological and societal evils she is supposed to combat. Among the "fundamentalists," in contrast, God's revealed truth often serves as a wall to block the church off from the live issues and compelling challenges of a world in crisis. Relevance without truth, or truth without relevance: these dual schizophrenias go far in explaining why contemporary man finds it easy to ignore the Christian message.

"Evangelical Perspectives" is a series of books designed specifically to overcome these false dichotomies. Historic Christian theology—the Christianity of the Apostles' Creed, of the Protestant Reformation, and of the eighteenth-century Evangelical Revival—is taken with full seriousness and is shown to be entirely compatible with the best of contemporary scholarship. Contributors to this series are united in rejecting the defensive posture which has so often created the impression that new knowledge poses a genuine threat to the Christian gospel. Axiomatic to the present series is the conviction that new discoveries serve but to confirm and deepen the faith once delivered to the saints.

At the same time, those participating in this project find little comfort in the reiteration of ancient truth for its own sake. Our age faces staggering challenges which can hardly be met by the repetition of formulae—certainly not by the negativistic codes of a fundamentalism which tilts against windmills that have long since fallen into decay. The race problem, social revolution, political change, new sexual freedom, the revival of the occult, the advent of the space age: these are areas of modern life that demand fresh analysis on the basis of the eternal verities set forth in the Word of One who is the same yesterday, today, and forever.

Out of the flux of the current theological situation nothing but flux appears to be emerging. What is needed is a firm foundation on which to build an all-embracing and genuinely relevant theological perspective for the emerging twenty-first century. The authors of the present volumes are endeavoring to offer just such a perspective—an *evangelical* perspective—a perspective arising from the biblical evangel—as the one path through the maze of contemporary life.

It is the hope of the editor that upon the solid Reformation base of a fully authoritative Scripture, the present series will offer its readers the Renaissance ideal of the Christian as "uomo universale." Such an orientation could revolutionize theology in our time, and ground a new age of commitment and discovery comparable to that of the sixteenth century. As in that day, new worlds are opening up, and just as a religious viewpoint reflecting the dying medieval age was unable to meet the challenge then, so today's "secular theologies" are incapable of pointing the way now. The Christ of the Bible, through whom all without exception have been created and redeemed: He alone is Way, Truth, Life—and Perspective!

JOHN   WARWICK   MONTGOMERY
General Editor

Introduction

When Benjamin Franklin submitted his design for the reverse side of the Great Seal of the United States, he suggested the following:

Pharaoh sitting in an open chariot, a crown on his head and a sword in his hand, passing through the divided waters of the Red Sea in pursuit of the Israelites. Rays from a pillar of fire in the cloud, expressive of the Divine presence and command, beaming on Moses, who stands on the shore and, extending his hand over the sea, causes it to overflow Pharaoh. Motto: "Rebellion to tyrants is obedience to God."

Our nation was born out of a revolutionary spirit of idealistic vision and religious zeal. At that time, as well as at present, Christians struggled with how our faith relates to man's quest for a "New World" . . . for justice, dignity, and liberation from oppression.

Today we are also living in an age of revolution. It is hard to know what form the revolutionary ferment in our society and throughout the world will take, or what the ultimate consequences will be. But the pulse of our time indicates more than the ordinary rebellion of youth, more than the normal restlessness of any age.

In our own land it is common to analyze our problems as certain concrete issues such as the war, the racial and poverty crisis, the threats to our environment, and the alienation from our political system. Yet, I believe that the fundamental nature of our crisis goes far deeper than those isolated problems, as grave as they all are. Those issues, it seems to me, are largely symptoms of a much deeper crisis—the growing irrelevance of the values that are held by our society, and the groping search for new values, and a new vision to guide us as a people. Throughout developed society—both East and West—and even among the developing world, contemporary youth share in common intensity of vision and hope. The ferment we see reflected all about us is not normal discontent; it could reflect the birth pangs of a new age.

In large part it is a cultural revolution that we face. Our time may well prove to be synonymous with the era of the Protestant Reformation, or the Copernican Revolution. It is likely to be a time when the major values and cultural understandings that have guided us in the past will be proven inadequate for the future. History may come to regard our time as one of those pivotal moments of our civilization when the decisions, choices, and actions that occur will have a decisive effect on future decades.

Beneath much of our world's groping and tension lies a spiritual restlessness. The search for new values, and for a new vision of the future, inevitably touches the spiritual nerves of man. A part of the cultural revolution engulfing us includes a new and refreshing curiosity about transcendent experience.

The Christian in particular must not remain insulated from the pace of revolutionary change that confronts us. Moreover, he need not be threatened by the appearance of instability in our social institutions.

Somehow, many Christians have assumed that faith places them in a mandatory alliance with the political status quo. But this is not the message of the Bible. We are instructed never to place our security in the world's existing political and social institutions. Christ, in fact, said, "Heaven and earth will pass away, but my words will not pass away." (Matthew 24:35) It is Christ Himself—He who has overcome the world—who provides the one and only basis for our security and our hope in the future.

The quest for fundamental change is borne out of impatience with injustice. If we are truly motivated by the love of Christ we must understand the depth of suffering lying at the roots of the world's ferment. Our call to bring Christ's life to others means that we must involve ourselves with the needs of other men. To bear witness to the Good News of new life in Christ means that we must incarnate His love for all men.

Like so much of its past, the Church today is deeply divided on these issues. On one hand, there are those sincere believers who wrap their Bibles with the American flag, and suggest that the missing clause of the Apostle's Creed should read: "I believe in the omnipotence of the Presidency and in the righteousness of the American Way."

Set against these are the political Messiahs of our day, who baptize contemporary revolutionary ideology as though it were all divinely inspired. Their intolerance for the injustice they see leads them to advocate revolutionary social change, with little regard for the means or the cost, as the primary mission of the Church.

The evangelical community is deeply indebted to Vernon Grounds' analysis of these issues. He understands the passion of those who cry out for the world to be made anew. And he explains how the Christian can approach today's turbulent world with undaunted hope and burning vision. Yet, Dr. Grounds reminds us that faith in Christ is most revolutionary because it believes that man himself—not just his society—stands in need of radical transformation. Taking this evangelical truth, he forms discerning perspectives on the contemporary quest for revolutionary change.

As this onslaught of change besieges us all, we are tempted to race from reality, and content ourselves with the false security that comes from social blindness. This superb book reminds every Christian that Christ's love thrusts us into the suffering of the world, and that His life shows us the way to meet the social, political and spiritual ferment of our age.

MARK O. HATFIELD
United States Senator

Preface

Reactionary governments in the Western world may once have considered Christianity their subservient ally against revolution. But today, when unpredictable change is a sort of predictable constant, there are some theologians who keep urging Christianity to abandon its role as the docile supporter and sanctifier of the *status quo*. They urge, instead, that it join forces with left-wing radicalism in the fight for a remade society. Thus a new movement, the theology of revolution, is emerging within the orbit of Christendom. While not yet a homogeneous school, it holds that the chief function of Christianity is to spearhead radical change for the sake of freedom and justice. Not all the theologians who can be fairly classified as revolution*aries*, or advocates of radical change, can also be fairly classified as revolution*ists*, or advocates of radical change by violence. But as a group they are tending more and more to be revolution*ists*, justifying violence if change cannot otherwise be effected quickly or deeply enough.

In this study, therefore, my purpose is to sketch the background against which this theology has emerged, particularly here in the United States. I have sought to let the critics of the Establishment, Christian and secular alike, present in their own words the case for revolutionary change. I have also sought to let the revolutionary theologians set forth their interpretation of Christianity in detail. Quite literally, I have allowed them to speak for themselves. I have sought, further, to let Christian scholars who dissent from this new theology engage its proponents in debate. Very heavily I have drawn upon the work of Jacques Ellul, the towering French sociologist who is rapidly gaining in the United States the attention and respect which his rare fusion of professional distinction, intellectual power, and biblical commitment deserves. I shall feel amply rewarded if through these pages he wins a wider readership among American evangelicals.

An additional purpose has been to confront my own ecclesiastical tradition, that of Protestant orthodoxy, with the inexpressibly pressing need of permitting the anguish of our world to drive theological conservatism back to a New Testament discipleship which is nothing less than revolutionary.

I appreciate deeply the kindness of my seminary colleagues in bearing increased burdens to grant me a semester's sabbatical for research and writing. My secretary, Mrs. Harald Krokaa, and my typist, Miss Elaine Potter, have been uncomplainingly cooperative and personally interested. My wife has been a helpmeet in every way. One therefore regretfully wishes that with such encouragement and assistance he might have produced a more significant contribution to the cause of that redemptive revolutionary, his Lord and Saviour, Jesus Christ.

Vernon C. Grounds

Revolution
and the
Christian Faith

Surely I live in the dark ages!
An anger-free word is absurd. An unwrinkled brow
Hides a hard heart. That laughing man
Has simply not discovered
The dreadful news.

What sort of time can this be, when
Speaking of trees is almost criminal
Because it does not speak against so much injustice!
Is not he who caimly crosses the street
No longer available to his friends
Who are in need?

—Bertolt Brecht

I. Total Revolution

Halford Luccock, for long years professor of homiletics at Yale Divinity School, once pointed out that Rip Van Winkle of Sleepy Hollow fame was a prototype of some twentieth-century Christians. He dozed off with George III ruling the colonies and woke up to find George Washington serving as the first President of the United States. While a revolution raged around him, Rip was fast asleep. During the relatively quiet decade of the 1950's many a Sunday morning congregation smiled agreeably as its pastor, like Luccock, warned against the danger of a somnolent complacency in an era of change and crisis. I speak from my own preaching experience.

Today, however, as we move into the 1970's reeling from the turbulence of the 1960's, it seems impossible that any American Christian is still asleep, torpidly unaware that a revolution has been taking place. But perhaps even wide-awake Christians do not realize as yet the nature and depth of that revolution. They may not realize, either, that perhaps we are on the verge of literal revolution—the deliberate use of terror and violence in an attempt to disrupt, subvert, and destroy the whole established order, replacing it with some new form of government and way of life. As Christians, busy with their own routine occupations and preoccupations, they probably are not hearing and reading the discussions which more and more dominate the forefront of theology. They would no doubt be shocked to learn that participation in the revolutionary movement—not only in theorizing and propagandizing but, if necessary, in guerrilla warfare as well—is being seriously advocated as the contemporary mode of following Jesus.

It is to this situation that American Christians, especially those of evangelical commitment, must be alerted. Once shock has snapped them out of stupor, they can decide on the proper reactions and actions which their faith demands. What follows, then, is a tocsin. Let me add, though, that I shall be inexpressibly grateful if, in the providence of God, I turn out to be a false alarmist rather than a prophet.

When I was a student at Rutgers University in the mid-30's, one of my professors assigned to us for a critical review Everett Dean Martin's book *Farewell to Revolution*. With irresistible cogency that scholarly liberal draws upon the resources of history and logic to demonstrate that only irrational fanatics would ever urge *"a faction in the community without sanction of law"* to engage in *"armed hostilities in the attempt to constitute itself the governing force in society."* Revolution, Martin argues, is "a social earthquake ... a barbarian invasion and conquest ... the supreme exhibition of mob behavior." As such, it is a futile tragedy and a tragic futility. After reviewing "the ten great revolutions of history—revolutions which are popularly supposed to have achieved for mankind its liberties and progress," Martin concludes:

I think that the realistic view shows that every one of these revolutions was a drama of delusion. Not one accomplished its aim. All were irrelevant and quixotic efforts to achieve by sudden violence what was really being achieved by the advance of culture. This advance was set back by each revolution and civilized men and women were obliged, after the earthquake, to pick up the debris of the great emotional debauch and begin again the building of the republic of free men. [1]

So that, I thought with considerable relief, takes care of all the flaming rhetoric about revolution. Only a moronic sadist would dream of fomenting armed insurrection in our day. If not safe for democracy, at least the world is secure against revolution. But events since 1935 have punctured the wistful illusion of a young American who idealistically had hoped that his century might see the advent of a peaceful, unified, global fraternity of nations.

Of course, revolution—armed insurrection with a view to overturning the *status quo*—is an age-old phenomenon. Marx, indeed, calls it "the locomotive of all history." But Hannah Arendt in her

[1]Everett Dean Martin, *Farewell to Revolution* (New York: W. W. Norton & Co., Inc., 1935), pp. 26, 28-38, 347.

magisterial work, *On Revolution*, correctly contends that "the revolutionary spirit of the last centuries, that is, the eagerness to liberate *and* build a new house where freedom can dwell, is unprecedented and unequalled in all prior history."[2] While she does not minimize the epochal significance of the eighteenth-century revolutions in the United States and France, nor the frequency and significance of the nineteenth-century revolutions, Miss Arendt remarks: "No historian will ever be able to tell the tale of our century without stringing it 'on the thread of revolutions.'"[3]

Hence in my student days if I had read Paul Hutchinson's 1931 analysis of world revolution and religion, I might not have been quite so optimistic about the renunciation of revolutionary violence as a final tactic for changing an order of things adjudged tyrannical and oppressive. That journalist, who edited the *Christian Century* with notable competence, reported in the pre-Hitler era that wherever he traveled he came upon "the ghastly reality of revolution"; and revolution, he said, "is all that the word implies."

It is taking this world of ours—this nice little settled comfortable world, with all the jimcracks of our civilization so nicely placed upon the mantels of our complacent enjoyment—and turning it upside down, so that that which has been on the bottom stands on the top, and so that

[2] Hannah Arendt, *On Revolution* (New York: The Viking Press, 1962), p. 28.
[3] *Ibid.*, p. 259. "The word 'revolution' was originally an astronomical term which gained increasing importance in the natural sciences through Copernicus's *De revolutionibus orbium coelestium*. In this scientific usage it retained its precise Latin meaning, designating the regular, lawfully revolving motion of the stars, which, since it was known to be beyond the influence of man and hence irresistible, was certainly characterized neither by newness nor by violence. On the contrary, the word clearly indicates a recurring, cyclical movement; it is the perfect Latin translation of Polybius's anakyklosis, a term which also originated in astronomy and was used metaphorically in the realm of politics. If used for the affairs of men on earth, it could only signify that the few known forms of government revolve among the mortals in eternal recurrence and with the same irresistible force which makes the stars follow their preordained paths in the skies. Nothing could be farther removed from the original meaning of the word 'revolution' than the idea of which all revolutionary actors have been possessed and obsessed, namely, that they are agents in a process which spells the definite end of an old order and brings about the birth of a new world." *Ibid.*, p. 35.

all our expensive and fragile bric-a-brac falls into fragments and forms part of a vast debris.

Revolution is a smashed, overturned, pulverized world. No other understanding of the word is sufficient for our present needs.

For the next hundred or two hundred years the world will be in the grip of revolution. [4]

Hutchinson saw and foresaw revolution occurring politically, industrially, socially, racially, and religiously. Thus had I been acquainted with his prediction, I might have guessed that the watchword of my lifetime would not be "Farewell to revolution!" It would be, instead, "On to the barricades!" For as the twentieth century zooms toward its twilight, revolution keeps growing into vaster and vaster proportions. To speak of it as worldwide, writes George Celestin, is no longer to engage in hyperbole. [5] Already in 1954, lecturing at Harvard University, Adlai Stevenson had declared:

Great movements and forces, springing from deep wells, have converged at this mid-century point, and I suspect we have barely begun to comprehend what has happened and why. In the background are the opaque, moving forms and shadows of a world revolution, of which Communism is more the scavenger than the inspiration; a world in transition from an age with which we are familiar to an age shrouded in mist. [6]

Now as we move into the 1970's, the professor of ecumenics at Princeton Theological Seminary, Richard Shaull, tells us that since a "social revolution is the primary fact with which our generation will have to come to terms," it follows that, regardless of our escapist wishes, "revolution is to be our destiny." [7] And in the words of André Philip, whom Shaull in another article quotes approvingly, that destiny lays upon us a responsibility which we may long to sidestep but simply cannot evade:

We no longer dream about a future revolution, because we are already

[4] Paul Hutchinson, *World Revolution and Religion* (New York: Abingdon Press, 1931), pp. 14-15.

[5] "A Christian Looks at Revolution," *New Theology No. 6*, Martin E. Marty and Dean G. Peerman, eds. (New York: The Macmillan Company, 1969), p. 93.

[6] *Ibid.*, p. 95.

[7] Richard Shaull, "Revolutionary Change in Theological Perspective," *The Church amid Revolution*, Harvey Cox, ed. (New York: Association Press, 1967), pp. 28, 30.

living in one, in a continual process of destroying existing structures and rebuilding them; and man's role is to influence events in such a way as to turn them in the direction he considers favorable.[8]

Yes, particularly if we are Christians, the reality of revolution, theologians of Shaull's viewpoint maintain, is summoning us to play a new role, that of insurrectionists in the name of God. Thus William Sloan Coffin, Jr., in a personal letter to Dr. John A. T. Robinson of *Honest to God* fame, declares:

I am afraid we are gradually moving towards that situation where citizens will have to choose between options no citizens should have to confront—namely, between change forced by violence and the repression of violence forced by no change. To me this means that the marching order for the church should read: twice as nonviolent, and twice as militant.[9]

Or listen to this account of the address which an eloquent Colombian, Dr. Castillo-Cardenas, delivered at the 1966 W.C.C. Conference on Church and Society held in Geneva:

He said that if Christians are coming more and more to realize that the present order is "an affront to God because it is an affront to man"; and when they realize how many forms of force are employed in order to protect this unjust order against the underprivileged and oppressed, the poor and the weak, then (if they really love their neighbor) they cannot content themselves with "certain isolated reforms equivalent to social anesthesia." What is required is "to take power away from the privileged minorities and give it to the poor majorities." "Therefore, revolution is not only permitted, but is obligatory for those Christians who see it as the only effective way of fulfilling love to one's neighbor."[10]

Such statements should shake drowsy Christians wide-awake. Revolution is evidently assuming the status of a required course in the curriculum of New Testament discipleship.

But really, as before God, is revolution the Christian's obligation today? Sharp and unequivocal is the opinion of Lutheran pastor and editor Richard John Neuhaus: "We are for revolution.

8 Quoted by Richard Shaull, "Christian Faith as Scandal in a Technocratic World," *New Theology No. 6*, p. 125.

9 Quoted by John A. T. Robinson, *Christian Freedom in a Permissive Society* (London: SCM Press, Ltd., 1970), p. 239.

10 Quoted in J. M. Lochman, "Ecumenical Theology of Revolution," *New Theology No. 6*, pp. 111-12.

A revolution of consciousness, no doubt. A cultural revolution, certainly. A non-violent revolution, perhaps. And armed overthrow of the existing order, it may be necessary. Revolution for the hell of it or revolution for a new world, but revolution, yes." [11] To be sure, Neuhaus is referring specifically to adherents of the so-called Movement, that disjointed conglomeration of New Leftists who are *"acting in radical judgment upon the prevailing patterns, political, economic, social, and moral of American life."* [12] But he makes it clear in his essay "The Thorough Revolutionary" that the concerned Christian can fulfill his discipleship only in the ranks of the Movement. In short, while Neuhaus is using the indicative, his indicative is in effect a hortatory imperative: "You, my fellow-Christians, ought also to opt for revolution."

Is anybody, having read this far, still asleep? The tocsin clangs out so stridently that it might well cause commotion in a mortuary. I, for one, as an American evangelical, admit that I listen with bewilderment and anxiety. Revolution may be the world's destiny as our century marches on. Yet is revolution, even if relatively bloodless, a sheer necessity in order that a juster society may be achieved? And—how incredible it sounds!—is revolution a Christian responsibility? Here are issues which compel hard thought—and maybe a radical reappraisal of positions held with easy conscience up to now.

To attain a clarifying perspective on the explosive situation which is rapidly evolving today, suppose we set the problem of social and political change within the larger framework of twentieth-century culture. For social and political change is simply one phase of what Heinz-Dietrich Wendland calls "total revolution," [13] that interlocking series of profound and planetary upheavals triggered in a sort of chain reaction by the progress of science and technology. Since this revolution is total, no area of human life lies outside its orbit. In that wryly amusing line from *Green Pastures,* "Everything dat's fastened down is comin' loose."

11 Richard J. Neuhaus, "The Thorough Revolutionary," Peter L. Berger and Richard J. Neuhaus, *Movement and Revolution* (Garden City, N. Y.: Doubleday & Company, Inc., 1970), p. 127.

12 *Ibid.*, p. 90.

13 Quoted by J. M. Lochman, *op. cit.*, pp. 104-05.

The turbulence of the twentieth century, however, its total revolution, can be understood only as we take into account the catalyzing influences of the scientific revolution. The theories and discoveries of creative geniuses like Sir Isaac Newton and James Watts produced an industrial revolution as well as a technological revolution, which in turn have produced social and political revolutions. That astute and philosophical commentator, Walter Lippmann, has italicized the all-inclusiveness of the change induced by the growth and progress of science.

This revolution is the transformation of the human environment and of man himself by technological progress which, beginning about two centuries ago, has now acquired enormous momentum. It is changing the way men live, not only their work and their houses, their food and their communications and their pleasures, but it is changing also the structure of the human family and the chemistry of the human personality. These changes are bewildering. [14]

The phenomenon of total revolution has been brilliantly analyzed by John McHale in his book *The Future of the Future*. Applied science, he reminds us, has set man free from a struggle merely to survive and put at his disposal limitless resources for controlling and creating the shape of human existence. McHale cites Boris Pregel's graphic summary of what has happened in modern times, the astonishing consequence of applied science, to which Lippmann has likewise called attention.

The first great changes came with the advent of the Industrial Age, based on engines that used energy stored in coal beds, which built cities and navies, wove textiles, and sent steam trains across the widest continents. Since then, with energy from petroleum and other sources, changes have come more swiftly. Today, radar telescopes scan the universe to record galactic explosions that occurred billions of years ago; oceanographic ships explore the undersea; electronic devices measure the earth's aura of unused energy and similar equipment traces inputs and outputs of single nerve cells; television cameras orbiting the earth send back photographs of entire sub-continents; electron microscopes photograph a virus; passenger planes fly at almost the speed of sound; and machines set type in

---

[14] Quoted by Fred J. Cook, *What So Proudly We Hailed* (Englewood Cliffs, N. J.: Prentice-Hall, Inc., 1968), pp. 255-56.

Paris when a key is tapped in New York. These are only a few of the changes.[15]

So science and technology have been transforming the face of the globe and the life of humanity. New modes of communication and transportation, for instance, have reduced our earth to the dimensions of Marshall McLuhan's global village, a fact which Ritchie Calder brings out strikingly.

Eskimo children who have never seen a wheeled vehicle can identify the types of aircraft which fly overhead. The young Dyaks in the conghouses of the equatorial jungle of Borneo listen to the Beatles, and the wandering Bedouins with transistor radios, bought by selling dates to the oilmen of the Sahara, hear Nasser's radio telling how American planes are bombing Vietnam children half the world away.[16]

Though shrinking in some respects, our world is exploding in others. We talk, therefore, about the population explosion and the knowledge explosion on a planet threatened by the ghastly possibilities of thermonuclear explosions. Indeed, one sometimes feels as though he is living on the outside skin of a soap bubble, swelling bigger and bigger, glistening as it inflates toward sudden disintegration.

Technological development has not, therefore, eliminated difficulties, making life utopian for most of mankind. Quite the reverse! Difficulties seem to multiply rather than diminish. What about the alarming depletion of resources and the more alarming pollution of the environment? The UNESCO Biosphere Conference held in Paris during September, 1968, warned in its final report:

Pollution is one of the major problems facing humanity at present and ... it may ultimately be important in limiting the earth's population through deterioration of man's physical and mental health. ... If mankind is prepared to make a determined effort, to support much more research to make that effort effective, our descendants may not be condemned to live on an impoverished planet devoid of so much of the varied life which has made it so interesting and so beautiful.[17]

15 Quoted by John McHale, *The Future of the Future* (New York: George Braziller, 1968), p. 6.

16 Quoted in *ibid.*, p. 270.

17 Quoted by Hugh Montefiore, *The Question Mark: The End of Homo Sapiens* (London. Collins, 1969), p. 25. *Cf.* McHale, *op. cit.*, pp. 156-57.

In a 1961 seminar George Keenan had issued a similar warning, declaring that, even if nuclear war is avoided, the human race by depleting and defiling its planetary home may render it uninhabitable.

It is the thoughtless, extravagant, destructive attitude of modern man with regard to his natural environment, from which he has himself grown and on which his existence depends, his remorseless, greedy plundering of the treasures of this environment, his eagerness to defile it forever with his industrial and human waste products, of which the by-products of atomic installations are only one among many, to defile them to such an extent that perhaps not even our own children, let alone future generations, will be able to live there.[18]

Shifting now to other problems, what about urbanization, militarization, and depersonalization, which are concomitants of mushrooming scientific and technological development? Ulf Goebel, who teaches political science at John Carroll University, indulges in a discouraging commentary.

The world has gone wrong. There's no room left for man. We suffer from the crisis manager mentality. In Moscow, London, Washington, Paris, Bonn and any number of other world capitals sit the builders of balancing systems of blood, steel, and blackmail. Missiles breed counter-missiles and cluster warheads. Executives fire cyborges. Statesmen make room for systems analysts. The evil spirits that inhabit the Pentagon are machines that depend on men to program them intelligently. But the power we have created here has far outdistanced our ability to control it. The demon of mechanized inertia has infiltrated the very marrow of our society.[19]

Again, what about hunger, not just malnutrition but actual starvation? What about the masses of people who have little food now and who in the foreseeable future will have less and less until they are reduced to the heartbreaking plight of those famished multitudes already without a crust of bread or a fistful of rice? William G. Pollard, who is both physicist and theologian, predicts the oncoming of ghastly disaster.

[18]Quoted by Helmut Gollwitzer, "The Demands of Freedom," *The Revolutionary Imperative*, Alan D. Austin, ed. (Nashville, Tenn.: National Methodist Student Movement, 1966), p. 87.

[19]Ulf Goebel, "Revolution and Hope for the Future," *Worldview*, April, 1968, p. 17.

By 1970 famine of catastrophic proportions seems inevitable in India, Pakistan, and China. It will be a calamity unparalleled in human history, involving death by starvation for numbers running into the hundreds of millions. We have somewhat longer in South America, but, unless major projects can be initiated in the next few years, famine of comparable proportions will occur there by 1980. ... In the long run, say thirty or forty years, we have the technological means to provide enough food. But the immediate needs are so pressing and are increasing so rapidly that there seems no possibility of avoiding short-term catastrophe.[20]

This possibility—Pollard views it as an inevitability—prompted Lady Barbara Ward Jackson to exclaim in her commencement address at the University of Pennsylvania in May, 1969:

Let it be clear that we're not just asking for something to stop. *We're asking for something to begin. That beginning is a strategy for the modernization of our planet in such a way that every child has a modest chance to live a fully human life. This is not true now; it is getting less true by the hour.* By the 1980's it will be so hideously untrue, that when Mr. Lin Piao, the likely successor of Mao Tse-tung, gets up and says, "The great masses of the world will surround the corrupt and wealthy white minority"—in which he includes, I need hardly say, the Russians —his prophecy, of the revolt of the world, of the hungry '70's leading to the revolutionary '80's, is not just a threat. It could be built into the existential situation that we face today.[21]

It is within this context, then, that we must see the emergence of today's crusading insurrectionists. Unquestionably, science and technology have been transforming the world, effecting a total revolution. But the lot of humanity has not yet been noticeably improved, nor is it likely to improve. On the contrary, Professor John Holt of Yale University wonders pessimistically if we have not reached a stage of immobilized bafflement.

Nobody seriously believes that we are likely to solve, or are even moving toward a solution of, any of the most urgent problems of our times—war, the proliferation of atomic, chemical, and bacteriological weapons, over-population, poverty, the destruction of the earth's biological environment, the fossilization and depersonalization of his political and economic institutions, his increasing alienation, boredom, anger. We do not think any more that we can really make the world a fit and happy and beautiful place for people to live: we scarcely think that we can keep it a place where people can live at all.[22]

Which is precisely why the crusading insurrectionists are convinced that a social and political revolution is imperative, a revolution which, if necessary, will use force and violence, shatter the old order, and make the world "a fit and happy and beautiful place to live in."

Since we are struggling to understand the reasons for the New Leftist Movement which is enlisting the sanction and support of some serious-minded Christians, we need to stifle our sense of boredom at more of the same and ponder seriously what has been said by John R. Seeley of the Center for the Study of Democratic Institutions:

The thrust of the movement's critique, and that which lends force to the action and the sense of irreconcilability to the issues, is that these—and larger matters such as the drift of war toward biocide; the mindless spoliation of nature and probable poisoning of the environment; the total corruption of men's minds by mass propaganda in small matters and large; the progressive alienation, constriction, and truncation of the human being in such a society; the dominance of technological thoughtways in which means float free of or determine ends—(all these) are the climactic, characteristic, and inseparable results (and, in a sense, aims) of the existing order. The indictment is drawn not in terms of reversible deviations from a right path, but in terms of persistence to a path so patently bound for hell on earth that a fresh beginning by new men, based on entirely new assumptions and with entirely different aims, is required—and inescapable.[23]

We need to ponder Seeley's conclusion very seriously. The New Leftists are persuaded that twentieth-century culture, that of the West in particular, is persistently following "a path so pa-

[22]Quoted in an editorial, "The Recovery of Purpose," *Christianity Today*, January 30, 1970, p. 21.

[23]"Youth in Revolt," in *Britannica Book of the Year, 1969* (Chicago: Encyclopedia Britannica, Inc.), p. 315.

tently bound for hell on earth that a fresh beginning by new men, based on entirely new assumptions and with entirely different aims, is required—and inescapable." In brief, many Americans are convinced that revolution will be total only when it overthrows the *status quo*, by force if necessary, and establishes a new order in which the resources of science will be used peacefully and productively.

In Latin America people die of old age at twenty-eight, the vast majority of the population does not eat more than 500 calories a day, illiteracy is higher now than ten years ago, and fewer people have potable water today than yesterday. That kind of poverty is an abstraction for us whites. No matter how much we see it around us we really can't understand what poverty is because we do not suffer it; at least not like an Indian peasant I once met in Bolivia. This peasant woman had four bowls of rice and five children. She gave her four eldest children a bowl, but not the youngest one sitting in the corner. I asked her, "Why aren't you feeding that child?" She said, "He's the weakest, he's the youngest, he's going to be the first to die anyway. I don't have enough food for all five so I have to make a choice, and I'm not going to feed the one that's going to die first." ... The peoples of the underdeveloped world will rebel because they are hungry, because they are exploited, because they are dominated by foreigners.

—John Gerassi

II. Third World Revolution

Utopia—who does not realize this discouraging fact?—still lies a long distance off in the uncertain future. To admit the truth, it is probably Samuel Butler's fictional Erewhon—Nowhere spelled anagrammatically! Yet leaving out of account the Communist World, it must be admitted that life in the Western World is, by and large, enviously utopian when contrasted with human existence, by and large, in the Third World. Almost anywhere in that ill-defined entity known as the West, there is a level of opulence that makes Europe and North America, to say nothing of Japan or Israel, a kind of Shangri-la in a global slum. So what happens when the have-nots who comprise the exploding masses of the underdeveloped nations, "the wretched of the earth," in Frantz Fanon's unforgettable phrase, learn about the glittering realities of the utopian Western World? The reaction is an explosive compound of astonishment, envy, anger, longing, and hope. Thus the communications revolution, offspring of the technological revolution, helps to foment another revolution, a revolution in dreams and desires and demands. Third World expectations are radicalized, rising from the nadir of fatalistic resignation to wildest heights of fantasy. Thomas and Margaret Melady are thus not guilty of exaggeration in describing a typical reaction to the growing awareness that human existence can be astonishingly upgraded.

The average woman in West Africa today is dead before forty after about nine pregnancies. She has a life that any observer would have to classify as miserable. She is not living any longer than her mother; the average woman of West Africa of twenty or twenty-five years ago was dead at thirty-six. The same was true at the beginning of the century. But there is a turbulent difference between the woman in West Africa today and her mother, grandmother, and great-grandmother. She has been hit by what sociologists call the impact of rising expectation. She knows—thanks to the little wireless set in her hut—that women in Europe and the United States have one great problem: how not to get too fat, while her problem remains to live beyond forty. Unlike her grandmother and mother, she realizes there are people in other parts of the world who are living until seventy or seventy-five and who are living a life that is free from the miseries she still has. She now has an obsession, the obsession to end the curse of poverty, illiteracy and disease and to end it dramatically —overnight regardless of the means. [1]

Consider, too, the daily experience of the exploited Algerian for whom Frantz Fanon, the black psychiatrist turned African revolutionary, serves as eloquent spokesman: "famine, eviction from his room because he has not paid the rent, the mother's dried-up breasts, children like skeletons, the building-yard which is closed down, the unemployed that hang about the foreman like crows." Consider that for the victim of exploitative colonialism a stolen piece of fruit does not represent a violation of morality but a victory in his ceaseless struggle to stave off death: "To live means to keep on existing. Every date is a victory: not the result of work, but a victory felt as a triumph for life." Consider Fanon's unforgettable vignette of "men and women for weeks at a time going to get earth at the bottom of the valley and bringing it up in little baskets. The fact is that the only perspective is that belly which is more and more sunken, which is certainly less and less demanding, but which must be contented all the same." [2]

What happens, therefore, when people who are victims not only of hunger but likewise of disease, illiteracy, and oppression hear about wheat plowed underground in the United States and the payment of government subsidies to American farmers for refraining from the cultivation of their fields? What happens when "the wretched of the earth" begin to perceive the abysmal difference between their own world and that of the West? What happens when they slowly realize that Europe, for example, is

[1] Thomas and Margaret Melady, *House Divided: Poverty, Race, Religion and the Family of Man* (New York: Sheed & Ward, 1969), p. 7.

[2] Frantz Fanon, *The Wretched of the Earth* (New York: Grove Press, Inc., 1968), pp. 307-09.

opulent precisely because, vampirelike, it has drained Africa of its vitality?

Today, national independence and the growth of national feeling in underdeveloped regions take on totally new aspects. In these regions, with the exception of certain spectacular advances, the different countries show the same absence of infrastructure. The mass of the people struggle against the same poverty, flounder about making the same gestures and with their shrunken bellies outline what has been called the geography of hunger. It is an underdeveloped world, a world inhuman in its poverty; but also it is a world without doctors, without engineers, and without administrators. Confronting this world, the European nations sprawl, ostentatiously opulent. This European opulence is literally scandalous, for it has been founded on slavery, it has been nourished with the blood of slaves and it comes directly from the soil and from the subsoil of that underdeveloped world. The well-being and the progress of Europe have been built up with the sweat and the dead bodies of Negroes, Arabs, Indians, and the yellow races.[3]

What happens when the awakening and aroused inhabitants of the Third World decide "not to overlook ... any longer" the contrast between their underdeveloped Third World and the exploiting Western World? What happens when the wretched of the earth realize that starvation and poverty and injustice and illiteracy and degradation need not be—and ought not be!—man's inescapable plight because it is not the plight of the utopian Western World? Then what? An explosion is inevitable. And, says Jean-Paul Sartre, "We are living at the moment when the match is put to the fuse."[4] There must be, Fanon announces to the dehumanized denizens of the Third World, a "radical transformation of society" even if it means "being caught up in a veritable Apocalypse."[5]

Revolution is blowing in the wind among the peoples of the Third World for another reason. Dedicated members of their own intelligentsia, of whom Fanon is a notable example, have been zealously nurturing it. They have lost all hope in the transforming influence of Christianity, humanitarian reformism,

[3] *Ibid.*, p. 96.
[4] Quoted in *ibid.*, p. 20.
[5] *Ibid.*, pp. 251, 310.

and political action. Revolution, they have decided, is the sole route by which the Third World can ever be free from famine, racism, and exploitation. Some of these indigenous insurrectionists are single-minded nationalists. Some are militant Marxists. But others have been and are Christians, both Catholics and Protestants.[6] Christians! Certainly not Christians! How, an American evangelical may wonder, is it possible for Christians to conclude that the Third World has no recourse but revolution in order to change an intolerable situation, leaping the gap between existence as it is and existence as it might be in our technological age?

Having already glanced at Africa in our allusions to Frantz Fanon, we turn now to Latin America. Dr. Lara-Braud, director of the Hispanic-American Institute in Austin, Texas, explains why nationals in that continent are abandoning the illusion of reformism for the realism of armed revolution.

They marvel at the naïveté of national and foreign defenders of the status quo who recoil in horror at the prospect of violent revolution. Is not the present situation itself the result of legal violence, legitimized by the language of stability, democracy, Pan-Americanism and anti-communism? Is it not violence that a man should die of old age at 28, that a woman should not feed the weakest of four children because there is just enough for the three who may survive, that 500 out of 1,000 children should die in the countryside before the age of two, that a maimed mine worker and his family should starve on the pittance of their indemnity, that student protesters should be tortured, that political prisoners should be shot, that half the children of school age should have no school to attend, that millions should be landless while one family owns acres by the millions, that more than half of the adult population should be illiter-

---

[6] Consider the case of "the priest turned guerilla," Camilo Torres, who "was ambushed and killed as he tried to man the machine gun of his ill-fated band. It was a painful and tortuous spiritual odyssey that finally brought Camilo to an unmarked grave. As his program for social reform tended more and more toward violence, Camilo was estranged from his aristocratic family and friends, became an enemy of the government and finally rejected by his ecclesiastical superiors. ... With the corrupt government bureaucracy incapable of effective social reform, Camilo became convinced that only a violent revolution could change things. 'The people,' he wrote, 'do not believe in elections. The people know that legal means are at an end. ... The people know that only armed rebellion is left. The people are desperate and ready to stake their lives so that the next generation of Colombians may not be slaves.'" George Celestin, *op. cit.*, p. 94.

ate, that one-third of the national budget should be spent for late-model weaponry, that 80 per cent should live on a yearly per capita income of $80? Active resistance to this pervasive violence should be called by its right name: counter-violence. How much of it shall become necessary so that nationalists may claim their future shall largely depend on how protracted may be the struggle between them and the Herodians. The longer the delay in the radical transformation of the present structures the larger shall be the explosion of repressed aspirations.[7]

Evidently, therefore, the Latin American situation is so pathological that we can at least sympathize with the advocates of violence as an *ultima ratio*, a last and desperate recourse.

Our sympathy may deepen as we review the sensational case of Thomas and Arthur Melville, who had been working with the Maryknoll Fathers in Guatemala. Thomas later married a former nun, Marian Bradford, who had also been working in that country. These three had tried to help the Indians who comprise 56 percent of the population, but at every turn they met frustration. William O. Douglas, Associate Justice of the Supreme Court, reports that between 1966 and 1967 they saw 2,800 assassinations by the entrenched forces of the reactionary *status quo*. "Social disturbers," struggling to eliminate some of the crying evils of their society, were simply liquidated. The Melvilles themselves assisted Indians in getting

a truck to transport lime from the hills to the processing plant, an operation historically performed by Indians who carried one hundred pound sacks on their backs. A truck would increase the production of the Indians and help raise their standard of living. But the powers-that-be ran this truck off the road into a deep canyon and did everything else possible to defeat this slight change in the habits of the Indians.

What could the Melvilles do in face of such brutal, irrational injustice? Thomas, writing for himself and his brother, describes the course of action they elected to pursue.

Having come to the conclusion that the actual state of violence, composed of the malnutrition, ignorance, sickness and hunger of the vast majority of the Guatemalan population, is the direct result of the capitalistic system that makes the defenseless Indian compete against the powerful and

---

[7] "We Claim Our Future," *Tempo*, January 5, 1970, p. 5.

well-armed landowner, my brother and I decided not to be silent accomplices of the mass murder that this system generates. We began teaching the Indians that no one will defend their rights if they do not defend them themselves. If the government and oligarchy are using arms to maintain them in their position of misery, then they have the obligation to take up arms and defend their God-given right to be men. ... Our response to the present situation is not because we have read Marx and Lenin, but because we have read the New Testament.[8]

In further self-defense of what he and his brother had done, Thomas quotes from the pastoral letter issued by the conference of Guatemala's Roman Catholic bishops:

No one can deny that our social and economic reality is terribly unjust and unbalanced, that change in our vitiated structures is mandatory, and that it is necessary first of all to change the mentality of our fellow citizens. The inequitable distribution of the national revenue; the disparity in the scale of salaries (some dispose of emoluments which are an insult to the poverty of the country, while the immense majority receives a miserable pittance); the fact that a bare two per cent of the active population own seventy per cent of the arable land; the system of recruiting our agricultural laborers, who do not even enjoy legal status; the fact that hundreds of thousands of school-age children lack basic education; the disintegration of the family; the growing immorality everywhere—all this demands bold and definitive change.[9]

Can "bold and definitive change" be effected by peaceful means? The Melvilles, while not personally involved in violence, have voted in favor of guerrilla action as the only means of effecting "bold and definitive change" in Guatemala.

For years a missionary to Colombia and Brazil, Richard Shaull holds unequivocally that revolution is the only route by which the Latin American peoples can move from their dehumanizing *status quo* to a higher plane of life. Thus he asks some painful questions, his own answers being plainly implied:

Will the guerilla *foco* be the only live option, or will Latin Americans discover and find it possible to follow another road to the same goals?

---

[8] Quoted in William O. Douglas, *Points of Rebellion* (New York: Vintage Books, 1970), pp. 89-91.
[9] Quoted by Jacques Ellul, *Violence: Reflections from a Christian Perspective* (New York: The Seabury Press, 1969), p. 64.

Will the U.S. fight to the bitter end against national revolution in Latin America, or will it wake up in time to avoid disaster—the total social breakdown and complete disruption of relations between North and South America?[10]

He then proceeds to discuss a book by one of Brazil's leading educators, Paulo Freire, whom Shaull terms a "Christian humanist." It discusses a possible "program of *conscientizacao*," and *conscientizacao* may be defined as "the task of creating critical awareness of a people's situation of oppression and their responsibility to do something about it." In other words, Freire wonders "how the depressed masses can move toward full human existence as persons." According to Shaull, he believes this

can happen only as they are enabled to cut the umbilical cord with nature and with a sacralized social order and thus discover themselves as participants in a concrete historical process open to the future. As this discovery occurs, they begin to assume a critical attitude over against their world, begin to make decisions about their future, and become creators. This leads them to see that they can be human only as they have an opportunity to participate in a society that is open. Given the condition of Latin American society today, this means that *conscientizacao* leads to radical politics.[11]

But *conscientizacao* may mean bloodshed. As it generates a liberating movement which disrupts "a static and closed society," *conscientizacao* leads, of course, to the creation of new political instruments. It therefore will probably result in violence since, in Freire's opinion, any attempt to suppress the "awakened masses is thoroughly dehumanizing, and can only be met by counter-violence."[12]

Shaull also discusses a book by Colombian sociologist, Orland Fals Borda. This Christian scholar thinks that Latin America is in a state of crisis which requires "the use of subversion as a category of sociological analysis." His study leads him to advocate a five-point subversive strategy, summarized by Shaull:

[10] Richard Shaull, "National Development and Social Revolution: Part I," *Christianity and Crisis*, January 20, 1969, p. 347.

[11] Richard Shaull, "National Development and Social Revolution: Part II," *Christianity and Crisis*, February 3, 1969, pp. 9-10.

[12] *Ibid.*

(i) A struggle for eventual control of the "mechanism of power," which includes a careful study of the points of political weakness of the system in order to take advantage of them; the formation of new political instruments; and where essential, the use of violence.

(ii) The formation of cadres who are well trained and disciplined, prepared to take the initiative and offer leadership in subversion. This involves the development of a "counter-elite," capable of resisting the pressures for integration into the system, at the same time that they are dispersed throughout the structures of society.

(iii) An organized effort to create wide awareness and diffuse new ideas within those organizations of the community which offer a significant opportunity for it.

(iv) Emphasis upon the mastery of technology, as a means of "imposing subversion," keeping control of the process and building a new order.

(v) Over against the international conspiracy of the friends of the *status quo*, it is necessary to have a new international relationship among those dedicated to subversion.[13]

In still another article, "How to Cause a Revolution," Shaull quotes an anonymous Latin American, apparently a Brazilian, who is merely identified as "the intellectual leader of one of the new Roman Catholic movements." His appraisal of the Hispanic situation, given in "a group of rather prominent middle-class professional people of deep religious conviction," was unflinchingly forthright. It had been our hope, he said, to produce economic, social, and political change, "by the democratic political process. As this is no longer possible, the only road open before us is armed struggle. And let us have no doubts about one point: in this struggle American military power will be the major force working against us." Shaull comments that "not one person in the group challenged his basic argument. The question they discussed was whether, given their comfortable bourgeois life and their reluctance to adopt violence, they could respond to the challenge presented to them."[14]

We must assume, consequently, that some Christians in the

---

13 *Ibid.*, p. 11.
14 Richard Shaull, "How to Cause a Revolution," *Tempo,* January 15, 1970, p. 6.

Third World have reluctantly and yet decisively come to Fanon's conclusion: "Radical transformation of society" is imperative even if it involves "being caught up in a veritable Apocalypse."

I cannot escape the uneasiness of mind of one who hears the kind of distant thunder that is the prelude to the breaking of a major storm, all the while a relatively surface calm offers an assurance that is deceptive. A gifted historian of our time has expressed in a different simile the haunting thought that accompanies me in these days. Writing of the city of Angers located in the Loire River Valley not too many miles from France's Atlantic Coast on the eve of the great revolution, he stated that in these last days of the ancien regime *one could study what he called "not great events, but great survivals, history of a special kind, the history of things which had endured." Then he observed: "It is a story, not of the sea with its waves and storms, but of a reed-grown river winding majestically through a monotonous plain. Even so, the scenery was changing and, perhaps, the current was imperceptibly quickening. There were tensions and oppositions in society; the stream was beginning to divide and subdivide to form the delta which marks the river's end. If men had cared to listen, they might have heard ahead of them the long slow murmur of the inconstant and ruthless sea."*

Will the men who control the destinies of . . . the United States, one may rightly ask, "care to listen" so that the "long slow murmur of the inconstant and ruthless sea" may prove a profitable warning before it is too late? Or must the drama be acted out after the fashion of a Greek tragedy to its inevitable end?

—*John Tracy Ellis*

III. Another
American Revolution?

In view of the circumstances we have been considering, it is
understandable why desperate people in the Third World are
more and more opting for revolution as a last resort in their struggle for a decent existence. Though as Christians we may shrink
from both lawlessness and violence, deep inside we can feel something of the compulsion which drove a Camilo Torres to join the
guerrilla forces in Colombia and die with a machine gun in his
hand. Given the seeming hopelessness of reform and the brutal
use of force to maintain an iniquitous *status quo*, what is there to
do but become a subversive and even an insurrectionist?

But here in the United States of America the situation, we
reassure ourselves, is different, providentially and—we think
with perhaps a touch of unctuous superiority—blessedly different.
This is a nation "under God, with freedom and justice for all."
This is a democracy in which the ideals of the French Revolution—
liberty, equality, and fraternity— have found fulfillment. This is
a model republic where peace and plenty and even piety abound.
With somewhat forgivable pride we sing:

> O beautiful for spacious skies,
> For amber waves of grain,
> For purple mountain majesties
> Above the fruited plain!
> America! America!
> God shed His grace on thee,
> And crown thy good with brotherhood
> From sea to shining sea!

To be sure, we have our problems and tensions; they are relatively minor, however, despite all the rhetorical exaggeration of Communist-inspired agitators and misguided malcontents, especially among the under-thirty generation. So regardless of riots in ghettos and on campuses, we are able to sleep tranquilly at night. While less fortunate countries tremble on the brink of revolution, it can't happen here.

But if a rising chorus of criticism is prophetic, it can. Disturbing as it may be, then, we must compel ourselves to listen as empathically as possible while the critics carry on their vivisection of our society. Large drafts of restraint and patience are required to do it, but we had better steel ourselves to listen and keep on listening. For their indictment is severe, sweeping, and sometimes savage. Thus Michael Novak, whom *The New York Times* has called "the most exciting of young American Catholic theologians," fires a withering broadside against American complacency:

It becomes increasingly difficult to see how a Christian can live in these United States and not protest with every fibre of his being against the militarization of American life, the appalling mediocrity of American imagination and sensibilities, and the heedlessness and irrationality of merely technological progress.... If we may paraphrase Nietzsche: What are these cloverleaves, these napalm factories, these university-industrial complexes, these selective service regulations, if they are not the tomb and sepulchre of man? [1]

In the eyes of a critic like Novak, our vaunted way of life is actually a complicated dehumanization which denies the revolutionary premises on which it was built by Washington, Adams, and Jefferson. As an experiment in democracy, the United States is not a shining model; it is, instead, a sad and sordid failure. It has degenerated into a tyranny,

the tyranny of an immoral majority—a majority that would prefer to wage war upon a mythical enemy embodied in other races and other nations rather than to face its own rotten core and incipient civil war at home. The state of American cities, the relationships between Americans of differing races, the general pursuit of mere expertise and the wealth

---

[1] Michael Novak, *A Theology for Radical Politics* (New York: Herder & Herder, 1969), p. 17.

that flows from it—these grave moral illnesses are not met by a majority with the will to alter its way of life.[2]

Novak's indictment is indeed sweeping and severe. But the indictment gains in sweep and severity until, as these critics single out specifics, it becomes lethally savage. For one thing, they declare, there is the unsolved problem of poverty in the world's most affluent nation, a problem which is quite literally disgusting because we refuse to solve it—somewhat as if a man allowed his face to remain covered with repulsive sores when he had available a medicine which would infallibly heal that noxious condition. So, when in 1937 Franklin Delano Roosevelt was inaugurated as President for the second time, he told his fellow Americans:

In this nation I see tens of millions of citizens—a substantial part of its whole population—who at this very moment are denied the greater part of what the very lowest standards of today call the necessities of life.

I see millions of families trying to live on incomes so meager that the pall of family disaster hangs over them day by day.

I see millions whose daily lives in city and on farm continue under conditions labeled indecent by a so-called polite society half a century ago.

I see millions denied education, recreation, and the opportunity to better their lot and the lot of their children.

I see millions lacking the means to buy the products of farm and factory and by their poverty denying work and productiveness to many other millions.

I see one-third of a nation ill-housed, ill-clad, ill-nourished.[3]

Those 1937 conditions have not improved dramatically. The simple fact is that the Great Society hides vast areas of wretchedness behind its glittering façade of technological wizardry. Michael Harrington is a sensitive, articulate, probing critic, concerned to heal the running sores of our society. Well-known for his book *The Other America*, a devastating exposé of poverty in the United States, he has written more recently *Toward a Democratic Left*. In it, like a compassionate surgeon, he has again laid bare the malignancy which lurks beneath our unprecedented prosperity. He notes, for instance, that the Department of Labor in its 1966 Manpower Report

[2] *Ibid.*, p. 78.
[3] Quoted by Fred J. Cook, *op. cit.*, pp. 4-5.

graphically demonstrated how, despite the theoretical achievement of full employment, people in the central cities were still living in the middle of the Depression. .... Perhaps the most chilling factor given consideration in the sub-employment index is the existence of non-persons among the poor. In the slums, the Department of Labor discovered a "fifth or more of the adult men expected to be a part of the population . . . were not located by the November surveys." The Bureau of the Census has recognized this similar problem of "under-counting" and is trying to devise a method to deal with it. No one knows the full story. But it does seem clear that there are people in the other America who are so marginal that they do not have even minimal contacts with the society, such as a regular address, and therefore are not socially visible enough to become a statistic. This suggests that there are more Negroes, more unemployed, and more poor people in the United States than we think. [4]

Harrington also quotes the finding published by the Council of Economic Advisers: "One-fourth of the nation's children live in families that are poor"—an estimated fifteen million of America's future citizens. And he stingingly asserts that the United States is "the stingiest welfare state in the Western World." [5]

Needless to say, poverty means hunger, not only hunger but likewise indignity and despair. Thus not long ago the *Boston Globe* printed a back-page story under the headline "Starvation No Stranger Here." A team of doctors had visited Mississippi and discovered that thousands of our future citizens are starving. "They saw children for whom hunger is a daily fact of life . . . sickness in many forms an inevitability." Hence they told the press:

We do not want to quibble over words but malnutrition is not what we found. Boys and girls we saw were hungry, weak, in pain, sick, their lives being shortened . . . they are, in fact, visibly and predictably losing their heath, their energy, their spirit. They are suffering from hunger and disease, directly or indirectly they are dying from them, which is exactly what starvation means. [6]

That report could be matched by similar ones from all over the

[4] Michael Harrington, *Toward a Democratic Left* (New York: The Macmillan Company, 1968), pp. 60-61, 63, 68.

[5] *Ibid.*

[6] Quoted by Truman Nelson, *The Right of Revolution* (Boston: Beacon Press, 1968), p. 115.

United States regarding Northern ghettos, rural areas of the South, Indian reservations, old people as well as children. Justice Douglas quotes some revealing statistics on the situation national- ly: "Families that make less than three thousand dollars a year number thirteen million. Families making less than two thousand dollars a year, eleven million. Families making less than one thousand dollars a year, five million." Pointedly he warns us, "The specter of hunger that stalks the land is likely to ignite people to violent protest."[7]

Poverty means not only hunger however; it means, in addition, poor housing, living quarters which are indescribably filthy and crowded and for which exorbitant rents must be paid. In multi- plied instances it even means rat-infested tenements. Fred J. Cook, in a special issue of *The Nation* entitled "The Shame of the Cities," focused attention on the appalling condition of our number-one metropolis:

New York is a sprawling, voracious monster of a city. It covers 315 square miles; it is crammed with some eight million people. At least a million, a full eighth of its total population, live in a packed squalor, six and ten to a room, in some tenements whose mere existence is a nause- ous stench on the air—tenements so rat-infested that, on an average, one hundred persons a year are badly chewed and, so far this year, two have actually been gnawed to death. Symbolically, perhaps, there are in New York more rats than people—an estimated nine million of them.[8]

As of 1968, Cook affirms that these conditions were unchanged. Mayor John Lindsay, testifying before a Senate subcommittee in Washington, underscored the plight of the metropolis he serves as mayor.

In New York City nearly two million people live in poverty...about 350 thousand (dwelling) units are in buildings built before 1900. We estimate that 800 thousand dwelling units, representing over one-fourth of our total housing supply, are substandard and need either replace- ment or major rehabilitation. One in four of our schools is more than fifty years old and is generally located among other scarred and broken buildings. The condition of many of our twenty-one municipal hospitals

---

[7] Douglas, *op. cit.*, p. 71.
[8] Cook, *op. cit.*, p. 87.

is disgraceful. It is estimated the city must spend a minimum of 400 million dollars to renovate or rebuild obsolete hospital facilities. [9]

Besides substandard diet, substandard housing, and substandard education, poverty means substandard, if any, medical service. Once again, Cook gives us a sharply etched picture.

To the despair and indignity of poverty, of slum housing and rat-infested tenements, of education that leaves pupils virtually illiterate, there must be added one final ingredient in the evil litany of the ghetto—bad health care. There is a reason for the statistics that show only a handful of Negroes over 65 on the welfare roles compared to more than four million whites; and the reason is that health care in the ghetto is so bad the Negroes are killed off faster. Infant mortality rates (the number of babies who die in the first year of life) are usually considered the most accurate barometer of the state of a nation's health. In the first six months of 1967 these statistics showed, for example, that the infant mortality rate in New York's Central Harlem was 44.4 and in East Harlem 42.6—some five times the 8.2 rate in a Bronx district that had the best record in the city. Throughout the range of New York's ghettos, the infant mortality rates ran three to four times as high as they did in the better-class white districts. [10]

Poverty means, moreover, a lack of opportunity, little or no hope for young people trapped in a situation from which they are unable to escape. At the Ribicoff hearings, Bayard Rustin, executive director of the A. Philip Randolph Institute, discussed the despair and desperation of ghetto adolescents:

There are 77,000 young people between 16 and 25 in New York for whom Mayor Wagner said there is no work in New York. Mayor Lindsay has not created any work for them, but I am not blaming him. . . . Why should there not be dropouts when young people know for one thing that the school system giving them a general diploma is preparing them for absolutely nothing? . . . Or how can they be excited if the likelihood of the best jobs many young Negroes in New York can get is pushing a hand-truck through the garment district, a job which has no future, a job which does not provide them with the necessary things of life, particularly in a society where the mass media tell them that they must have the things they do not need? Imagine a pimply-faced 15-year old boy being

9 Quoted in *ibid.*, pp. 13-14.
10 *Ibid.*, pp. 178-79.

told by television that if he doesn't use X perfume he will not get a girl.
... There is not only among Negroes but among all youth a feeling of
"What is the use? You will not make it anyhow. There are no jobs out
there anyhow."[11]

Poverty, therefore, does more than render the subproletariat
sick and illiterate; it stunts and shrivels personhood. This, Paul
Henly Furfey begs us to bear in mind, is "the essential tragedy
of the slums. To be fully human, one's spiritual and mental   capacity must attain a certain fruition. The life that falls short of this
goal is, to that extent, a failure. In the slums, this human failure
is usually overwhelming, withering, disastrous."[12]

So far, we have failed to touch upon an excruciating problem
intertwined with that of poverty—America's dilemma, Gunnar
Myrdal termed it years ago—the problem of racism. To be white
and poor is bad enough; to be black and poor is to compound
misery and frustration. Yes, statistics are boring, and we are busy
people, busy with the pastimes of a luxury liner that may soon
have gaping holes in its hull. Nonetheless, these boring statistics, cited by Justice Douglas, ought to grip our attention:

In recent years two out of three Negro families have earned less than
$4,000 a year, as opposed to only 27 percent of the Whites. Only one out
of five Negro families has made $6,000 or more as opposed to one out of
two White families. The chance of a Negro, aged 24, making $3,000 or
more a year is 41 percent while the chance of a 24-year-old White is 78
percent. In April, 1968, only 3.5 percent of the general population were
unemployed, while for those in the slum areas it was 7 percent, with 5.7
percent for Whites and 8.7 percent for Negroes. The national White unemployment rate has been about 3.1 percent and the national Negro
unemployment rate 6.7 percent. [13]

Or shall we let Truman Nelson's description of Harlem, with
its counterparts in Detroit and Watts and Newark, occupy our
attention for a little while?

A day in the life of Harlem is enough to convince most Americans that
there are no answers to this degradation in any present political appara-

11 Quoted in *ibid.*, 157-58.
12 Paul Henly Furfey, *The Respectable Murderers: Social Evil and Christian
Conscience* (New York: Herder & Herder, 1966), p. 101.
13 Douglas, *op. cit.*, p. 45.

tus. It has been a sociological disaster area for generations, and it is getting worse at a frenzied rate. There are certain fixed conditions that everyone knows about. Five hundred thousand black people in one of the most congested areas in the world, with one hospital, grossly inferior schools, the highest rents in the worst buildings, the highest prices for the worst food, the highest rate of unemployment, the lowest grade of service from public agencies, and lately a refusal from the Congress of the United States to seat the Congressman the people in Harlem elected by an overwhelming majority. These, and other visible human indignities, have become the standard description of the Harlem area. [14]

Add to all of this the horrifying injustice which has been and still is the experience of the American Negro. Shall we take still some more time to let Nelson, who, by the way, is a well-known novelist and historian, help us catch a glimpse of black reality through the eyes of Negro militant Robert Williams when he was living in Monroe, North Carolina?

He saw a white man escaping a Grand Jury indictment in the face of the brutal fact that this man had kicked a Negro chambermaid down four flights of stairs because she had made a clatter with her wash pail when he was trying to sleep . . . kicked and cuffed her down the stairs and across the landing so roughly that she had to remain in the hospital several months. He saw an epileptic black man given two to five years for attempted rape for touching the wrist of a white woman during an argument over a tractor. He heard a white woman testify that she saw a white man come into a corn-field drunk and attempt to rape a black woman eight months pregnant, in her presence. Williams heard the white jury acquit the assaulter almost without stirring in their seats. He saw, transpiring before his eyes, acts of atrocity which in other lands, other times, and even in this land, move men to the breaking point. [15]

Can those of us who are busy, bourgeois, and well-meaning whites feel the resentment, the bitterness, the hate which well up in blacks trapped in a quagmire of poverty and injustice in our free, opulent, equalitarian society? Can we empathize with the excruciating emotions produced by the contradiction they experience between possibility and reality? Cook catches something of the mood which eventually inspires revolution.

[14] Nelson, *op. cit.*, p. 55.
[15] *Ibid.*, pp. 87-88.

You can sit before your television set and watch Jim Dooley wave his arms and call, "C'mon down to sunny Florida." You can see a golden Yellow Bird take off into an encarmined sky. You can see the waving palms and the sunlit blue water of Hawaii or the isles of the Caribbean, and you can listen to the pitch that tells you it is a beautiful, beautiful world—and come on, don't be an old stick-in-the-mud, have yourself a wonderful vacation on your American Express credit card. Enjoy now, pay later. You see all this, you hear all this, and you live in Watts or Hough or the ghetto of Newark; you cannot get a job and, if you could get one, it pays less than relief. The world of affluent America, the world of all those happy people "out there" who have it "made," swears at you and mocks you. And if it is pure inescapable hell, it is no wonder.[16]

So even those of us who are busy, bourgeois, and well-meaning whites may now be starting to realize why another Negro militant, William Epton, says, "We will go on and do all these things that we can do till we hope there's a revolution in this country and we do have socialism."[17]

Perhaps we are also starting to realize why a revolutionary mood has been developing among a surprisingly large number of American whites, adult as well as young, Christian as well as secular. They agree with Henry Clark: "The outrageousness of the injustice that pervades this society is enough to justify a literal war on poverty, and anyone who does not see this is either a fool or a knave."[18] John Gerassi may deepen our empathy with their bitter antagonism toward the Establishment.

What bugs the New Left is that it knows no one *needs* to go hungry; that it is precisely institutionalized greed which keeps so many millions hungry. The New Left understands that our system, based on profits, must by necessity exploit some to make others rich, and that this exploitation leads inevitably to Viet Nam, the Dominican Republic, the Congo, South Africa, Indonesia, Watts, Detroit, the assassination of Martin Luther King, etc.[19]

But the indictment against American society to which we have

---

[16] Cook, *op. cit*, pp. 141-42.

[17] Quoted by Nelson, *op. cit.*, p. 73.

[18] Henry Clark, "The Student Revolt as a Just War," *Perspective*, Spring, 1969, p. 40.

[19] John Gerassi, "Violence, Revolution, and Morality," *Perspective*, Spring, 1969, p. 55.

been listening is not yet through. Thus far it has been limited to domestic difficulties and internal issues. It reaches out beyond our shores, however, to the ends of the earth. Our country, the charge runs, is guilty of ruthless, bloody imperialism on a planetary scale. Uncle Sam is Uncle Sham, perpetrator of injustice, enemy of freedom, a self-seeking, self-righteous tyrant whose tyranny is camouflaged by professed commitment to freedom, morality, and religion. Take, for instance, the article by Dr. Gerassi which has just been quoted. Now professor of international relations in San Francisco State University, he is a responsible scholar, formerly Latin-American editor for *Time, Newsweek,* and *Ramparts,* as well as Latin-American correspondent for *The New York Times.* "One could logically infer," he alleges, "that the United States is responsible for the unnatural or premature death of 100 million people every year on this planet." Hence he maintains that

to the world at large, especially to the 'Third World,' to the ghettos of America, to the unemployed or underemployed Chicanos of New Mexico, the bastion of injustice is the United States. Thus it resorts to more violence than ever before and thus too the revolutionaries who must try to bring it down use more counter-violence than ever before.[20]

In its crusade against Communism—really in defense and development of its own interests or at least the interests of economy-controlling industrial and commercial combines—our country, we are told, has built up the most formidable military establishment in history. This vast power is being deployed in keeping with what Carl Oglesby singles out as "the central preoccupation of American statecraft."

And that prime problem—the main nut and kernel of the American foreign policy from its earliest days onwards—is to ensure the availability of fertile frontiers to American business. The economic doors must be open; the survival of our system depends upon it. . . . Put it roughly: For us peace finally exists when the world is finally safe for American businessmen to carry on their business everywhere, on terms as favorable as they can be made, in settings managed preferably by native middle-class governments, but if need be by oligarchic and repressive ones, by the old

[20] *Ibid.,* pp. 53, 51.

foreign grads of Fort Bragg, or if the panic hits in a pivotal place, by our own Marines.[21]

In support of his contention that American policy is that of deploying its military power to protect and promote its economic interests, Oglesby quotes "three outbursts of exemplary candor":

First, from a 1938 report authored by the United States Office of Naval Intelligence: "Realistically, all wars have been fought for economic reasons. To make them politically and socially palatable, idealogical issues have always been invoked. Any possible future war will, undoubtedly, conform to historical precedent."

Second, Senator Arthur Vandenberg's belief that to win their acceptance of a militant and expensive Cold War policy it would be necessary "to scare hell out of the American people."

Third, the testimony of General Douglas MacArthur:

Talk of imminent threat to our national security through the application of external force is pure nonsense. ... Indeed, it is part of the general pattern of misguided policy that our country is now geared to an arms economy which was bred in an artificially induced psychosis of war hysteria and nurtured upon an incessant propaganda of fear. While such an economy may produce a sense of seeming prosperity for a moment, it rests on an illusory foundation of complete unreliability and renders among our political leaders almost a greater fear of peace than is their fear of war.[22]

In brief, Oglesby contends that the United States is not a global benefactor, doling out largess to encourage underdeveloped nations in attaining their own levels of affluence. On the contrary, our country is a self-appointed planetary policeman, intervening at will by financial pressure or armed force in the internal affairs of smaller countries and doing this solely for the sake of *Realpolitik*. Itself born of revolution, it now opposes revolution under the pretense of preventing Communist take-overs. Meanwhile it supports reactionary governments which are oppressing their own people—the Franco regime in Spain, to mention a notorious case.

[21] Carl Oglesby, "Vietnamese Crucible," in Carl Oglesby and Richard Shaull, *Containment and Change: Two Dissenting Views of American Society and Foreign Policy in the New Revolutionary Age* (New York: The Macmillan Company, 1967), pp. 70-71.

[22] *Ibid.*, pp. 165-66.

Oglesby does not stand alone in his indictment of America's imperialistic arrogance, disguised as anti-Communist. World-renowned historian Arnold Toynbee levels the same indictment, an indictment to which his unbiased perspective and immense prestige lend compelling significance.

America is today the leader of anti-revolutionary movement in defense of vested interests. She now stands for what Rome stood for. Rome consistently supported the rich against the poor in all foreign communities that fell under her sway: and, since the poor, so far, have always and everywhere been far more numerous than the rich, Rome's policy made for inequality, for injustice, and for the least happiness of the greatest number. America's decision to adopt Rome's role has been deliberate, if I have gauged it right. ... Since 1917, America has reversed her role in the World. She has become the arch-conservative power instead of the arch-revolutionary one. ... Affluence is estranging America from her own ideals. It is pushing her into the position of being the leader of the very opposite of what America's World Revolution stands for. It is pushing her into becoming the policeman standing guard over vested interests. ... So, on the issue of social justice, where does the United States stand today? This question is a world-wide one. ... Beneficiaries ask themselves every time that the United States makes a motion to aid them, "Is the United States a sincere convert to the cause of social justice, or is this just another transparent maneuver in defense of the vested interest of the United States herself and the rest of the tiny affluent and satiated minority of mankind? Is the United States perhaps just doling out a minimum installment of alimony to us as a less unpleasant alternative than 'the wrath to come'?"[23]

If the criticism of a British outsider is resented, what about the criticism of an insider, our own distinguished historian, Henry Steele Commager, testifying before the Senate Foreign Relations Committee?

We think we are better than other nations and doubtless in some respects we are. ... Yet even in domestic affairs we have not been beyond criticism; when we speak, as we often do, of communist slavery we might remember that we retained legal slavery after other civilized nations had abandoned it. ... We are distinctly parochial in our attitude toward expansionism, aggression, and imperialism. ... In the eyes of the 19th-

[23] Arnold J. Toynbee, *America and the World Revolution* (New York: Oxford University Press, 1962), pp. 92-93, 102, 210; *cf.* pp. 214-30.

century world, the U.S. was pre-eminently an expansionist and aggressive nation, ... trebling our territory at the expense of France, Spain, Mexico and Britain. Our President, through the Monroe and Polk Doctrines, proclaimed American hegemony in the Western hemisphere. If China today should put on a show of this kind we might truly be alarmed ... we claimed a vital interest in Vietnam but did not tolerate a Soviet claim to vital interest in Cuba or a Chinese claim to vital interest in South Vietnam. We assert a sphere of influence in the Caribbean but will not concede to China a comparable sphere of influence in South-east Asia. We feel justified in intervening in the domestic affairs of Guatemala and the Dominican Republic but would be surprised if Cuba intervened in Florida or Mexico or Texas. Our President called it a "dark day" when China exploded a nuclear bomb. We forget that so far we are the only nation to use the atomic bomb in anger, though it must not be supposed that the Japanese have forgotten—or that the Chinese will forget our 17 years of implacable hostility, or the Vietnamese our bombing. We have allowed ourselves to drift into the position of champion of the status quo ... most of the world looks upon us today as the leading opponent of revolutionary change. ... The revolt of Asia and Africa against the West and the emergence into modernity of two-thirds of the world's peoples is probably the greatest revolution since the discovery of America.[24]

Thus the critics of twentieth-century America, in constructing their case for revolutionary change, point out that our country has come under the domination of a military-industrial complex which controls education, science, and government for its own ends, and those ends involve injustice, war, and the threat of genocide. Which is to say that the United States has fallen victim to the very danger against which President Eisenhower warned in his 1961 Farewell Address:

We annually spend on military defense alone more than the net income of all U.S. corporations. ... This conjunction of an immense military establishment and the large arms industry is new in the American experience. The total influence—economic, political, even spiritual—is felt in every city, every statehouse, every office of the Federal Government. ... We must not fail to comprehend its great implications. ... In the councils of government we must guard against the acquisition of unwarranted influence, whether sought or unsought, by the military-industrial complex.

[24] Quoted by N. Emorey, *A Serious Call to an American (R)Evolution* (New Haven, Conn.; Bulldog Books, 1967), pp. 59-60.

The potential for the disastrous rise of misplaced power exists and will persist.[25]

Which is to say, moreover, that we are squandering astronomical sums on the Pentagon's death machine and by comparison pennies for the agonizing needs of our society.

All the criticism to which we have been listening moves toward one upsetting conclusion. America is getting ripe for revolution. It is to be hoped that this revolution will be what Justice Douglas is pleading for, "a vast restructuring of our society" by an aroused public utilizing our political resources. But Douglas warns us that armed violence is not improbable if no "vast restructuring" occurs:

George III was the symbol against which our founders made a revolution now considered bright and glorious. George III had not crossed the seas to fasten a foreign yoke on us. George III and his dynasty had established and nurtured us and all that he did was by no means oppressive. But a vast restructuring of laws and institutions was necessary if the people were to be content. That restructuring was not forthcoming and there was a revolution. We must realize that today's Establishment is the new George III. Whether it will continue to adhere to his tactics, we do not know. If it does, the redress, honored in tradition, is also revolution.[26]

Richard Shaull has little hope, however, that the American Establishment will turn out to be a far-sighted, repentant George III.

What makes the present situation so revolutionary among the younger generation is their discovery that when they begin to work for change at any specific point, they are confronted by a total system—a complex of attitudes, institutions, relations, and power alignments—which block fundamental changes in society. Under these circumstances we should not be surprised if the new revolutionaries conclude that the established order is incapable of bringing about the changes now demanded and no longer trust in the traditional means of working for social transformation.[27]

Michael Novak shares Shaull's pessimism. The "mainstream

[25] Quoted in *ibid:*, pp. 56-57.
[26] Douglas, *op. cit.*, p. 95; *cf.* p. 56.
[27] Richard Shaull, "Revolution: Heritage and Contemporary Option," *Containment and Change*, pp. 188-90.

of American opinion," he fears, is complacently "racist, counter-revolutionary, and militarist."

More exactly, American opinion seems in recent years to be showing signs of uneasiness—and symptoms of a bad conscience—but the policies espoused by government officials of nation, state, and city seem to be policies of repression. What many Americans see as the matter of great urgency is to silence "outside agitators," "pseudo-intellectuals," and "other troublemakers." Few seem willing to face matters as they are, and to begin the necessary changes. .... The conclusion of this line of reasoning is that evolution is not sufficient; there must be a fundamental change in direction. Those who propound this more radical analysis wish to differentiate it from the liberal pragmatic analysis which is evolutionary. The only word which remains at hand, once evolution is rejected, is "revolution."[28]

Richard Neuhaus is likewise persuaded that some kind of revolution must be engineered. He personally endorses the slogan repeated "by devotees of flower power and gunpowder alike," the slogan "preached at the pulpits of prestigious churches by black men demanding reparations and in the pulpits of student revolutionary caucuses," the slogan which "infiltrates itself into the literature of organizations founded for liberal uplift." That slogan is "The System itself must be radically changed." Revolution is imperative because reform, Neuhaus suspects, is impossible.

The decision for revolution is made at the point where it becomes inescapably clear that no amount of political activism, protest or pressure—legal or extra-legal—can make this constitutional order work to the benefit of American citizens and millions of others who are under the sway of American power.[29]

He himself thinks that our society does not have the capacity for radical change. So melodramatically he declaims, "The stage is set and the casting offices have announced auditions for the event of the season, 'Revolution'."[30]

If Neuhaus' conclusion is not melodramatic enough—though

---

[28] Novak, *op. cit.*, pp. 69-70.
[29] Neuhaus, *op. cit.*, p. 194.
[30] *Ibid.*, pp. 96, 194, 132. Cf. pp. 128-29, 195-203 where Neuhaus attempts to justify his skepticism concerning America's capacity for reform.

we must realize that he writes in grim seriousness—here is John Gerassi's manifesto, issued ostensibly in the name of under-thirty insurrectionists:

America ... is a dictatorship. It is a closed society. It is an oppressive society. It is a violent society. ... American "democracy" with its "free" speech and "free" press is part and parcel of American society, a society based on greed, competition, oppressions, and, increasingly more evident, murder, invasion, occupation. It must be stopped precisely because of its inherent violence. It must be destroyed. And the only way to do that is by smashing it through counter-violence.[31]

[31] Gerassi, *op. cit.*, pp. 58-59.

The American Revolution has made a declaration of the spiritual rights of Man. But this American shot would not have been heard round the World if the charge of powder had not been a mighty one. What is this mighty force that has sent that sound rolling round and round the circumference of the planet? The impetus behind the American Revolution is the spirit of Christianity; the sound is the voice of God which speaks not only through Christianity but through all the historic religions which have preached their gospels to all the World and which, between them, have reached almost the whole of mankind. . . .

What, then, is America's relation to the World Revolution? It is her revolution; it was she who launched it by firing that shot heard round the World. What about America's recently acquired affluence? It is a handicap, and a formidable one, but it is a handicap that can be overcome. Can America rejoin her own revolution? In my belief, this is still within her power. America's destiny is, I believe, still in America's own hands.

—Arnold Toynbee

IV. A Revolutionary Tradition

With the tocsin sounding in our ears we who are Christians may be motivated piously to beseech God that it will prove a false alarm. For revolution, we know, is not a tidy, bloodless affair; it is not a surgically implemented *coup d'état* with no killing and horror. One may argue that the gruesome butchery of the Terror in Paris under Robespierre was a ghastly exception, but the argument fails to convince. Terrorism is as characteristic of revolution as saltiness is of the sea.

Shrinking back, then, from the cruelty and carnage of insurrectionary struggle, we may wish that we could somehow rewrite history and, without losing any of our present privileges, blot out our nation's revolutionary past. Of course, it is possible to present a plausible case that our War of Independence was entirely atypical of revolutions, the sole revolution in all history which has carried the divine imprimatur. Thus the late Donald Grey Barnhouse in his multivolume commentary on the Letter to the Romans questions whether or not a Christian in 1776 should have supported George Washington, a lawbreaking rebel, and opposed George III, a legitimate monarch. After all, the inspired apostle solemnly instructs his readers that God commands submission to the powers that be. What solution does Barnhouse, an evangelical, propose to this spiritual problem which faced our forefathers?

A Christian in France or Russia could never have sympathized with the godless upheavals in those countries. What part could a believer in Christ have had in the riots of Paris, the enthronement of a nude harlot as goddess on the altar of the church, and the murders of 1793? Or what part could a believer have had in the purges of millions by the Communists in Russia, the Ukraine, and Hungary?

In the American colonies there were godly men who did not move without prayer and waiting on the Lord. As late as July 1775, the Congress sent another address to the King which has been called "The Olive Branch." In this the leaders of the colonies expressed dismay at the disturbance of peaceful relations by the forces of Parliament.[1]

In his argument Barnhouse appeals to Frederick Von Gentz's essay, "The French and American Revolutions Compared," which John Quincy Adams translated from the German. Gentz says,

The revolution of America was, therefore, in every sense of the word, a revolution of necessity: England, alone, had by violence effected it: America had contended ten long years, not against England, but against the revolution; America sought not a revolution; she yielded to it, compelled by necessity, not because she wished to extort a better condition than she had before enjoyed, but because she wished to avert a worse one, prepared for her.[2]

So Barnhouse concludes that the American Revolution was a providential breakthrough.

Undoubtedly, God so ordered events in England that the creation of a new nation was forced upon the Colonists in America. The founders of our nation were believers in the Lord Jesus Christ and followers of the Christian ethic. They reached decision with deep agony of soul lest they should veer from moral righteousness. But we must have equal sympathy for those true believers who held that it was their Christian duty to remain faithful to the King.[3]

In other words, the colonial revolutionists were the agents of a supernatural wisdom and power; they "were forced" to create a

---

[1] Donald Grey Barnhouse, *God's Discipline: Romans 12:1-14:12, Exposition of Bible Doctrines*, vol. 9 (Grand Rapids, Mich.: William B. Eerdmans Publishing Co., 1964), pp. 110-11. Gentz' essay was reissued by the Henry Regnery Company of Chicago in 1959. The gist of his position may be found on pp. 35, 52, 63, 67, 75, 81, 84, 85, 99. No Christian and no theist, Hannah Arendt approaches the American Revolution from a standpoint antithetical to that of Barnhouse, yet she too avers that it was astonishingly unique. *Cf. op. cit.*, pp. 62-63, 90, 108, 114-15, 124-25, 131-32, 145 ff., 155-57, 267.

[2] Quoted in *ibid.*

[3] *Ibid.*

republic "dedicated to the proposition that all men are created equal."[4]

A providential breakthrough perhaps, the War of Independence was nevertheless a bloody insurrection, and as such it postulated the right of revolution as the ultimate foundation of all civil rights. That right which lies, then, at the origin of our national existence is a right which in the revolutionary twilight of the twentieth century we may wish to deny, forget, or minimize. But if, as Rap Brown claims, violence is as American as cherry pie, so too is revolution. It is our birthright—our basic right. In the words of Arthur Schlesinger, among America's benefactions to the world.

First and foremost stands the concept of the inherent and universal right of revolution ... proclaimed in the Declaration of Independence: the doctrine that "all men are created equal ... possessing inalienable rights to life, liberty and the pursuit of happiness" with the corollary that governments derive their just powers from the consent of the governed, and that therefore the people have the right to supplant any government "destructive of these ends" with one they believe most likely to effect their safety and happiness. True, the history of England provided precedence to the men of 1776, and the Age of Enlightenment supplied intellectual support; but the flaming pronouncement, followed by its vindication on the battlefield, made the doctrine ever afterwards an irrepressible agency in the course of human events. [5]

Since 1945, this concept, Justice Douglas laments, has "become almost subversive,"[6] yet to repudiate the right of revolution is to repudiate the heritage in which we as Americans glory. We cannot deny this right without drastically overhauling much of our own secular hagiography. Who, for example, said this? "The tree of liberty must be refreshed from time to time with the blood of patriots and tyrants. It is its natural manure." That was said by Thomas Jefferson, the third president of the United States, who also said, when the news of Shay's uprising reached him in Paris,

---

[4] *Ibid.*

[5] Quoted by Nelson, *op. cit.*, p. 38.

[6] William O. Douglas, *The U.S. and Revolution, an Occasional Paper on the Free Society* (Santa Barbara, Calif.: The Center for the Study of Democratic Institutions, 1961), p. 8.

"God forbid that we should ever be twenty years without a rebellion." **7**

Jefferson's opinion was also that of another '76 insurrectionist, John Adams, who preceded Jefferson in the Presidency. "It is an observation of one of the profoundest inquiries into human affairs that a revolution of government is the strongest proof that can be given by a people, of their virtue and good sense." **8**

John Quincy Adams, who later succeeded his father in the Presidency and who had earlier in his life served as Jefferson's secretary, spent sixteen years in the House of Representatives following his term as Chief Executive from 1825 to 1829. There he fought valiantly against the freedom-denying institution of slavery. At the age of seventy-four he was accused of high treason by his Southern opponents. With admirable courage and over-whelming logic he defended himself. What follows is a much-abbreviated transcript of his speech during the second session of the Twenty-seventh Congress in 1842.

I am not surprised that the charge has been brought against me of high treason. What is high treason? The Constitution defines what high treason is, and it is not for him or his puny mind, to define what high treason is and confound it with what I have done. Sir, the first volume of the laws of the United States will show what it is. I desire the clerk to read the first paragraph of the Declaration of Independence. [Raising his voice.] The first paragraph of the Declaration of Independence. [Raising his voice to a still higher pitch.] The first paragraph of the Declaration of Independence! **9**

The clerk then read that paragraph, and Adams continued his address.

"The right of the people to alter or to abolish it." Now, Sir, if there is a principle sacred on earth and established by the instrument just read,

---

7 Quoted by Arendt, *op. cit.*, p. 236. In his later years, Arendt reminds us, Jefferson was more likely to speak, however, about "the dreadful necessity of revolution" (*ibid.*, p. 321). But D.W. Brogan's verdict seems indisputable: until he died, Jefferson "continued to hold his semi-anarchical views, to hold that the dead could not bind the living, that revolutions were always respectable and prob-ably necessary political activities." D.W. Brogan, *The Price of Revolution* (New York: Harper & Brothers, 1951), p. 4.

8 Quoted by Nelson, *op. cit.*, pp. 46-47.

9 Quoted in *ibid*.

it is the right of the people to alter, to change, to destroy the Government if it becomes oppressive to them. There would be no such right existing, if the people had not the power, in pursuance of that right to petition for it.

When I come to make my defense before the House, I shall show other oppressions, not only actual, but intended. I shall show that the portion of the country from which the gentleman comes are endeavoring to destroy the right of habeas corpus, the right of trial by jury, and all the rights of which the liberty of this country exists ... and that there is a continued system and purpose to destroy all the principle of civil liberty in the free states, not for the purpose of preserving their institutions within their own limits, but to force their detested principles of slavery into all the free states. I will show that measures are systematically pursued or projected to force this Country into war. This is the state of things that exists and it is provided for in the Declaration of Independence; and if there is no other remedy for it, it is the right and duty of the people of that portion of the Union to take that remedy. [10]

A still later President, Abraham Lincoln, acknowledged the right of revolution in his first inaugural address: "This country with its institutions, belongs to the people who inhabit it. Whenever they shall grow weary of the existing government, they can exercise their constitutional right to amend it, or the revolutionary right to dismember or overthrow it." [11]

General U. S. Grant, also one of our Presidents, repeated Lincoln's dictum:

The right of Revolution is an inherent one. When people are oppressed by their government, it is a natural right they enjoy to relieve themselves of the oppression if they are strong enough, either by withdrawing from it, or by overthrowing it and substituting a government more acceptable. [12]

This right, then, stated explicitly in the Declaration of Independence, and restated by a succession of eminent Americans, repeatedly has been accorded legal status. Thus the Maryland Declaration of Rights affirms:

Whenever the ends of government are perverted, and public liberty

10 Quoted in *ibid.*, pp. 128-30.
11 Quoted in *ibid.*, p. 45.
12 Quoted in *ibid.*, p. 47.

manifestly endangered, and all of the means of redress are ineffectual, the people may, and of right ought to, reform the old or establish a new government: the doctrine of non-resistance against arbitrary power and oppression is absurd, slavish and destructive of the good and happiness of mankind.[13]

The Pennsylvania Court has similarly asserted that a change in government of that state may be effected in one of three ways:

The words "in such manner as they may think proper" in the declaration of rights, embrace but three known recognized modes by which the whole people, the state, can give their consent to an alteration of an existing lawful frame of government, viz:
1) The mode provided in the existing constitution.
2) A law, as the instrumental process of raising the body for revision and conveying to it the powers of the people.
3) A *revolution*.
The first two are peaceful means through which the consent of the people to alteration is obtained, and by which the existing government consents to be displaced without revolution. The government gives its consent, either by pursuing the mode provided in the constitution, or by passing a law to call a convention. If consent be not so given by the existing government the remedy of the people is in the third mode—revolution.[14]

In 1950 Supreme Court Justice Jackson reasserted and reemphasized this right as grounded in the Declaration of Independence.

We cannot ignore the fact that our own government originated in revolution, and is legitimate only if overthrow by force can sometimes be justified. That circumstances sometimes justify it is not Communist doctrine, but an old American belief. The men who led the struggle forcibly to overthrow lawfully constituted British authority found moral support by asserting natural law under which their revolution was justified, and they bravely proclaimed their belief in the document basic to our freedom. Such sentiments have also been given a rather extravagant expression by Americans of undoubted patriotism.[15]

This litanylike recital may seem unduly repetitious, but the sheer multiplication of such pronouncements may serve to keep in the forefront of our thinking a fact we might prefer to forget.

[13] Quoted in *ibid.*
[14] Quoted by Douglas, *The U. S. and Revolution*, pp. 7-8.
[15] Quoted in Nelson, *op. cit.*, p. 48.

America is founded not simply on the Constitution but on the right to change that Constitution by revolution. So discussing the perfectibility of constitutions, Jefferson wrote, "Can they be made unchangeable? I think not. ... Nothing is unchangeable but the inherent and unalienable rights of man." And among these Jefferson unquestionably included the right of revolution.[16]

Let a distinguished British scholar, Lord Acton, instruct us as Americans concerning the unique foundation of our democracy:

The story of the revolted colonies impresses us first and most distinctly as the supreme manifestation of the law of resistance, as the abstract revolution in its purest and most perfect shape. ... It teaches that men ought to be in arms even against a remote and constructive danger to their freedom; that even if the cloud is no bigger than a man's hand, it is their right and duty to stake the national existence, to sacrifice lives and fortunes, to cover the country with a lake of blood, to shatter crowns and scepters and fling parliaments into the sea. On this principle of subversion they erected their commonwealth, and by its virtue lifted the world out of its orbit and designed a new course to history.[17]

This foundational principle of our national existence did not, however, spring up full-blown on American soil by a kind of spontaneous generation. It was a transplant from England, the product of a deep-rooted political and theological tradition. One of its sources was Enlightenment rationalism, French and German as well as English. Thus in arguing their case against the repressive actions of George III, colonial apologists quote profusely from Voltaire, Rousseau, Beccaria, Montesquieu, Grotius, Pufendorf, Burlamaqui, and Vattel. As Bernard Bailyn remarks, "The pervasiveness of such citations is at times astonishing."[18] Another of its roots was British common law as developed by justices like Edward Coke, Matthew Hale, John Vaughan, and John Holt, to say nothing of William Blackstone in his venerated *Commentaries*.[19]

But the chief and all-important root of colonial theory was sec-

[16] Quoted by Arendt, *op. cit.*, p. 236.

[17] Quoted by D. W. Brogan, *op. cit.*, pp. 268-69.

[18] Bernard Bailyn, *The Ideological Origins of the American Revolution* (Cambridge, Mass.: Harvard University Press, 1967), p. 27.

[19] *Cf.* Bailyn's discussion, *ibid.*, pp. 30-31.

tarian Protestantism as it flowered out in New World offshoots. During the revolutionary seventeenth century especially, interminable discussion of political issues went on among English subjects who are by no means uncritically loyal or docilely obedient. There were debates, pamphlets, sermons, and more sermons. It has been estimated that in Welsh and English parishes 340,000 sermons, many dealing with public issues, were delivered from 1600 until the time of the Puritan Revolution, which began in 1642 and culminated with the execution of Charles I in 1649.[20] In the 1640's alone, two hundred homilies were given before Parliament and subsequently published. A sizable segment of this pulpiteering was devoted to the exploration of a multifaceted problem: to what degree does compliance with divine law require compliance with the laws of a *de facto* monarchy? Using theology polemically, Levellers, Fifth Monarchists, Quakers, Ranters, Independents, and Puritans attacked the established church. Though these radical Protestants differed among themselves on a host of points, they agreed that Anglican ecclesiasticism was biblically aberrant, grossly so. Their attacks against the sacerdotal order rapidly broadened to include the political order. Hence the sovereign who was patron and protector of the sacerdotal order became inevitably the focus of attack. Thus in a 1641 sermon Samuel Faircloth made a bold assertion: "The divine policy and heavenly remedy, to recover a commonwealth and church ... endangered, is that those that have authority under God totally abolish and extirpate all the cursed things whereby it may be disturbed."[21] As to who might "have authority under God" to destroy illegally legal saboteurs of the order scripturally revealed, that was scarcely an issue. Obedience to the divine Ruler endowed believers with the right of disobedience to any human ruler.

Three years later, Stephen Marshall, preaching before both Houses of Parliament, commanded soldiers to remember that in battling against their king they were actually doing combat against the forces of Antichrist:

---

20 *Cf.* Michael Walzer, *The Revolution of the Saints: A Study in the Origins of Radical Politics* (Cambridge, Mass.: Harvard University Press, 1965), p. 32.

21 Quoted in *ibid.*, p. 296.

Go now and fight the battles of the Lord ... for so I will not now fear to call them ... although indeed at the first nothing clearly appeared but only that you were compelled to take up arms for the defense of your liberties. ... All Christendom ... do now see that the question in England is whether Christ or Anti-Christ shall be lord or king. [22]

It was Marshall, again, who in 1649 exhorted his fellow believers to support the holy crusade of the Cromwellian Roundheads or suffer God's wrath: "All people are cursed or blessed according as they do or do not join their strength and give their best assistance to the Lord's people against their enemies."[23]

That same year John Goodwin argued analogically that Parliament might justly be purged and a king legitimately brought to trial:

When the pilot or master of the ship at sea be either so far overcome and distempered with drink or otherwise disabled ... so that he is incapable of acting the exigencies of his place, for the preservation of the ship, being now in present danger ... any one or more of the inferior mariners, having skill, may, in order to the saving of the ship and of the lives of all that are in it, very lawfully assume, and act according to the interests of a pilot. [24]

Appealing, therefore, not alone to logic but primarily to the Word of God, these Puritan seditionists mounted a sustained onslaught against a government which, as they saw it, had forfeited divine sanction. Dedicated to the overthrow of an unbiblical, unjust, ungodly tyranny, saints could be seditionists. Indeed, in the face of tyranny, to be a saint one must be a seditionist. Thus Walzer thinks Protestant sectarianism, and Puritanism particularly, "made revolution available to the minds of seventeenth-century Englishmen as it had never been before."[25]

It was this tradition, then, which decisively influenced the

[22] *Ibid.*, p. 295.
[23] Quoted in *ibid.*, p. 294.
[24] Quoted in *ibid.*, p. 181.
[25] *Ibid.*, p. 290. Thomas Hobbes, reflecting on the savagery of civil war, was prompted to inquire: "Had it not been much better that these seditious ministers, which were not perhaps one thousand. had been all killed before they had preached? It had been, I confess, a great massacre, but the killing of 100,000 is a greater one." Quoted in *ibid.*, p. 114.

American colonists. They were descendants of ideological fore-
bears who, after executing Charles I, had in the Glorious Revolution of 1688 driven James II to France as an exile. They were not
ready to acknowledge supinely the divine right of a king to govern
wrong. On the contrary, they held that any regime which per-
sisted in flagrant wrong lost its right to remain in power.
Furthermore, it was the divine right of a people suffering wrong
to oppose and depose a regime which by wrongdoing had become
illicit. Obedience to God, they contended, might demand action
beyond passive disobedience to an ungodly ruler, it might demand revolution. So in 1750 Jonathan Mayhew in his notable
"Discourse Concerning Unlimited Submission" summarized the
philosophy which led eventually to the Boston Tea Party, the
battle of Concord, and the Declaration of Independence. Lucidly
he stated the issue under debate: "Whether we are obliged to
yield an absolute submission to our prince, or whether disobedience and resistance may not be justifiable in some cases." To be
sure, he said, submission is required, but it is not absolute and
unqualified. God does not require submission "to all who bear
the *title* of rulers in common, but only to those who *actually*
perform the duty of rulers, by exercising a reasonable and just
authority for the good of human society." Instead of rendering
absolute and unqualified submission to any *de facto* government,
we sometimes may be constrained to disobey: "A regard to the
public welfare ought to make us withhold from our rulers that
obedience and subjection which it would, otherwise, be our duty
to render to them." To obey tyranny is to promote "slavery and
misery."

For a nation thus abused to arise unanimously and to resist their prince,
even to dethroning him, is not criminal, but a reasonable way of vindicat-
ing their liberties and just rights; it is making use of the means, and the
only means, which God has put into their power, for mutual and self-
defense. And it would be highly criminal in them not to make use of this
means. It would be stupid tameness and unaccountable folly for whole
nations to suffer *one* unreasonable ambitious and cruel man to wanton
and riot in their misery. And in such a case it would, of the two, be more
rational to suppose that they who did NOT resist (rather) than that they
who did, would *receive to themselves damnation* [26]

[26] Quoted by Bailyn, *op. cit.*, pp. 92-93.

In a word, Mayhew argued and his fellow colonists with him, revolution is a right and even more than a right. In the ongoing of events it may become a God-required responsibility. John Bradshaw put this philosophy in an epigram: "Rebellion to tyrants is obedience to God." And of necessity resistance may sometimes be armed and violent.

As twentieth-century Americans, particularly if we are of evangelical belief, we may regard this component of our national heritage, grounded deeply in Protestantism, as a skeleton in the family closet. Defenders of our comfortable way of life, we may recoil in fear and horror from the thought of subversion. Yet, unless we dishonestly manipulate the historical data, we cannot deny that revolution, both as right and responsibility, is a foundational principle of this republic "under God."

Must I not rather accept and understand Christian love as an unconditioned and selfless will and an unquestioning resoluteness for justice and freedom for others? ... Revolution is not at all a question of the relation of one person to another, but of structures and relations within society, which in themselves can be objectively unjust; and in cases where a social situation contains at least as much injustice as may be expected to arise if the situation is gotten rid of by revolution, such a revolution for the removal of the unbearable misery of the other, the least among the brethren, cannot be against Christian love. To this moralizing of the phenomenon of revolutionary violence there corresponds indeed likewise an individualizing of Christian virtues, above all that of love. Christian love comes to be seen for the most part as a strongly interpersonal something, only to be found in the I-Thou relation, or as a form of charitable helping of the neighbor. But must it not also and above all be conceived ... as the unconditioned will to procure justice for others; and is it not also oriented as such directly toward the changing of relations and structures? ... How then does it stand today, I would like to ask, when it is not an individual brother, but many, indeed all who have something against us, whole social groups, whole peoples and countries trapped in their condition of misery? Must we then not mobilize our Christian love in the form of such an unquestioning, unconditioned resolution for justice for others? Must we then not finally give up that petty form of Christian love of neighbor which makes us keep fastidiously asking ourselves "Who then is my neighbor?" and which continually tempts us to encounter as our neighbor only him whom we have in each case already chosen and admitted as such? Finally, must we then not take revolution and revolutionary violence into consideration as an imposed form of Christian love under certain circumstances?

—Johannes Metz

V. The Theology
of Revolution

It is Alan Austin who in *The Revolutionary Imperative* talks about the "strange odyssey of the church—from the Bible to the picket line."[1] Strange, indeed! It is even more so because, fantastically, the odyssey gives evidence that it may move on from the picket line to the barricade, from the seminary lecture hall to the guerrilla hideout. Traumatic for rank-and-file church members is the discovery that reputable, reflective, and responsible Christian leaders are advocating the overthrow of established governments. Convinced that reform is impossible, these leaders—and their number is evidently growing—argue that radical change—nonviolent if possible but violent if necessary—must be engineered in God's name. Reluctantly but openly they have become insurrectionists. The evolution of their thinking has brought some of them to the definite conclusion that the twentieth-century disciple of Jesus Christ may judiciously resort to killing, bombing, sabotaging, terrorizing, and torturing in order to implement reconciling love. Utterly bewildered by this position, though it would not have unduly shocked the majority of Protestants in England and the colonies during the seventeenth and eighteenth centuries, church members today may wonder how Christianity, once stigmatized as a religious opiate, has been changed into a political crusade. They may wonder what has happened to the pacifism which in the earlier decades of our century was the stock-in-trade of theological liberalism. They may wonder, too, how biblical sanction can be invoked for attacking the *status quo* when historically that sanction has been invoked to hallow existing authorities.

[1] Alan D. Austin, ed., *The Revolutionary Imperative: Essays Toward a New Humanity* (Nashville, Tenn.: The Board of Education of the Methodist Church, 1966), p. 59.

Such bewilderment, however, is readily understandable. For the emergence of this new position within the matrix of Christianity could scarcely have been predicted when World War II ended in 1945. To explain it, then, will require a detailed study.

Let us recall at the outset that for long centuries the Church has taken a very conservative stance. Luther opposed the rebelling peasants of his era; Abraham Kuyper, one of Calvinism's greatest champions in modern times, became prime minister of the Netherlands when he led his antirevolutionary party to victory;[2] and to a latter-day German theologian like Julius Stahl, the Church is "the last stronghold of legality and divinely appointed authority," the incarnation of Kuyper's antirevolutionary spirit, and as such will triumphantly "outlive democracy and despotism, with which it has nothing to do."[3] Thus established religion, socially and sometimes officially allied with the political order, has, Gerald O'Collins writes, "for so long played a conservative role in culture that it would have been surprising to find the Christian churches producing or at least tolerating theological treatments of revolution."[4]

But with the world in upheaval and crisis, sensitive Christians are being compelled to rethink the problem of revolution. With Harvey Cox they have begun to perceive not only "the need for a theology of social change" but likewise the need for a theology of revolution. This need, Cox avers, ought to be given top priority: "The development of such a theology should be the first item on the theological agenda today."[5] Cox supports his averment with an illustration:

It is reported that during the initial stages of Castro's movement, before he came into power and even for a short time thereafter, there were a number of Cuban Baptists in high positions in his movement. But, when

[2] Frank VandenBerg, *Abraham Kuyper* (Grand Rapids, Mich.: William B. Eerdmans Publishing Co., 1960) is the definitive source. *Cf.* for the antirevolutionary philosophy, pp. 70 ff.

[3] Quoted by Lochman, *op. cit.*, p. 118, n. 16.

[4] Gerald O'Collins, *Man and His New Hopes* (New York: Herder & Herder, 1969), p. 139.

[5] Harvey Cox, *The Secular City: Secularization and Urbanization in Theological Perspective* (New York: The Macmillan Company, 1965), p. 107; *cf. ibid.*, p. 115.

they found a real revolution on their hands and wanted to make a Christian witness and contribution within a revolutionary situation, they were totally baffled. ... These Cuban Christians lacked the kind of theology of the world that we have begun to develop; perhaps if they had not retreated, the story in Cuba might have been different.[6]

Hence, only if this need is met can the Church be relevant to our revolutionary century. Only so, moreover, Carl Braaten reminds us, can the church atone for its contradictory role in the past: fomenting revolution, it has selfishly served as a reactionary force, sanctifying the *status quo* and squelching the legitimate aspirations of downtrodden people.

Indirectly the church has sponsored the revolutionary process by preaching a message which sets things in motion, stirring up the imagination, arousing new expectations, and stimulating a crusading zeal to translate hopes, whose realization some would postpone for heaven above, already into the social structures of this world. The simple fact of preaching the gospel is like putting sticks of dynamite into the social structure. The church is responsible for having planted many charges of dynamite into beloved structures that it at the same time had no desire to explode, since its own privileges were beholden to them.[7]

In other words, the Church must practice repentance and exercise responsibility by coming to terms with revolution. This, admittedly, is a task of staggering difficulty. It involves so drastic a revision of traditional formulations that one may seriously question whether biblical faith can survive the reconceptualization.

The young Brazilian theologian, Rubem A. Alves, frankly declares in his book *A Theology of Human Hope* that to perform this staggering task one must first "unlearn the language of theology," a language which sounds to contemporary secularists "like the voice of an alien and remote sphere." But some Christians— Alves himself, for instance—are wholly sympathetic with the revolutionary goals of secularism; they therefore are striving to remain loyal to their faith while recognizing that "its language must continually be going through a process of death and resurrection." Loyal to the deepest insights of the religious community

6 Harvey Cox, *God's Revolution and Man's Responsibility* (Valley Forge, Pa.: Judson Press, 1965), pp. 53-54.

7 Carl E. Braaten, *The Future of God: The Revolutionary Dynamics of Hope* (New York: Harper & Row, 1969), p. 143.

which is the center of their lives, they have nevertheless come to understand that its history "could be written as the history of the birth, death and resurrection of its languages." They have also come to understand that, if the language of faith remains "frozen as the world moves ahead," both the language and the faith "cease to be instruments of liberation and become structures of repression." Only if the old language is "forgotten and a new one created," only if there is radical "discontinuity," a break between the faith and its formulations, can the faith itself be "kept alive." "Language as such," these Christians have come to realize, has only "a secondary import ... a footnote function." It is "nothing more, but nothing less than a footnote to the events which, in any specific moment, provide the vector and thrust of the possibilities of human liberation amid history." Thus the language of faith is "iconoclastic, subversive and humorous." It is "an expression of imagination." Secular critics may contend that "it is not verifiable, that it is not falsifiable, and that consequently it is meaningless, a sort of fictionism, not willing to come to terms with the facts as they are." It is possible for Christians, however, to reply that the language of faith—iconoclastic, subversive, humorous, imaginative, unverifiable, and changeful—serves as a vehicle for the profoundest understanding of existence and history.[8]

What does Alves have in mind by this discussion of language? His purpose, rather plainly, is to show that our traditional theology must be radically recast, our traditional theology derived by painstaking exegesis of what was assumed to be a fixed, final, and "frozen" revelation of truth which God had given once for all. No, his purpose is even more radical than that. Since the old language of faith must die, daringly new conceptualizations must be essayed, conceptualizations which are discontinuous with the historic conceptualizations. Alves, then, is not simply proposing that the old wine of Christianity be put in new wineskins. He is actually proposing that by the chemistry of a sophisticated hermeneutic the old wine of redemptive supernaturalism be changed into the new wine

---

[8] Rubem A. Alves, *A Theology of Human Hope* (Washington, D. C.: Corpus Books, 1969), pp. 29, 71-73, 161, 165.

of a secularized revolutionism and still dispensed as Christianity.[9]

Richard Shaull, who is Alves' mentor and friend, shares the same perspective and purpose. In his opinion, traditional theology must die the death of radical reconceptualization; otherwise Christianity itself will die. A Draconian either/or! Either the old language of faith dies or in our desacralized world Nietzsche's prophecy, "God is dead!" will come to pass.

Most of the categories for describing God's action in the world are so identified with the "religious" or metaphysical understanding of transcendence that they do little to point to the "beyond in the midst of life." And the whole religious framework in which our talk about God is set identifies Him with the order which must be repudiated if man come of age is to move toward meaning and fulfillment in contemporary terms.

Our contention here is that in this situation it no longer makes any sense for us to work out, in theological isolation, a systematic interpretation of *Heilsgeschichte* and from that try to deduce what God is now doing in our world. The alternative open to us is to be fully involved, as theologians, in this historical moment, and from within it work out the terms for a fruitful dialogue with the heritage of faith. Whatever these terms turn out to be, they should represent a description, in secular language, of the possibilities open for the renewal of man and for the transformation of society that can be perceived as we look at our world through the eyes of faith. If God is at work in this revolutionary situation, this type of dialogue should not only provide us with some clues to his actions but also lead us eventually to a new language, new imagery, and new concepts for speaking authentically about Him.[10]

[9]"If the language of the community of faith is, on the one hand, totally historical but, on the other hand, does not refer to history as a divine process, it is a language expressive of a secular world. A secular world means two things. First, it is totally historical. It does not look for metahistorical points of reference or values to organize itself. It 'does not look beyond the stars first in order to find a meaning for the earth.' History is the horizon within which it moves, the language of the community of faith is therefore expressive of man's courage and determination to remain historical. And second, a secular world is an experimental world, a world that does not have a navel, a world that leaves behind possibilities which are negated and marches toward horizons which are still open. It lives in a constant elimination of absolutes because all absolutes are idols. The language of the community of faith is thus secular and secularizing." *Ibid.*, pp. 163-64.

[10] Richard Shaull, "God and the Human Revolution," *Contemporary Religious Issues,* Donald E. Hartsock, ed. (Belmont, Calif.: Wadsworth Publishing Co., Inc., 1968), p. 204.

So the Christian theologian has no option but to involve himself—become identified with some revolutionary program?—in "this historical movement and in the midst of his involvement work out the terms for a fruitful dialogue with the heritage of faith." Is anything, then, to be salvaged from this wholesale abandonment of traditional theology? What will survive after the old language, imagery, and concepts have been interred in some academic mausoleum? Fortunately, Shaull assures us:

We have at our disposal a wealth of biblical and theological images and symbols, of myths, parables, and stories, which can give new insight into human and social reality, call attention to dimensions of that reality that are often overlooked, provide us with clues as to what is most important, and make possible a clear vision of the whole. Our task, accordingly, is clear. We must rediscover the meaning and wealth of our Christian imagery especially of those clusters of myths and symbols which help us to discern the nature and direction of God's humanizing activity in the world.[11]

If we courageously accomplish our task, "myth and symbol can become the basis for a new *logos*." But, Shaull concludes, "the new *logos* that may emerge from the confrontation of the biblical images with contemporary reality will not necessarily be a *Christian logos*." Why, though, be troubled over that? Alves is correct in his controlling purpose. At this explosive juncture in history the theologian must do more than provide new wineskins. He must go beyond Harry Emerson Fosdick's attempt to give abiding truth a fresh formulation. Today he must use the chemistry of a sophisticated hermeneutic to change the old wine of redemptive supernaturalism into the new wine of a secularized revolutionism which can still be dispensed as Christianity. "In fact, the primary concern of the theologian should be to contribute as much as possible to the broadening, deepening, and revitalization of *secular* thought."[12]

Why be troubled, either, if the new *logos* demands a new *logic*? Ernst Bloch is a Marxist philosopher whose *Das Prinzip Hoffnung* has decisively influenced some of today's major theologians. He sees no reason for sticking to old-fashioned logic.

[11] *Ibid.*
[12] *Ibid.*, pp. 206-07.

This is Cox's significant commentary on Bloch's cryptic sentence "S is not yet P."

Does this mean that for Bloch the venerable law of identity in classical logic is passé? Yes it does. For Bloch's ontology, to claim that S must be S and nothing else is to fall into a static view of reality, a condition which can only result in hindering and slowing down the onward march of history, though it can never halt it. In short, Bloch is suggesting a logic of change, a new logic appropriate to a time when we have discovered at last that change itself is the only permanent thing we have.[13]

After this lengthy orientation to the methodology of the revolutionary theologians, we are ready to examine in detail their deployment of specific categories. To start with the very fountainhead of theology, God is postulated in this reconceptualized Christianity. Transcendence is affirmed, not simply transcendence as man's capacity to rise above what is, envisioning what ought to be, but transcendence as an other-than-human reality, a power beyond history at work in history. Immediately, however, qualification is called for. One must not equate the other-than-human transcendence of the revolutionary theology with old-style supernaturalism. Alves endorses John A. T. Robinson's repudiation of the transcendence which in traditional terminology is referred to by "ups" and "outs," a transcendence which "is literally or physically up there" or "a spiritual and metaphysical reality which is out there."[14] The God or transcendence of revolutionary theology is, therefore, hazy and indefinite, an elusive X which defies any linguistic precision. Its view of God or transcendence, so far as that concept can be articulated, is more that of a process than a person, more that of a becoming than a being. At best, God is that ground of being which sustains becoming. But the notion of a finished deity, "One and the Plenum and the Unmoved and the Sated and the Permanent," as Nietzsche sneers, dehumanizes man and fatalizes history. Alves concurs with Nietzsche regarding the "inhumanity of theological languages. ... How could man find his vocation in the creation of the world, if the world is un-

---

[13] Harvey Cox, "Ernst Bloch and 'The Pull of the Future,'" *New Theology No. 5*, Martin E. Marty and Dean G. Peerman, eds. (New York: The Macmillan Company, 1968), p. 194.
[14] Alves, *op. cit.*, p. 28.

real? And how could he ever create something new, if everything is already finished in God?"[15]

Fortunately, however, the God of the Bible is not the finished deity of orthodox dogma. He is the God Who, according to Exodus 3:14, discloses Himself as "Eh'je ascher eh'je." Traditionally, this name, translated as "I am that I am," has been construed as a proof text for ontologizing God, defining Him as "being itself." But biblical scholarship now suggests that a futuristic rendering is preferable: "I will be that I will be." Carl Braaten comments with respect to this name, "The passage is ambiguous, and it is doubtful that anything can be clenched for theology by the underlying verb itself, *haja*. The Revised Standard Version is correct in allowing for both translations."[16] But in his monograph *Prediction and Fulfillment in the Bible*, Gordon C. Oxtoby points out that "these two suggestions by no means exhaust the possibilities. It could also mean, 'I have been what I am,' or 'I will be what I have been,' or 'I am what I will be.' There are other possibilities as well."[17] The implications of this divine self-disclosure are drawn out by Jürgen Moltmann who, without mentioning Ernst Bloch explicitly, leans heavily upon him.

The God of the exodus and of the resurrection "is" not eternal presence, but he promises his presence and nearness to him who follows the path on which he is sent into the future. YHWH, as the name of the God who first of all promises His presence, and His kingdom and makes them prospects for the future, is a God "with future as His essential nature," a God of promise and of leaving the present to face the future, a God whose freedom is the source of new things that are to come. His name is not a cipher for the "eternal present" nor can it be rendered by the word EI, "thou art." His name is a wayfaring name, a name of promise that discloses a new future, a name whose truth is experienced in history inasmuch as his promise discloses its future possibilities. He is therefore, as Paul says, the God who raises the dead and calls into being the things that are not (Romans 4:17). This God is present where we wait upon his promises in hope and transformation. When we have a God who calls into being the things that are not, then the things that are not yet, that

15 *Ibid.*, p. 32.

16 Braaten, *op. cit.*, p. 48.

17 Gordon C. Oxtoby, *Prediction and Fulfillment in the Bible* (Philadelphia: Westminster Press, 1966), p. 126.

are future, also become "thinkable" because they can be hoped for.[18]

Together with his fellow German, Wolfgang Pannenberg, who is another of today's significant theologians, Moltmann has been developing in his own distinctive way an interpretation of Christianity which has as its deepest foundation the idea that futurity is a divine mode of being. God is not essentially *summum ens* or *ens perfectissimum*; essentially He is *primum movens*, the power of the future. Thus Pannenberg affirms, "As the power of the future God is no thing, no extant object ... He appears neither as a being among others nor as the quiet background of all things."[19] Operating out of the future, therefore, He impinges upon the present, luring it forward to new possibilities. He is God on the move, the God of action, the God of promise, the God of hope. Alves sums up the meaning of this concept common to both Pannenberg and Moltmann:

If God is future in his essential nature, we cannot meet him either as an "intra-worldly" or as an "extra-worldly" reality. He cannot be grasped as a "being." He reveals himself as one who is absent, always pointing to the future. His appearance is thus grasped as the uttering of the word of promise. He "encounters us in his promises for the future." We cannot therefore "have Him." We can "only await in active hope."[20]

Much as he appreciates this approach, though, Alves finds fault with it for so stressing the future as virtually to deny God's present reality and activity.

The pure futuricity of God is a new form of Docetism in which God loses the present dimension and therefore becomes ahistorical. The messianic possibilities of history for both the Old and the New Testaments depend on the fact that God has a present. For the Old Testament one can hope because "the Lord your God is in the midst of you" (Deut. 8:21) [Deut. 7:21]; for the New, hope is derived from the historicity, the incarnation of God. A God who is always future is a God who does

---

[18] Jürgen Moltmann, *Theology of Hope: On the Ground and the Implications of the Christian Eschatology* (London: SCM Press, Ltd., 1967), p. 30.

[19] Quoted by Braaten, "Toward a Theology of Hope," *New Theology No. 5*, p. 108.

[20] Alves, *op. cit.*, p. 56.

not become historical in terms of power but who remains ahead, attract-
ing history to himself by means of eros.[21]

Yet Alves, too, believes that God "has not yet arrived." Rather,
He is working with man in "historical dialogical cooperation" to
create a future which is still open, unfinished, experimental, and
fraught with possibilities of freedom and justice.

If creation is a joint enterprise, the God who is involved in the politics
of liberation remains open. He does not look at history from his future
nor does he pull history from his future. In history, with man, their
future is engendered. This is so because the future is created historically
with man. It is not simply a future created by God for man, but by God
and man in historical dialogical cooperation. This is the necessary implication of his incarnation: that he remains open to man. But openness
implies unfinishedness, it implies that one is still in an experimental
stage. The incarnation of God means thus that he remains historical
and is adding to himself everything that is human. ... His incarnation
cannot thus become a "take off" point from which God builds an onto-
logical reality separated from what is going on here and now. He remains
historical. He has not yet arrived.[22]

In other words, those of Harvey Cox in his foreword to *A Theology of Human Hope*, "For Alves, the name of God is not a cipher
for some extrahistorical entity; it is faith's way of speaking about
what is required to make him keep life human. Hope grows out
of historical experience, especially the experience of liberation
that occurs where there is no evidence that it could."[23] Alves,
consequently, is at one with Moltmann in denying that God is
"some extrahistorical entity." Both of them retain the traditional
name for the future-producing and history-creating power chiefly
because it symbolizes hope, in the case of Alves, hope against hope
for a future of liberation, hope which inspires revolutionary
action in the present. It would seem, therefore, as though Alves'
criticism of Moltmann on the ground that his God-concept dis-
courages revolutionary activity is not well taken. For in Moltmann's opinion traditional theology which preached a *God
without future* paved the way for a messianic atheism—in
Marxism, notably—which proclaimed a *future without God*. But

21 *Ibid.*, p. 94.
22 *Ibid.*, p. 144.
23 *Ibid.*, p. x.

this dilemma, he argues, can be resolved if Christianity recovers its revolutionary message of a God with a future and thus a future with God.

In the past two centuries, a Christian faith in God without hope for the future of the world has called forth a secular hope for the future of the world without faith in God. Since the Christians, the Churches, and theology believed in a *God without future*, the will for a future of the earth has joined itself to an atheism which sought a *future without God*. The messianic hopes emigrated from the church and became invested in progress, evolution, and revolution. In the church only a half-truth remained. We have arrived at a moment in history that provokes the question: Should there now be a parting of ways in history, so that faith aligns itself with the past and unfaith with the future? I think that we can overcome this present dilemma only if Christians begin to remember the "God of hope," as he is witnessed to in the promissory history of the Old and the New Testaments, and thus begin to assume responsibility for the personal, social, and political problems of the present.[24]

24 Jürgen Moltmann, *Religion, Revolution and the Future* (New York: Charles Scribner's Sons, 1969), pp. 200-01. Shaull is highly appreciative of Moltmann's contribution: "Recent developments in theology, centering around a theology of hope, seem to me especially important. As Professor Moltmann (*Theology of Hope*) has worked this out, the Christian symbols point to a God who goes ahead of us and who is bringing a new future into being. His word is essentially a word of promise, that awakens in us the hope for a new future. It is a word that upsets old stabilities, arouses dissatisfaction with the old order, and frees us to expect and serve the things that are to come. Professor Moltmann has done such a masterful job that I need say nothing more about this." "Christian Faith as Scandal in a Technocratic World," *New Theology No. 6*. p. 130. Rolland F. Smith also has high praise for Jürgen Moltmann and his Catholic counterpart, Johannes Metz, both of whom interpret Christian theology as eschatology, "the straining after and anticipating the future of Christ which is the future of the world ... a revolutionizing and transforming of the present. ... The future of Christ is a mission for the future of the world. Hence it is a continual criticism and transformation of the present because it is open towards the universal future of the kingdom. The church, then, is an exodus church which is both creative and militant. It is that body of Christians who, relying on the promise expressed in the cross and resurrection of Christ, and hoping for its fulfillment, engage themselves in the world to attack and call the world into its history, its transformation in Christ It is easy to see from this latter point why both Moltmann and Metz consider the theology of hope a theology of revolt." "A Theology of Rebellion," *New Theology No. 6*, pp. 144-46. Cox, though, together with Peerman, has some reservations about the theology of hope: "Will it be understood in a sick society which confuses hoping with a craving for things—the second car, the first boat, more cholesterol in which to wallow? Most of all: is its doctrine of God ('I will be

It follows from what the revolutionary theologians tell us about God that He is the tireless activist Whom the ancient Psalmist extols because He never slumbers or sleeps. God is the unwearying worker of Whom Jesus speaks: "My Father worketh hitherto, and I work." His very being is a matter of doing. "The Hebrew," N. H. Snaith comments, "does not say that Jehovah is, or that Jehovah exists, but that He does."[25] God is struggling in the present with man as His partner to create a new future in keeping with His promise. Theology, then, if faithful to its biblical sources—so runs the argument—must be a theology of politics.

It is Paul Lehmann, who perhaps more than anyone else, has systematically interpreted or reinterpreted Christianity from this perspective.[26] He holds that only within the context of faith and the community it begets—the church or *koinonia*, "the *fellowship creating reality* of Christ's presence in the world[27]—can the purposes of God be clearly apprehended and appreciated.

From within the *koinonia* it makes sense to say that what God is doing in the world is His will. It makes sense because in the *koinonia* the will of God is no pious platitude but a clear and concrete matter of politics. In short, 'the God of the church' *is* 'the God of politics'! ... the present adoption of the word 'politics' as applied to the activity of God has to do, not with these pragmatic and passing manifestations of political behavior, but with that to which the word 'politics' fundamentally and centrally refers. In this precise and basic sense, it is possible to say that God, if he is denotable by one phrase more characteristically than by another, is a 'politician'.[28]

And why is God characteristically a politician? Quoting Aristotle,

who I will be'), with its temporal transcendence in place of spatial transcendence, an evasion, an illusive way of keeping theology going without saying much of anything at all?" "Christian Hope and Human Futures," *New Theology No. 5*, pp. 17-18.

25 Quoted by Alves, *op. cit.*, p. 90.

26 Shaull commends Lehmann because he especially "has provided a number of theological categories for dealing with revolution; and, not surprisingly," has attracted the attention of "those who are involved in revolutionary struggles." "Revolutionary Change and Theological Perspective," *The Church amid Revolution*, p. 35.

27 Paul L. Lehmann, *Ethics in a Christian Context* (New York: Harper and Row, 1963), p. 49.

28 *Ibid.*, pp. 82-83.

Lehmann contends that "the Good of man must be the end of the science of Politics." But man's good is determined by man's nature as *politikon zoon*, a political animal, a creature who finds fulfillment in community.[29] Hence God's will, as interpreted within the context of the Christian community, is at bottom no different from the purpose of politics as defined by Aristotle: it is "to make and keep human life human in the world." And this statement of faith's ultimate purpose echoes like a leitmotif throughout the writings of Lehmann's *epigonoi*. Alves, for instance, repeats it frequently. Indeed, for him, Christianity is "the answer to the question: 'what is necessary to make and keep human life human in the world?'"[30] But that very question prompts a further question: how is humanization understood by revolutionary theology?

Appropriating a passage from Paul's Ephesian Letter, Lehmann very precisely discriminates between a definition and a description of what is ideally human. According to the Pauline description, then,

What it takes to make and to keep human life human in the world is "the unsearchable riches of Christ ... the plan of the mystery hidden for ages in God who created all things; that through the church the manifold wisdom of God might be made known to the principalities and powers in the heavenly places ... until we all attain to mature manhood, to the measure of the stature of the fullness of Christ."[31]

Here, accordingly, we have a description of true humanization, and it turns out to be a Christocentric image, a complex metaphor which in terms of a body and its parts pictures that community which is the new humanity. This concept of maturity, borrowed

[29] Lehmann cites the relevant pages from Aristotle on pp. 84-85. In his essay "The Shape of Theology for a World in Revolution," Lehmann repeats himself: "Now, if one is careful enough to understand that, as Aristotle said, 'Politics is the art of human community' then we may say that politics is the art of what it takes for man to be a human being in the world. The Bible describes the characteristic way that God has of being God in political images. Political imagery is used in the Bible to proclaim and describe God as the architect of the humanity of man, to put Christian faith into the middle of the revolutionary environment of man, and to make Christian faith itself the catalyst of authentic revolution." *The Revolutionary Imperative*, pp. 67-68.

[30] Alves, *op. cit.*, p. 98.

[31] Lehmann, *Ethics in a Christian Context*, p. 85.

from Paul, is so crucial in his ethics that Lehmann explicates it as exactly as possible. In the New Testament, he says, maturity means

human wholeness, the full or complete development of man as an individual and of all men in their relationships with one another. ... For Christianity, what is fundamentally human in human nature is the gift to man of the power to be and to fulfill himself in and through a relationship of dependence and self-giving toward God and toward his fellow man. Thus, maturity is *self-acceptance through self-giving.*[32]

Maturity, Lehmann says later on,

is the full development in the human being of the power to be truly and fully himself in being related to others who also have the power to be truly and fully themselves. The Christian *koinonia* is the foretaste and the sign in the world that God has always been and is contemporaneously doing what it takes to make and to keep human life human. This is the will of God "as it was in the beginning, is now and ever shall be, world without end."[33]

But we must not mistakenly conclude that only professing members of the *koinonia* or individuals who consciously accept the Gospel are included in the new humanity en route to maturity. Since God has elected all men in the Second Adam,

Both believer and unbeliever are being confronted in the environment being shaped by Christ's royal and redemptive activity, by the decision to accept or to reject the conditions of the new humanity on Christ's terms, not their own. The difference is that for believers as members of the *koinonia*, the kingship of Christ "is revealed; in the world (that is, among unbelievers) it is hidden. The church lives as the people who know that the victory has been won. The world lives on as though nothing had happened. The church realizes that the powers which militate against God's plan are under control. The world lives on as if these powers were still able to shape the ultimate destiny of men." The difference between believers and unbelievers is not defined by church membership, or even, in the last analysis, by baptism. The difference is defined by imaginative and behavioral sensitivity to what God is doing in the world to make and to keep human life human, to achieve the maturity of men, that is, the new humanity.[34]

32 *Ibid.*, p. 16.

33 *Ibid.*, p. 101; *cf.* p. 131.

34 *Ibid.*, p. 117; the interior quote is from W.A. Visser't Hooft, *The Kingship of Christ: An Interpretation of Recent European Theology* (New York: Harper & Brothers, 1948), p. 124.

On Lehmann's assumption of universalism, belief is relatively incidental; behavior is the crucial factor: "Those who start with and from within the *koinonia* find themselves, on the behavioral level, involved in situations and with people who start from outside the *koinonia* yet whose behavior makes the recognition inescapable that they are sheep belonging to the same fold."[35] So Lehmann's *koinonia* ethic eliminates any sort of spiritual segregation "by including the unbelievers among the other sheep of the Holy Spirit of God" and affirming that the entire family of man is divinely destined for maturity and community, personal and universal wholeness.[36]

Granting, then, that the purpose of God *ex hypothesi* is true humanization, what are the components of this ideal which addresses a galvanizing word of judgment and hope to man in his present inauthenticity? Freedom is the mark which Alves underscores. "Rob a man of freedom to shape his own tomorrow and that of his world, and you rob him of manhood. Humanization, in point of fact, exists to the extent to which man, as free subject, creates his future, the future which liberates him from the passivity under which the master keeps him."[37] Thus Christianity, a humanistic religion, shares with political humanism "a passion for and vision of human deliverance."[38] Together with political humanism, it speaks the "language of hope, freedom and liberation."[39] It, too, endorses the contention that "only as the creator of history does man find his authentic life" and that "authentic life cannot be separated from the objective possibility of transforming the earth."[40] So Christianity agrees with political humanism that liberty, maturity, and authenticity are inseparable components of humanity as it ought to be. Freedom, Alves insists, "takes on flesh ... when we understand it in the context of this possibility of creating a new earth."[41]

[35] *Ibid.*, p. 157.
[36] *Ibid.*, p. 159; *cf.* pp. 155-59 for the complete presentation of Lehmann's position on this point.
[37] Alves, *op. cit.*, p. 15.
[38] Paul Lehmann, as quoted in *ibid.*, p. 85.
[39] *Ibid.*, p. 114.
[40] *Ibid.*, pp. 140, 141.
[41] *Ibid.*, p. 138

As a humanistic religion, Christianity differs, however, from political humanism in its belief that liberation is achieved in history "not as the result of the power of man" but by "grace, efficacy, 'in spite of.'" It is achieved by "the free action in history of the messianic power from beyond history."[42] God's gracious efficacy and efficacious grace are the dynamics which political humanism fails to recognize. Christian humanism, on the contrary, "drawing an inference from the historical experience" of the biblical community holds that "in spite of the collapse of all human resources," freedom is still achievable. How? Human freedom is grounded in God's freedom and the gracious exercise of His power: "determined by God's freedom for man and history, man finds the possibility of living as free man in and for history.[43] And when man becomes fluent in the language of faith, the grammar of which is action, he grows maturely free— free from the fear of the future, free from legalism, cynicism, despair, fantasy, and illusions, free from death and for death, free from the present, free for enjoyment and happiness, free even "from the concern about absolutes, about religion, about the immovable, and free to live as a permanent experiment."[44] Man is free to become himself; and only the exercise of his freedom will disclose the potentialities which he possesses. For, as Esdras B. Costa writes, humanization is really "an experiment in which the criteria of humanity are discovered and transcended by other better criteria, and applied to life by free men and women, in their faithfulness to their vocation as human beings."[45]

Responsibility is the mark of true humanization which Harvey Cox stresses. He mentions freedom and dignity as well but invariably in conjunction with responsibility. "Where is the new age breaking in?" he asks. "It is appearing," he answers, "wherever men are summoned to dignity and accountability, where defeat and resignation give way to freedom and responsibility."[46] He informs any of his readers who have not yet been cued in that

---

42 *Ibid.*, pp. 89, 93.

43 *Ibid.*, pp. 98, 99

44 These facets of mature freedom are developed in detail by Alves, *op cit.*, pp. 78 ff. The quotation comes from pp. 164-65.

45 Quoted in *ibid.*, p. 138.

46 Cox, *The Secular City*, p. 143.

"God is at work in history bringing man to adulthood and responsibility."[47] Christians, he tells us, find ground for this belief in those "New Testament images for conversion, for the
transformation of one's perception of reality" which denote "the
achievement of maturity, coming of age and adulthood."

"When I became a man," says St. Paul, "I put away childish things."
In the letter to the Galatians he compares the man of faith with the person who has been under the governance of a tutor during his minority
but now attains the age of accountability and becomes a full heir to his
father's estate. As a son, the heir must now bear full responsibility for
the administration of the estate.[48]

"These images of maturity and responsibility ... " Cox further
informs us, "are in no sense exceptional in the New Testament.
They appear for instance in several of the parables attributed to
Jesus in which he speaks of stewards who are given charge of an
estate while the master goes away."[49]

As Cox interprets the New Testament, maturity or a willingness to shoulder responsibility does not usually develop slowly
and steadily. As a rule, it is produced by some crisis, some catastrophe, which jolts people out of their catalepsy or "political paralysis," their "blindness," and "stupor"; this induces catharsis,
a *metanoia* that causes them "to change, to repent, to revolt, to
accept responsibility for the exercise of power." Freed, consequently, from "adolescent illusions," they then assume "the
status of sonship, maturity, and responsibility."[50]

Cox's emphasis upon the "category of responsibility" is by no
means atypical. Thomas W. Ogletree is of the opinion that this
category provides precisely "the most decisive one for charac-
terizing the shape of contemporary theology."[51] Ogletree
endorses Cox's view that the catalytic events of our time have
jolted us out of our blindness and stupor and enabled us to perceive appreciatively "certain neglected features of the Christian
gospel," especially its concept of redemption as man's "libera-

47 *Ibid.*, p. 215.
48 *Ibid.*
49 *Ibid.*, p. 119.
50 *Ibid.*, pp. 114-121.
51 Thomas W. Ogletree, "The Shifting Focus of Theological Reflection,"
New Theology No. 6, p. 60.

tion from alien powers and his elevation to a share in the power God exercises over things." We now see, Ogletree asserts, that "being a man—a mature man—involves the exercise of power, the act of assuming responsibility for your own life and the life of the world."[52] In a passage which brings together a number of important themes, he gives us the consensus of frontline theology:

The gospel does empower man to take responsibility for his own life and the life of the world, where it breaks the hold of those anxieties that keep him so preoccupied with his own well-being as to make him ineffectual in dealing with the critical issues of life. It does free man to move creatively into an open future, uninhibited by the limits of past and present conditions, because it continually mediates the future to him as the hope for overcoming the negativities of life in the realization of new levels of personal and social fulfillment. It does enable man to account for his life in openness because it calls him to that accounting with a word of forgiveness, forgiveness which does not simply excuse his irresponsibilities, but also transforms the distortions of his being into a new integrity and wholeness.[53]

Assuming, therefore, that true humanization includes maturity, freedom, and responsibility, what kind of world is the church, the *avant-garde* of the new humanity, to be creating in history as it collaborates with the power beyond history, the divine power Who from His future works in the present to achieve the future of integrity and wholeness which He desires? Obviously, that new world will be a world where true community obtains, a world where selfish estrangement has been overcome and the "atomic individual," as Michael Novak terms him, has virtually disappeared. For, to follow Novak's summary of psychology and sociology,

The primary reality of human consciousness is not the individual but the community; the individual person develops creatively only in the context of a community. Such a community, to be healthy, must respect the uniqueness of each person. Each person, to be healthy, must respect his brotherhood with all others. Community and person are interrelated and cannot be understood apart from one another.[54]

Thus true humanization means a true community, and such a

52 *Ibid.*, p. 53.
53 *Ibid.*, p. 63.
54 Novak, *op. cit.*, p. 27.

community, according to Novak, measures up to three criteria. First, "each person in the relationship has a basic *independence*; each is able to function apart from the given community; each person in the relationship is an end and not a means." Second, "*communication* between members of the community—verbal, emotional, symbolic, functional—must be clear and open; people must be able to mean what they say and say what they mean." Third, justice or fairness, a criterion which Novak borrows from John Rawls, prevails. This means that "all offices and functions ... must be equally open to every member of the community. ... The system of offices and functions is fair when it respects all persons equally, and when the differentiation according to offices and functions does not become a differentiation of opportunity for aspiring to those offices and functions."[55]

Within this context, then, every person will have an opportunity to work out the pivotal issue of his self-identity, being himself and becoming himself. The just or fair community will elicit genuine selfhood. For, Novak correctly asserts, "no man becomes himself in solitude. Men create one another; identity is a gift one man confers on another."[56]

This is Shaull's vision as well. In faith, revolutionary theology anticipates "God's world," a world where "justice and reconciliation belong together" and where there are "constant efforts toward reconciliation of conflicting interests and restoration of broken relationships," a true *koinonia* in which a person "can be fully human" because he "has opportunity to participate in the life of his community and in the decisions that shape his destiny."[57]

While he does not specify it as a criterion of true community, Novak evidently includes love among the qualities of the *koinonia* which allows man to be truly human. He writes that Stokely Carmichael was once asked, "When the world is the way you want it, what will it be like?" After brief reflection, Carmichael answered, "Men will love one another." Novak cites, in addition, Carl Oglesby's one-sentence summation of the revolutionary goal: "We want to create a world in which love is more possible."[58]

[55] *Ibid.*, pp. 41-43.
[56] *Ibid.*, p. 38.
[57] Richard Shaull, "Revolutionary Change in Theological Perspective," pp. 39-40.
[58] Quoted by Novak, *op. cit.*, pp. 45, 48.

Perhaps the nature of the hoped-for community has been better articulated by the New Leftists than it has by the revolutionary theologians. But why be surprised at that? Political humanists and Christian humanists, we must recall, speak dialects of a common language, the language of "hope, freedom, and liberation." Thus Novak refers to the Port Huron statement of the Students for a Democratic Society to illustrate the kind of "human community" which is "the goal pursued by the new radicals" and their religious comrades-in-arms:

We regard men as infinitely precious and possessed of unfulfilled capacities for reason, freedom and love. In affirming these principles we are aware of countering perhaps the dominant conceptions of man in the twentieth century: that he is a thing to be manipulated, and that he is inherently incapable of directing his own affairs. We oppose the depersonalization that reduces human beings to the status of things—if anything, the brutalities of the twentieth century teach that means and ends are intimately related, that vague appeals to "posterity" cannot justify the mutilations of the present. We oppose, too, the doctrine of human incompetence because it rests essentially on the modern fact that men have been "competently" manipulated into incompetence—we see little reason why men cannot meet with increasing skill the complexities and responsibilities of their situation, if society is organized not for minority, but for majority, participation in decision-making.

Men have unrealized potential for self-cultivation, self-direction, self-understanding and creativity. It is this potential that we regard as crucial and to which we appeal, not to the human potentiality for violence, unreason, and submission to authority. The goal of man and society should be human independence: a concern not with image of popularity but with finding a meaning in life that is personally authentic; the quality of mind not compulsively driven by a sense of powerlessness, nor one which unthinkingly adopts status values, nor one which represses all threats to its habits, but one which has full spontaneous fragmented parts of personal history, one which openly faces problems which are troubling and unresolved; one with an intuitive awareness of possibilities, an active sense of curiosity, and ability and willingness to learn.

This kind of independence does not mean egotistic individualism—the object is not to have one's way so much as it is to have a way that is one's own. Nor do we deify man—we merely have faith in his potential.[59]

Suppose we now succinctly restate our discussion of the true humanization which God in collaboration with men, whether believingly secular or secularly believing, is at work to effect— "What it takes to make and keep human life human in the world." The Pauline image of the new humanity in Jesus Christ reveals that God wants a community of justice and reconciliation and love in which individuals are free to become mature and responsible, free to become themselves in relationships which are mutually self-fulfilling. If this is written off as vague and redundant, let the critics of Lehmann and his school consider that, even with the illumination of the biblical symbols, we can scarcely conjecture all that self-fulfilling humanization embraces. At least we know, on Novak's authority, that as we move toward that alluring goal, anything distinctively Christian will merge into the as yet indefinably human.

The purpose of the Christian life is not to become more Christian but less so; not to become more parochial and special but less so. The purpose of the Christian life is to become all that the human being can become, to become more fully human. Man was made in the image of the Word, and through the birth, death and resurrection of Jesus yet more wonderfully restored in that same image. The outermost bounds of that image have never been explored. We do not yet know what it is that Christians, like other men, are capable of becoming. The old cocoons must give way to fresh life in every historical epoch. We are not yet human beings, only striving to become so.[60]

What, now, about some of the more specific categories which spell out the significance of the political paradigm that revolutionary theology takes as central and commanding? Like it or not, we must reckon with the fact, Lehmann informs us, that "the language of theology, in trying to describe the political images with which the Bible talks about God's humanizing activity in the world, is a code language," and it is imperative, plainly, that "we get our code language straight."[61] We cannot do this, however, unless we keep in mind that theological talk, whatever the imagery employed, "does not mean many things, it means one thing." Whether the imagery is that of incarnation, atonement,

[60] *Ibid.*, pp. 120-21.
[61] Paul H. Lehmann, "The Shape of Theology for a World in Revolution," *The Revolutionary Imperative*, p. 68.

or resurrection, whether the imagery has to do with "change and stability, decay and fulfillment," it illustrates and illuminates the same story: "God's humanization of man through revolutionary social change in whatever form it takes."[62]

Shaull stands on the same hermeneutical platform. In italics he declares that *"The Biblical symbols and images stress discontinuity, judgment, the end of the world and the emergence of the radically new."* These symbols and images, when properly understood, enunciate the backbone principle of theology: "History often moves ahead by leaps; the social order does not stand open to the future; again and again it has to be broken open." Among these symbols and images, Shaull instances

—those describing man's pilgrim existence, on the road from Exodus to Promised Land, from Exile to the New Jerusalem;
—those describing life as a gift, as response to the surprises of grace;
—the great symbols of crucifixion and resurrection and their implications for man's historical existence;
—those which give us a basis for iconoclasm, for an attitude of radical transgression and transcendence in relation to every established order;
—those which describe the dialectical relationship between conflict and reconciliation, stability and change;
—the images that point to signs of hope in the midst of the social struggle in which we are involved.[63]

Through these symbols and images, therefore,

Christian faith can provide resources for being authentically revolutionary. It can produce the type of person whose own inward experience of death and resurrection equips him to let the old die when its time has come, and frees him to give form to the new possibilities open before him. This is what we most desperately need today; men liberated for creativity, participating in a community in which they are forced to die daily in order to create new ideas, new perspectives, new experiments, new institutions, new political possibilities.[64]

Take, for one, the category of messianism. This term denotes God's revolutionary action in history, judging, overthrowing, destroying, changing, bringing out of the stultifying present a

[62]*Ibid.*, pp. 68, 63, 70.
[63] Richard Shaull, "God and the Human Revolution," p. 207.
[64] Richard Shaull, "Christian Faith as Scandal in a Technocratic World," pp. 130, 131.

new and open future. Bruce O. Boston explicates for us the significance of this vital category. As the result of their historical
experience

the Israelites concluded that the God who had become present to them
was leading them toward a new day, a day in which they would discover
opportunities for fulfillment within the new social order. But they
further realized that the new order would not come about simply by
wishing for it, but that it had to be the "result of a disciplined and sustained effort of a particular people to whom this historic mission had
been entrusted." Thus the category of messianism carries with it three
characteristics: (1) the sense of liberation from old authorities, Pharaoh
or the technological ethos, (2) a sense of negation—the messiah negates
death, and (3) a sense of destiny or mission. ... the category of messianism means that: (1) those structures, institutions, and personages
which presume total power may be called into question, however benign
their form or rational their ideology; (2) the Given may be risked for the
sake of the future, regardless of the advantages which may accrue to man
in the familiarity of what-is, because the maintenance of freedom demands Exodus; and (3) historical experience is going somewhere, toward
the kingdom of God, and its direction depends in part on us, our decisions, our will.[65]

Shaull, in applying this category, acknowledges a debt to
Lehmann for highlighting the "messianic tradition and imagery
of the Bible that provide the real clue to what is going on in the
world."[66] Yes, the category of messianism provides the real clue
"to God's action," for

If we want to understand what is really happening in history at any

---

[65] Bruce O. Boston, "How Are Revelation and Revolution Related?" *Theology
Today*, July, 1969, pp. 148-149. The interior citation is from Shaull's essay "Revolution: Heritage and Contemporary Option."

[66] Richard Shaull, "Revolutionary Change and Theological Perspective," p. 35.
At the heart of the biblical "outlook is what can best be described as thorough-
going *messianism*. As the people of Israel reflected on the meaning of their experience, they came to the conclusion that history was going somewhere. Their entire
life as a nation was oriented toward the coming of the Messiah, a ruler whose
appearance would mean the establishment of a new order in the world. Thus,
history is not merely a constant struggle for human liberation; it is a struggle that
is moving toward its goal. ... In the messianic perspective, new possibilities for
human life appear in history after all human possibilities have been played out."
Shaull, "Revolution: Heritage and Contemporary Option," p. 217.

particular moment, or to assess correctly the impact of the future upon it, we should focus our attention at those points where *messianic movements are arising and challenging the power structures of society.*[67]

But Shaull, as he joins forces with Lehmann in rehabilitating and revising this concept, is aware of its semantic difficulties; he is cognizant that authentic messianism may be confused with non-biblical varieties of revolutionary hope.[68] Helpfully, therefore, his disciple, Rubem Alves, differentiates sharply between a non-biblical humanistic messianism, on the one side, a messianism that does not recognize the being and activity of God; and, on the opposite side, a biblical messianic humanism which believes "the achievement of humanization comes by the reality and power of a deliverance which occurs in history from beyond history and refuses to abandon history."[69] Distinguishing again between these two types of messianism, Alves claims that humanistic messianism "starts with man. Because man is the only resource it has at its disposal, he is the object of its trust and hope. It stands or falls with the transcending powers of man."

Messianic humanism, on the contrary, believes, from its historical experience, in the humanizing determination of the transcendent. When it pronounces the name "God," it is referring to the power for humanization that remains determined to make man historically free even when all objective and subjective possibilities in history have been exhausted.[70]

Utilizing biblical symbolism, then, humanistic messianism rejoices that destruction is the prelude to liberation and that out of destruction, by the grace of transcendence, a new creation emerges. "Because God's politics negates the natural unfolding of the old, room is made for the new. And one can truly say that it is created *ex nihilo*, since the new cannot be explained in terms of the logic of natural causality."[71]

Thus, to turn from Alves back to Lehmann, messianism is "the crucial image which illuminates what God is doing in the world. Consequently, theology, as reflection upon the Biblical

---

67 *Ibid.*, p. 219. For Shaull's application of this principle *cf. ibid.*, pp. 223-25.
68 *Ibid.*, p. 217, n. 4.
69 Alves, *op. cit.*, p. 87.
70 *Ibid.*, pp. 98-99.
71 *Ibid.*, p. 127.

witness to revelation, acquires a messianic character. Christian theology is *ex animo* theology of messianism."[72]

Take, next, the category of exodus, a category which, more often than not, is linked with the category of resurrection. Moltmann, for instance, alludes to them as "creative symbols of freedom: the exodus of Israel from bondage in Egypt and the resurrection of the crucified Christ into the coming kingdom of God—a deliverance *in* history and a deliverance *from* history."[73]

Cox likewise links these categories together as forming a comprehensive symbol of divine action.

Exodus and Easter remain the two foci of Biblical faith, the basis on which a theology of the church must be developed. The Exodus is the event which sets forth "what God is doing in history." He is seen to be liberating people from bondage, releasing them from political, cultural and economic captivity, providing them with the occasion to forge in the wilderness a new symbol system, a new set of values, and a new national identity. Easter means that the same activity goes on today, and that where such liberating activity occurs, the same Yahweh of Hosts is at work.[74]

Let us consider the exodus by itself, though, and under Braaten's tutelage learn its value as a paradigm for the theology of politics.

The features of this story became landmarks on the way to an eschatological hope with messianism at its core. A people are in slavery, groaning under their burdens. A leader arises to lead a revolution. At this moment religion is used no longer to soothe the suffering but to transform it into action on the way to freedom. Religion becomes exodus from slavery and oppression. God reveals himself along the way by signs his people cannot control, a cloud by day and a pillar of fire by night. The God of the exodus does not yet reveal him*self*, but rather he reveals the way in the direction his people should go. He does not give religion a center in a sacred place, but he gives a goal whose reality can be known only by trust and hope in a promise.[75]

So important is the paradigmatic value of the exodus that it can be called, Shaull suggests, an "archetype for interpretation."

---

[72]Lehmann, *Ethics in a Christian Context*, p. 104.
[73]Jürgen Moltmann, *Religion, Revolution and the Future*, pp. 66-67.
[74]Cox, *The Secular City*, p. 132.
[75]Braaten, *The Future of God, op. cit.*, p. 47. *Cf.* Harvey Cox, *God's Revolution and Man's Responsibility*, p. 29.

He appropriates the position of Swedish theologian, Bishop Einar Billig,

that the Exodus should provide the central category for interpreting not only the Old Testament, but the work of Jesus and the mission of the church as well. ... The Exodus was an event in which a people experienced unexpected deliverance from bondage; it came about through the breaking of the power of the oppressor and meant the opening up of an until then impossible future for those who had been oppressed.[76]

In Shaull's opinion, if theology were to follow Billig's seminal insight, it would substantially contribute "to the present political struggle" by holding out the hope that "we, too, are embarked on an Exodus and that we move toward the future as we participate in the negation of the given order and the creation of a new one on the other side of change."[77]

We turn now to an even more dramatic paradigm of political theology, Jesus' resurrection. The overwhelming value of this symbol cannot be grasped, however, if it is isolated from the whole Christ-event, that sequence of divine acts which began with the incarnation and terminated with the ascension. It is this segment of history which climactically discloses the reality and efficacy of grace. With Luther, therefore, revolutionary theology is concerned about no theology but the theology of the God Who in Christ has "given himself historically to man." It is persuaded, Alves declares, that "to speak correctly about God is to speak about One who does not have any other mode of determination save that of being for man." Hence Luther and Barth were penetratingly right: the language of theology is "simply the description of a historical person who exhausts the self-determination of God: Jesus Christ." In Him, accordingly, we have the convergence of history, messianism, and humanism. He, to be properly understood, must be understood "as the power and as the norm of God's historical politics of human liberation."[78]

---

[76] Richard Shaull, "Liberal and Radical in an Age of Discontinuity," *Christianity and Crisis*, January 5, 1970, p. 343.

[77] *Ibid.*, p. 344.

[78] Alves, *op. cit.*, pp. 99-100. Rolland F. Smith countersigns Alves. He interprets the Christ-event as "the central promise and basis of hope for this world. It is a historical event because by promise, hope, and contradiction it makes the reality of man historic." He then adds this: the Christ-event "does not fulfill all promises but itself becomes promise." *Op. cit.*, p. 145.

As for the atonement, we are implicitly advised to forget the old ideas of propitiation and justification, the legal legerdemain which viewed the cross as somehow satisfying the righteous demands of God and by so doing staving off His wrath. A fresh formulation is called for. Actually, the "life of Messiah was an intense conflict with the powers of domination"; His cross, accordingly, had "the character of confrontation," and thus "Christ was killed as a subversive," by the religious and political establishment, those authorities and powers which embodied, as they almost invariably do, "the dynamics of the politics of the Anti-Christ, one who wants to kill the Messiah, the presence of the future." The cross, then, when properly construed, "becomes the central point for the understanding of the possibilities of liberation in history...the power which, in every situation, negates the power of what is, in order to make possible the creation of the new."[79]

Lehmann, too, taking the cross as a profound symbolism, gives a dramatically and drastically new formulation.

When theology talks about atonement, it does not mean many things; it means only one thing. It means that in this act, wherein Jesus of Nazareth allowed himself to die in obedience to God's way of working in the world, the focus and locus of man's secret in the world was exhibited. The secret was that the suffering of man in the revolutionary environment in which God has put him is the power of redemption.[80]

Forgoing now any criticism of this dogmatic and egregious reduction of the cross to nothing but—after all, "it means only one thing"—a mere image of any man's suffering on behalf of revolutionary freedom at any time in history, let us ask about the resurrection. What about that consummate event in the series of events which form the Christ-event? Need it be said, Moltmann wonders, that "by 'resurrection' the earliest Christians did not mean a return of the dead Christ into mortal life or a restoration of the fallen creature"? But in case it need be said, Moltmann says it for us: "The inbreaking of a qualitatively new future, the entrance of something completely unexpected and the appearance of a life which is no longer 'life toward death' but 'life out of death.' In

79*Ibid.*, pp. 113-14, 131.
80Paul Lehmann, "The Theological Roots of Revolution," p. 68.

the historical *novum Christi* they saw the anticipation in the already effective promise of that which was ultimately and universally new." Given this understanding of the resurrection, it involves nothing less than "the transformation and fundamental revolution of the world"; yes, nothing less than the "new future of God, of the world, and of man." Hence, when Christianity is resurrection-oriented and resurrection-motivated, it refuses to "be the 'honey' of an antagonistic and repressive society." On the contrary, it becomes "provolutionary"—a neologism Moltmann coins and defines as repudiating the reactionary implication of the "re" in revolution and turning the human dream forward to a new future in which man directs "the course of human history as well as the evolution of nature."[81]

Alves advances the same exegesis of the resurrection. Whatever traditional theology may have taught otherwise, this event "does not indicate either that a dead body was brought back to life again or how it happened." The term itself "was borrowed from Jewish apocalypticism to express the community's experience that the One who had been crucified was alive in history, as a power of liberation." Thus resurrection is "the language of the ongoing politics of God in history," describing His "activity that through the negation of the Suffering Slave, liberates history for the future."[82] Humanistic messianism, therefore, by properly interpreting this category can ally itself with messianic humanism. "Both hope for the resurrection of the body" if by that symbol is meant "the resurrection of nature, the elimination of repression, the triumph of the erotic sense of life." That reinterpreter of Sigmund Freud, Norman O. Brown, so understands it. In his extraordinary tour de force *Life Against Death*, he reinterprets the New Testament as adroitly as he reinterprets Freud:

The question confronting mankind is the abolition of repression—in traditional Christian language the resurrection of the body. The resurrection of the body is a social project facing mankind as a whole, and it will become a practical political problem when the statesmen of the world are called upon to deliver happiness instead of power.[83]

[81] Moltmann, *Religion, Revolution and the Future*, pp. 33-34, 32.
[82] Alves, *op. cit.*, pp. 130-31.
[83] Quoted in *ibid.*, p. 153.

Since Alves approves of this reinterpretation, provided God not be forgotten—a provision which Brown ignores—he can write:

Here, the social project of the resurrection of the body ceases to be only a hope given to those who are strong and alive and becomes the universal project of the resurrection of the dead: the universal liberation of the body for the erotic sense of life in a world given to man for his enjoyment and happiness.[84]

If this reinterpretation of the—in Moltmann's phrase—"Christian myths" is followed, Marx was profoundly mistaken. "The missionary proclamation of the cross of the Resurrected One is not," Moltmann strongly protests,

an opium of the people which intoxicates and incapacitates, but the ferment of new freedom. It leads to the awakening of that revolt which, in the "power of the resurrection" (as Paul expresses it), follows the categorical imperative to overthrow all conditions in which man is a being who labors and is heavily laden. . . . Proclamation, through its announcement of new freedom, brings the denunciation of the bondage and fettering of the present to the past. . . . The understanding of the Biblical proclamation is turned from the inner agreement of faith to bodily obedience and to political work in the liberation of mankind from present affliction.[85]

Take, once more, the category of exorcism to which Cox calls attention, primarily in *The Secular City*, the seventh chapter of which he entitles "The Church as Cultural Exorcist." In the ministry of Jesus, he reminds us, the casting out of demons was "in no way peripheral but stood at the heart of his work." In the twentieth century, to be sure, we no longer subscribe to such "prescientific" concepts as "spirits and demons," but this does not carry the corollary that we can ignore the realities they symbolized. Demythologizing these concepts for a youthful audience, Cox explains:

We don't believe in principalities and powers, because we identify them with demons, spooks, and goblins. But we can break through this language barrier. . . . What Jesus was talking about, these principalities and powers, these forces which pervert and distort, are still here today. We give them different names, but they are still among us. Not too long ago we smiled just a bit contemptuously at people who talked about *supra*-human or *sub*-human forces. Some things have happened, however, in Western history in the past fifty years that made us a little less sneering about the reality of such forces. ... Let us not think, therefore, that when the New Testament talks about "principalities and powers" it is a document that we can simply dispose of as not speaking the language of the day. It is talking about forces that we still have. Today we call them blood, or class, or statistical probability; only the names are changed. Perhaps all of these forces—this entire range of symbols denoting the control of man's life by something other than man—can be called fate.[86]

Addressing the readers of *The Secular City* Cox engages in essentially the same explanation. "These 'principalities and powers' actually signify all the forces in a culture which cripple and corrupt human freedom." In his very vivid style, Cox proceeds to update the apostolic allusions to "the weak and elemental spirits of the universe" which hold man in bondage: "Paul was using his own language to describe the forces which impair human responsibility, including genes and glands and early toilet training. He is saying that, although these things exist, no one *has* to be determined by them. Man may be free—if he chooses to be." Indeed, taking Christ as his example, man can be a revolutionary exorcist: "The kerygma comes to a people when they stop blaming economic forces or psychological pressures for social injustice and family strife and begin to do battle against the causes of woe." And if man will act in faith on the promise of the kerygma, "there are no powers anywhere which are not essentially tameable and ultimately humanizable." In Jesus Christ, therefore, God is calling man "to freedom *from* the powers and principalities," calling "him at the same time to responsibility *over* and *for* them." God is calling people "away from their fascination with other worlds—astrological, metaphysical or religious," calling them "to confront the concrete issues of this one, 'wherein alone the true call of God can be found.'"[87]

The ministry of the church, accordingly, is that of "social

---

[86] Cox, *God's Revolution and Man's Responsibility*, pp. 65-66.
[87] Cox, *The Secular City*, pp. 128-30, 154.

exorcism." It must do battle against "principalities and powers," all those structures which cripple and corrupt human freedom today. The revolutionary implications of this ministry are plain enough to require no comment.

Take, again, the category of prophetism. Confessedly, this is another very inclusive and, in some ways, elusive concept, aspects of which can readily be overlooked and distorted. But essentially prophetism was a message of divine demand, judgment, and hope. Its spokesmen were champions of God's righteousness and thus champions of mercy, equity, and faithfulness. Conversely, they were critics of injustice, cruelty, and exploitation. Fearlessly they denounced kings and rebuked priests, warning of Jehovah's imminent punishment in terms of political and social upheaval—famine, pestilence, rebellion, war, and conquest. Yet beyond destructive wrath they always foresaw the emergence, redemptively, of a new order which would embody and implement the divine righteousness; they foresaw, in the words of R. B. Y. Scott, "the end of oppression, injustice and helpless poverty, of inhumanity, and the hurt and destruction of war." So the prophets, taken as a whole, were viewed by the established authorities of their times as irritants and even subversives. Their message "concerning society" was, to quote Scott further,

Not evolutionist or reformist but revolutionary. And they were social revolutionaries because they were religious conservatives, seeking to revive the essential ethics and social creativity of historic Yahwism. Yahweh, Himself, they declared, is in the struggle for social justice. He is the great Ally of the wronged and dispossessed. But He is more, for He is the protagonist in the vast drama of creation, whose final purpose is the making of a people for Himself. His will is to create *community*, an order of relationships with and among men in which His righteousness can find fulfillment. [88]

Shaull appeals to the prophets as models for revolutionary theologians in the twentieth century. Drawing upon Von Rad's *Old Testament Theology*, he reminds us that "with extraordinary freedom," the prophets did not hesitate "to denounce and abandon not only the old social and political structures, but also

[88] Quoted by Melvin Gingerich, *The Christian and Revolution* (Scottdale, Pa.: Herald Press, 1968), pp. 195, n. 7; p. 159.

the fixed order of religion that the great majority still considered valid." In the same spirit of freedom, they were ready "to abandon normal social life and economic security." From their perspective, discontinuity is the earmark and consequence of divine activity.

God's judgment on Israel means the end of the established sacral order. Suddenly, in an instant, ruin will overtake the whole generation; God will destroy His own people, leaving only a pitiful remnant. The break is so deep that the new state beyond it cannot be seen as a continuation of what went before. In fact, this discontinuity applies to God's own work. He tears down His own work in history, "revokes His historical design." All this is seen, however, as opening the way for the creation of a new order. ... As Von Rad puts it, their whole preaching is characterized by an unrivalled ability to respond to new historical developments and to point toward the eventual appearance of the qualitatively new: a new entry into the land, the appearance of a new David, a new Zion, a new Covenant.[89]

A Roman Catholic theologian, Father Peuchmard, sets forth the explosive potential of this category when he exclaims, "One cannot *a priori* exclude the participation of Christians in revolution on the ground that it involves violence. We are called to restore prophetism—not a verbal but a responsible prophetism."[90] And responsible prophetism is patently revolutionary, even if revolution necessitates violence.

Take, as a final category, a highly suggestive and very inclusive symbol, the kingdom of God. Cox perceives it as "a kind of living picture of the character and composition of the true city of man," the new fellowship in which "tribal and town chauvinism are left behind along with their characteristic mythologies, and a new, inclusive human community emerges."[91] It is the ingroup which acknowledges "the Lordship of Jesus Christ over the world," and which, consequently—to borrow Ellul's summation of a view with which he disagrees—seeks to become an all-embracing outgroup:

If Jesus Christ is truly Lord, then all that happens in the world is under

89 Richard Shaull, "Liberal and Radical in an Age of Discontinuity," p. 343.

90 Quoted by Jacques Ellul, *op. cit.*, p. 49.

91 Cox, *The Secular City*, pp. 144-45; *cf.* all of chapter 6, "The Church as God's Avant-garde."

His Lordship. Therefore it is not in the church (with its rites and cere-
monies and prayers) or even through study of the Bible that we participate in His Lordship, but in the world. It is by communion with all men
(with men who know Christ and men who do not) that the kingdom of
this Lord is built—this Lord who is present incognito in even the least of
these (Matt. 25:40, 45).[92]

And what revolutionary implications does this concept carry?
Moltmann indicates them:

The kingdom which Jesus preached and represented through His existence is not only the soul's bliss but *shalom* for the body as well: peace on
earth and liberation of the creature from the past. "The body is meant ...
for the Lord and the Lord for the body" (I Cor. 6:13). If, however, the
body belongs to the Lord, the task of the Christian is to await and antici-
pate his dominion in the emaciated and exploited body. This is not just
Christian *charitas*, but a practical proof of hope in the redemption of the
body in this world. The social revolution against unjust circumstances is
the immanent reverse side of the transcendent resurrection hope. Only
because the Church limited itself to the soul's bliss and the heavenly beyond and became docetic did the act of hope of bodily salvation wander
out of the Church and enter into social-change utopias. ... Therefore,
the Church and Christians should recognize a spirit which is of the spirit
of Christ in the movement of changing social relationships. It is, of course,
not so much a matter of a "latent Church" or an "anonymous Christianity" that appears here. It is much more the latent kingdom, for which
the Church (in its own way) exists, that proves itself effective in these
movements.[93]

So we end our tedious survey and summary of the biblical
materials which the revolutionary theologians utilize to effect
their own Copernican revolution in reconceptualizing traditional
Christianity. Perhaps, though, it is only fair to have one of this
rather disparate and differing group state succinctly its consensus.
Here, then, are the seven theses which Moltmann explicates in
his essay "God in Revolution."

Thesis 1: We live in a revolutionary situation. In the future we shall
experience history more and more as revolution. We can be responsible
for the future of man only in a revolutionary way.

Thesis 2: The new revolutionary situation has brought Christianity into

[92] Ellul, *op. cit.*, p. 123.
[93] Moltmann, "Toward a Political Hermeneutics of the Gospel," p. 87.

a deep crisis of identity. Christians in the churches will rediscover their true self-consciousness only if they overcome their own religious aliena-tion and their own hindrance to the free self-realization of man.

Thesis 3: The eschatological (and messianic) tradition of hope can give rise to a new birth of Christian faith in the revolutionary present.

Thesis 4: The new criterion of theology and faith is found in praxis.

Thesis 5: The Church is not a heavenly arbiter in the world's strifes. In the present struggles for freedom and justice, Christians must side with the humanity of the oppressed.

Thesis 6: The problem of violence and nonviolence is an illusory prob-lem. There is only the question of the justified and unjustified use of force and the question of whether the means are proportionate to the ends.

Thesis 7: The presence of Christians in revolution can mean that revolu-tions are freed from the coercion of the law. [94]

One thing should by now be clear. Moltmann states it flatly. Christianity's "all-embracing vision of God must be linked with the economic liberation of man from hunger, with the political freeing of man from oppression by other men, and with the hu-man emancipation of man from racial humiliation." Christianity, in short, must become a proligion, as Moltmann chooses to style it, "the joining of faith in God with hope in the liberation of man on a new earth and under a new heaven." [95] Or, even more crisp-ly, loyalty to the Bible may lead to the barricades.

[94] Moltmann, *Religion, Revolution and the Future*, pp. 130-47.
[95] *Ibid.*, p. 41.

When we take seriously ... the impact of Jesus upon men and upon es-tablished attitudes of his time, we begin to realize how revolutionary Jesus and his gospel were and how natural it was that men who cher-ished the established order should want him silenced. Not only was he propagating an order of life which set in question the foundation princi-ples of a God-fearing society, firmly anchored in an infallible Scripture, but, even more seriously, he was shaking men at the point of their inmost security, concerning the basis on which they counted themselves accept-able to God. God's ruthless claim on man came to expression in Jesus in such a radical way that it must have seemed to make valueless and innocuous all the assurances of the long-established religious authorities. He could not offer to men the freedom and blessing of an unconditional openness to God without claiming from them an equally unconditional binding of their wills to the will of God. The consequent tension with the existing order must have been explosive. It disturbed even such prophetically-minded people as the followers of John the Baptist.

And yet this revolutionary character of Jesus and his gospel is fre-quently concealed from the minds of Bible-reading Christians. Because his revolution was a quiet revolution, with no loud public protests, with no program for the reform of existing religious institutions, with no strategy for the seizure of power, it is possible to miss the radical quality that was inherent in every part of it and to picture Jesus' ministry as such a gentle, peaceful religious program that not even the most con-servative religionist could be disturbed by it. So also those who think loud public protests and strategies for the seizure of power are essential for any effective Christian revolution may be deceived by the quietness of Jesus' approach into underestimating the subversive quality of his mission.

—*James D. Smart*

VI. Jesus the Revolutionary

We have been examining the case for a Christian radicalism which contends that in many parts of the world today, including the United States of America, oppression and injustice are so flagrant as to justify subversive change, violent change if necessary. As we have observed, the radicals who argue this case appeal to theology in order to show that God is on their side or, less presumptuously, that they are on God's side. They view the Bible as an arsenal which provides powerful weapons for their attack upon the institutions and authorities that are frustrating the divine purpose to make and keep human life truly human. As they interpret Christianity, it requires obedient disciples to become insurrectionists bent on a revolutionary transformation of our allegedly moribund society. To name Jesus as Saviour and Lord is to confess that Karl Marx, Mao Tse-Tung, Che Guevara, Fidel Castro, and Abbie Hoffman are really one's spiritual brothers, however mistaken some of their ideas and misguided some of their tactics.

But the mention of Jesus as Saviour and Lord introduces what to the mind of an evangelical is the absolutely decisive reason for rejecting the theology of revolution. It is impossible to believe in Jesus Christ as Saviour and follow Him as Lord while at the same time advocating social change by any method except peaceful reform. Here, for an evangelical, is the watershed which divides him from those Christian radicals whose militancy contradicts the teaching and example of the Master they acknowledge. Yes, they acknowledge with Ernst Käsemann that Jesus "is the object of our faith; for he is, and never ceases to become afresh, our

Lord." [1] But acknowledge that, an evangelical maintains, and one immediately stands outside the orbit of revolutionary theology.

Colin Morris, the British missionary who served as president of the United Church of Zambia from 1965 to 1969, meets this contradiction head on in his incendiary book, *Unyoung, Uncolored, Unpoor.* With utmost directness he answers the question of an African believer who, to quote from his letter to Morris, wants "to join the Freedom Fighters," but hesitates precisely because of his religious convictions. "Can a Christian," he inquires, "take up guns and sticks against his fellowman?" [2] To which Morris replies, "Yes, I believe a Christian is justified in using violence to win freedom in Rhodesia. ... I believe freedom fighters are justified in using any method short of sadistic cruelty for its own sake to overthrow the Salisbury regime." But, having forthrightly stated his opinion, Morris has on his hands the problem of reconciling that opinion with the teaching and example of Jesus. He admits very frankly, "my argument stands or falls by His attitude to violence." Just as frankly Morris admits that "the words and witness of Jesus stick in the throat of any Christian contemplating revolution. He who was a stumblingblock to Jews and foolishness to the Greeks is an Almighty Headache to the Christian activist." Hence Morris has on his hands a seemingly insoluble problem: "It is impossibly difficult to reconcile Christ's command that we should love our neighbor with the decision to destroy him." [3] The evangelical therefore advises the revolutionist to make a choice. Either give up Jesus and stick to revolution, or else stick to Jesus and give up revolution. But many Christian radicals, Morris among them, reject that either/or. They prefer to endure the painful tension of trying to perform a feat which is "impossibly difficult." As Samuel Dickey put it years ago, those Christians who covet Jesus' "prestige and sanction" for their own programs must reinterpret Him in terms of political revolution, proving that He was "primarily not a religious

---

[1] Ernst Käsemann, *Jesus Means Freedom* (London: SCM Press, Ltd., 1969), p. 36.

[2] Colin Morris, *Unyoung, Uncolored, Unpoor* (Nashville, Tenn.: Abingdon Press, 1969), p. 10.

[3] *Ibid.*, pp. 19, 83, 98, 97.

teacher but a social and political insurrectionist."[4] Yet how can they successfully do so? How can "the impossibly difficult" possibly be done?

A Christian insurrectionist might perhaps respond that, despite the contradiction between revolutionary violence and Jesus' love ethic, the Gospels may be so read as to interpret the iconoclastic carpenter of Nazareth in terms of political revolution. He was a rebel against the Establishment which controlled Palestine in His day. As far back as the eighteenth century, the German scholar Hermann Samuel Reimarus maintained that the preaching of Jesus was an "incitement to revolt against the government of Rome."[5] In 1908 Karl Kautsky "represented Jesus as a rebel engaged in a first-century Marxian class-struggle."[6] In our own time, Ewan MacColl, portraying Jesus as the organizer of a popular front, sings his "Ballad of a Carpenter":

> He became a wandering journeyman,
> And He travelled far and wide;
> And He noticed how wealth and poverty
> Lived always side by side.
>
> So He said come all you workingmen,
> Farmers and weavers, too;
> If you would only stand as one,
> This world belongs to you.[7]

One more example of this continuous attempt to radicalize Jesus will be enough. In December, 1968, divinity students, demonstrating during a church synod at Hessen, Germany, carried a placard which described Jesus as a revolutionary outlaw.

Reward. Who knows this man? Wanted for vagrancy, insurrection, political intrigue, carpenter by occupation, suffers from hallucinations,

---

[4] Samuel Dickey, *The Conservative Revolution of Jesus: A Study of Some of His Social Attitudes* (New York : George H. Doran Company, n.d.), p. 88.

[5] The words quoted are those of S. G. F. Brandon in his impressively erudite *Jesus and the Zealots; a Study of the Political Factor in Primitive Christianity* (New York: Charles Scribner's Sons, 1967), p. 22.

[6] *Ibid.*, p. 23, n. 1; *cf.* Dickey's comment, *op. cit.*, p. 88, n. 1.

[7] Quoted by Steve Weismann, "New Left Man Meets the Dead God," *New Theology No. 5*, p. 41.

in league with the common folk and the anti-social . . . probably Jewish,
calls himself at times "Son of the Lord." . . . [8]

Hence if one is minded to do so, there is the possibility of interpreting Jesus from a revolutionary perspective, unconventional
though this perspective may be.

But is such a perspective simply unconventional? Must we not
protest that the picture of Jesus as a radical represents an unwarranted eisegesis of the New Testament sources? Morris hesitates either to affirm or deny this allegation, despite his personal
opinion that the Gospels are compounded of unreliable and inconsistent materials which render any interpretation arbitrary. Referring to the "Jesus of History" Whom New Testament experts
have repeatedly attempted to discover, he writes sarcastically:

This Jesus of History some theologians chat about as though He were an
old pal is a lay-figure built up of myth, dogma, guesswork, and pious
supposition wrapped round a flimsy skeleton of fact. Hobbes said a
mouthful when he claimed that coming to terms with Christianity is like
taking a pill: if you swallow it in one gulp it will probably work, but
start to chew it and you end up retching all over the place. [9]

Morris, therefore, surrenders to agnosticism, not sure whether
to place Jesus "in the van of the revolution egging on the peasantry or to interpose him between the mob and the barricades, pleading with murderous men to turn the other cheek." [10] Agnostically
he suggests that the Gospels may be regarded as a sort of Rorschach test:

Our ideals about Jesus tell us more about ourselves than they do about
Him. I search the Gospels for a freedom fighter and Jesus strides out
sword in hand; the pacifist looks there for the great advocate of non-
violence and is rewarded by a glimpse of the triumph of suffering love. [11]

Fortunately, however, regardless of the complexities of New
Testament criticism, we are not left in such a dismally agnostic
impasse. If we were, then we could scarcely any longer be Christian in a meaningful sense. R. F. Aldwinckle, professor of

---

[8] Quoted by A. Basilea Schlink, *World in Revolt* (Minneapolis, Minn.:
Bethany Fellowship, Inc., 1969), p. 7.

[9] Morris, *op. cit.*, p. 100.

[10] *Ibid.*, p. 101.

[11] *Ibid.*, p. 133.

systematic theology at McMaster Divinity College, does not ex-
aggerate the predicament which such agnosticism would create.

The mind of Christ must presumably be taken seriously by anyone
claiming to be His follower. If, on the contrary, such knowledge is not
attainable, then there would seem to be no point in trying to establish
a religious position in which Jesus would have the central place. It is no
answer to this problem to insist that we still have the "faith" of the
church. Either the faith of the church has some foundation in the mind
and intention of Jesus or it has not. If it has not, then it is logical to claim
that the "faith" of the church is not self-created or simply a mythopoetic
activity of the worshiping community, but derives in the last analysis
from an understanding of the "mind" of Christ reliably known. On the
other hand, if the faith of the church is not rooted in any knowledge of
the mind of Christ, and the thought and intention of Jesus must inevitably remain a mere X, then the church is no longer bound, morally,
intellectually, or spiritually to its past or to Jesus, and can develop its
contemporary spiritual life in complete freedom. The Church might continue to use the term "Christ" to denote the Christ-idea or some con-
stellation of spiritual ideas and ideals, but these would have no necessary
connection with Jesus of Nazareth. Once again it could be argued that
Biblical criticism has left us with this option alone, but it must be asked
whether the result would still be Christianity in any intelligible and
recognizable form.[12]

Yet Aldwinckle in a scholar's guarded style refuses to endorse this
agnostic conclusion.

The constant reiteration in recent years that "the quest of the historical
Jesus" has failed is one of those oversimplifications which can seriously
mislead the uninitiated. If it is simply the claim that it is no longer possible to penetrate behind the New Testament documents to a purely
human Jesus who by definition could not be the "Christ of faith," then
the point is well taken. But is it possible that the authentic Jesus of
history was never such a figure stripped of all supernatural claims. It

---

[12]R. F. Aldwinckle, "Did Jesus Believe in God?" *New Theology No. 5*, pp.
76-78. It is not our purpose here to discuss the technical problems of New Testament criticism. It must be borne in mind that Brandon, to whose book Morris enthusiastically appeals as substantiating the revolutionary view of Jesus, is equally
agnostic. "We have no certain record of Jesus' teaching preserved in His own
words and accurately describing the context in which it was given." Brandon,
op. cit., p. 336; *cf.* pp. 147-48.

might just be the case that the Christ to whom the apostolic witness esti-
fies was in fact the real Jesus of history. [13]

With a touch of irony, he adds that "many who speak of the failure of the quest of the historical Jesus ... speak as if they knew with reasonable certainty a good deal about Jesus' thought." [14] Thus agnosticism with respect to the historical Jesus is wholly un-called for. The situation has not changed in any essentials since Harry Emerson Fosdick, after alluding to all the difficulties and problems the scholars must deal with, rightly affirms, "These Gospels are genuine historical documents ... vivid portrayals of a real personality of whom they are honestly trying to present a true picture." [15]

Choosing, then, to adopt an interpretation of Jesus which is in keeping with his own convictions and commitments, Morris attacks "the idea of a pacifist Christ," who "kept aloof from do-mestic political issues in loyalty to a higher destiny." He prefers to view Jesus as a "freedom-fighter," a Man of His times, a patri-otic Jew upon Whom "the vicious politics of his day" impinged agonizingly. Hence Morris chooses "to believe that Jesus was involved in seditious activity against Rome." Believing this, he sees no reason why Jesus "ought not to have believed that it was God's will for him in first-century Palestine to help release Israel from a heathen yoke." [16] "Why should we balk at the possibility in the New Testament that God willed his obedient servant to head the struggle to free Israel from Roman dominion?" Take into account the dovetailing pieces of evidence, and this supposi-tion is not as incredible as it first sounds. For one thing, Jesus was raised among a subject people who hated their Roman overlords and plotted rebellion against them. He "must have been educated as much on the legends of the Galilean freedom fighters as in Jewish law." [17] For another thing, in the Gospels He is recorded as scathingly denouncing the Pharisees, Sadducees, and Herodi-ans; but He is never recorded as saying a single word in criticism

[13] Ibid.

[14] Ibid.

[15] Harry Emerson Fosdick, The Man From Nazareth: As His Contemporaries Saw Him (New York: Harper & Brothers, 1949), p. 31.

[16] Morris, op. cit., pp. 113, 125, 133, 102, 121, 123.

[17] Ibid., p. 105.

of the Zealots, those fanatical, militant, violent Jews "who were prepared to fight and die for freedom."[18] In the third place, "he chose at least one Zealot to be a member of his inner circle, named Simon the Canaanite by Mark, but identified openly as Simon the Zealot by Luke."[19] Again, His reply to the "most explosive issue of his day," the payment of tribute to Caesar, "was clearly seditious":

It is as though members of the Underground in occupied Europe had asked a patriot whose judgment they respected whether they ought to help the Nazis ransack their country of its treasures, and had received the reply, "Give the Nazis what is coming to them!" A passing *gauleiter,* unfamiliar with the idiom, might find such an answer unexceptionable, but the questioners would recognize fighting talk when they heard it.[20]

Once more, Jesus' cleansing of the Temple

must have been seen by the people as a blow struck for the integrity of the Jewish people as well as a vindication of the righteousness of God. Who could blame either the Romans or the Festival crowds for reading into the Cleansing of the Temple a symbolic condemnation of any collaboration with the Romans? For every loyal Jew, freedom or servitude began at the Temple, and it was interesting that when the Zealots made their final fatal bid for freedom in A.D. 66, their first act was to repeat what Jesus had done and occupy the Temple, ejecting the quisling High Priest and his officials.[21]

The option, therefore, as Morris phrases it, was quite simple: "Jesus was either a responsible leader of the freedom struggle which had both political and religious implications, or else He was playing with fire and inviting others to be burned."[22] Still further, the triumphant entrance was a responsible bid for the leadership of the Jewish people, "with a view to throwing off the oppressor's yoke."

Jesus must have known the political connotations placed by ordinary Jews on the role of the Messiah, yet he chose to ride into Jerusalem solemnly acting out that role at a time when the mood of the people

18 *Ibid.*, p. 106.
19 *Loc. cit.*
20 *Ibid.*, pp. 111-12.
21 *Ibid.*
22 *Ibid.*, pp. 116-17.

was at its most militant and fervent and then, we are told, expected them to see the Suffering Servant through the garb of a political liberator. It takes some crediting. Again the question must be posed—was he a fool? If not, he would surely have avoided raising false hopes by sparking off a demonstration that was bound to misfire and possibly lead, through patriotic fervor, to a bloody confrontation with Roman forces.[23]

In addition, there are those strange references, in the closing stages of the Gospel drama, to the carrying and use of weapons. "How could a pacifist Christ permit his closest disciples to be armed?" What an irrational contradiction!

The Gospels unflaggingly portray a leader who would countenance only suffering love as the instrument of his will, yet apparently those whom he is grooming to carry on his work tramp around with swords clanking at their heels. The picture conjured up is as incongruous as that of a team of Quakers setting out on one of their missions of reconciliation with rifles slung over their shoulders. It is very odd. [24]

Add these pieces of evidence together, and one confronts a disjunction. Either Jesus "was a dangerous, blundering fool, doing ambiguous acts and saying provocative things that invited bloody retaliation upon His followers all the while protesting that He was being misunderstood," or "Pilate was right in putting Jesus to death for insurrection ... stirring up the people, refusing to pay tribute, and claiming political messiahship."[25]

Perhaps this is the appropriate place to note that Morris praises Brandon's book, *Jesus and the Zealots*, as a work of "massive and wide-ranging scholarship," which must hereafter be "the standard text for any Christian trying to make theological sense of the revolution of our time."[26] To review adequately this work of "massive and wide-ranging scholarship" lies beyond our present purposes. Brandon's thesis, however, which is elaborately and tendentiously worked out, can best be summarized in his own words:

Some Christian scholars have indeed given serious attention to the more obvious indications of a political element in the trial and execution of

[23] *Ibid.*, pp. 114, 115.
[24] *Ibid.*, pp. 117, 118.
[25] *Ibid.*, pp. 102, 110.
[26] *Ibid.*, p. 119.

Jesus; but their approach to the issue has always been too clearly made from a firm conviction that the Divine Saviour could not have concerned himself with contemporary Jewish politics—if he did touch upon them, it was only by way of warning and to urge his hearers to seek spiritual values beyond them. ... There is still a curious reluctance even to consider the possibility that Jesus might have had political views. Although the suggestion would be vigorously repudiated that Jesus was unpatriotic, the logic of what patriotism meant to a Jew living under Roman rule in Judea is never faced out. Yet it has to be recognized that the Roman domination was imposed and maintained by force; it was, moreover, a heathen administration closely associated with the worship of false gods; and its officers were frequently unjust, corrupt, and cruel. To tolerate, still less endorse such a rule, could by no conceivable interpretation of the word be judged patriotic. ... If Jesus had been regarded as the Messiah, indeed had himself claimed to be this long hoped-for deliverer of Israel, he could surely not have avoided pronouncing on the question of the legitimacy of the Roman rule over Israel. What his verdict would have been is surely obvious also. ... There is every reason, therefore, for assuming that Jesus, during his youth and early manhood, grew up with a close acquaintance of the Zealots and their aims and activities. ... It is likely that many Galileans had taken part in a revolt of A.D. 6, and Jesus would have known some of the survivors in the families of those who had perished. To a Galilean boy or youth those martyred patriots would surely have been heroes, and doubtless he would often have listened enthralled to tales of Zealot exploits against the hated Romans.[27]

Having filled in the background rather prejudiciously, Brandon proceeds to develop his case for a definite linkage between Jesus and the Zealots. These fanatical patriots comprised a movement which

was essentially religious in its inspiration and purpose. It found practical expression in armed action, even including assassination. ... Jesus must have known of the Zealot ideal, and of Zealot exploits and martyrdom from boyhood. Because he was a Jew, nurtured in the tradition of his people and believing in the absolute sovereignty of God, both his religious instincts and his sense of patriotism must have been affronted by the presence of the heathen Romans, who dominated his people by force of arms and demanded tribute to support their ungodly rule. It is, accordingly, difficult to see on *a priori* grounds why he should not have sympathized with the Zealots and felt hostile toward the Romans and

27 Brandon, *op. cit.*, pp. 24, 25, 66.

those Jews who, for wordly gain, cooperated with them. The possibility that he was so disposed is, moreover, confirmed by the fact that he chose a Zealot to be one of his inner band of disciples. It is also reinforced by the absence of any record of his condemnation of the Zealots. ... There seems to be nothing in the principles of Zealotism, enunciated by Judas of Galilee, that we have definite evidence for knowing that Jesus would have repudiated.[28]

What, then, is Brandon's conclusion? Rather than being "a quietist," Jesus was far more probably an insurrectionist who "must have reckoned with the fact that his mission would ultimately bring him into conflict with the Roman Government in Judea."[29] So we may assume "that the movement of Jesus and that of the Zealots converged in revolutionary action in Jerusalem."[30]

Of course, if one agrees with Brandon as Morris enthusiastically does, and if one therefore abandons, as Morris also does, "the idea of a pacifist Christ," he must "come to terms with a warlike one," engaging unflinchingly in a reconstruction of his Christology. He must abandon the traditional doctrine of Jesus' "moral perfection." He must insist, on the contrary, that Jesus, as a real man immersed in the extremist politics of His own time, had to be guilty of "shabby compromises, nasty but necessary actions, desperate decisions." As a result, He was less than impeccable and unsullied. "A great man might, in such circumstances, retain his integrity, but never his purity." Morris wonders, however, who really wants to retain the preposterous, ethereal concept of an impeccable, unsullied Jesus. "A sinless man would be a monster, a shapeless blur, lacking individuality." A sinless Jesus "would bypass history instead of experiencing it." Far better, consequently, to see in Him "a quality of integrity, a single-minded determination to do, in concrete situations, what he believed to be the will of God"—which in first-century Palestine meant rebellion against Rome.[31]

As for Christ's love-ethic, there is no reason to quarrel with Reinhold Niebuhr's appraisal of it: "The social idea of Jesus is

[28] *Ibid.*, pp. 326-27, 355.
[29] *Ibid.*, p. 344.
[30] *Ibid.*, p. 356.
[31] Morris, *op. cit.*, pp. 124, 121, 123.

as perfect and as impossible of attainment as his personal ideal."[32] There is no reason, either, to regard it as binding upon real people living in today's real world. In Morris' judgment it is an impossible ideal which he characterizes as self-defeating and paradoxical, an ideal which, if taken "to its limits will deny the Christian any participation in political life at all," an ideal which has burdened Christ's disciples "with an unresolvable dilemma." So why not confess that, as a real man, Jesus "may have had a whole jumble of ideas in his mind without wanting, or being able, to resolve them into some neat pattern"? Why impose on Him our Western modes of thought? No doubt "we cannot live with contradictory ideas; we must settle for one or the other, or else evolve a third which harmonizes the other two." But the Jesus of the Gospels is a prescientific Semite Who thinks "things totally inexplicable to our tidy minds ... holding contradictory ideas in tension without trying to resolve them ... acting upon whichever idea seems to fit the circumstances." Better by far, though, this inconsistent, roughhewn revolutionary than the anemic pietist, the "Church's Jesus ... a gleaming diamond of a man" Who is not "relevant to the life of our time," because "he was irrelevant to his own time."[33]

Two comments are now in order as we reflect on Morris' radicalization of Jesus, a messiah Whose view of His messianic role, though hopelessly confused, was in essence that of spearheading a this-world revolution rather than providing a next-world redemption.

First and crucially, Morris unabashedly confesses that the Jesus Whom he finds in the Gospels may be a projection of his own psyche. Himself a revolutionary, Morris—remember the Rorschach test analogy—imposes a revolutionary interpretation on the New Testament data. What he does, and Brandon likewise, is adopt a presupposition which, by dint of conjecture and extrapolation, he compels the materials to fit and fortify. Brandon, who is an outstanding authority in the field of comparative religion, does not deny that the Gospels present the traditional interpretation of Jesus, the very interpretation which Morris chal-

32Quoted by *ibid.*, p. 125.
33 *Ibid.*, pp. 127, 128, 134, 135, 136, 132, 102.

lenges. Brandon simply argues that the Gospel writers, hypothetically motivated by apologetic interests and needs, deliberately misinterpreted the real Jesus. Thus the Jesus of the Gospels is undeniably the pacifist Jesus Whose portrait Morris is eager to repaint. The Matthean and Lukan Gospels, Brandon tells us, "elaborated the Markan portrait of Jesus into that of the pacifist Christ, which became the established tradition of Christianity."[34] Matthew not only accepts the Markan thesis that Jesus had been "innocent of sedition against Rome," but develops it into the concept "of the pacifist Christ who renounced all resort to force, whether human or angelic," a Christ Who taught His disciples that "Zealot virtues and Zealot action must be repudiated and replaced by the idea of the 'poor in spirit,' the 'meek,' and the 'peacemaker.'"[35]

As for "Luke's portrait of Jesus as the pacifist Christ," it is "a more subtle elaboration." Striking at its outset a note of peace in the angelic chorus that heralds the Saviour's birth, this Gospel makes Him "the author of noble parables such as the Good Samaritan and the Prodigal Son." Besides this, Brandon points out, Luke represents Jesus as rebuking "his fierce disciples who wish to call down fire from heaven to consume certain uncooperative Samaritans and ... warning against the consequences of violence when told of Pilate's slaughter of some Galileans and those killed by the fall of the tower in Siloam."[36]

The Fourth Gospel is no different from the Synoptics, Brandon asserts, with respect to this "concept of the pacifist Christ." In point of fact, John 18:36-37 "attributes to Jesus a significantly formal repudiation of political ambition." John, moreover, includes a narrative which depicts Jesus as "specifically repudiating the armed support of his followers" in achieving the kingdom which He defines as not of this world.[37]

Brandon's very summary is, therefore, a refutation of any attempt by honest exegesis of the Gospels *as they stand* to metamorphose the New Testament Christ into a Palestinian freedom

---

[34]Brandon, *op. cit.*, p. 285.
[35]*Ibid.*, pp. 308, 310.
[36]*Ibid.*, pp. 316-17.
[37]*Ibid.*, pp. 318, 320.

fighter. "We see, then, that the authors of Matthew, Luke and John, each in his own way and for his own purpose, elaborated the Markan portrait of Jesus, as one innocent of sedition against Rome, into that of the pacifist Christ, who taught his followers to love their enemies and rejected all resort to armed force." This "representation of Him as living aloof or insulated from the political realities of first-century Judea" is one "which the Evangelists fabricated for their own particular apologetic needs."[38] So if Morris is to establish his contention that Jesus was a revolutionary, he cannot do so by an honest exegesis of the Gospels as they stand. He can do so only by assuming with Brandon that the Gospels, instead of faithfully reporting the life and teaching of the real Jesus, give us a portrait which is not only completely distorted but largely imaginative. He can do so only by assuming, as Brandon does, "that the author of Mark was not concerned to present an accurate historical record of the career of Jesus, but that he was moved by a definite apologetic motive." To shield the Christian community from persecution, Brandon speculates, "Mark" was forced to conceal the fact "that Jesus had had a connection with Zealotism which might fairly be interpreted as sympathetic." "Mark," accordingly, manufactured an account which Brandon adjudges "vague and imprecise'. . . self-contradictory on grounds of internal logic," an account which is "awkward and naïve," an account which is "incredible both on historical grounds and because of its intrinsic impossibility." [39] Hence to establish his contention that Jesus was a Revolutionary, Morris has no option but to embrace Brandon's reinterpretation of Mark and the other Gospels. But this reinterpretation is controlled by questionable canons of credibility and guided by some incidental information which gets shanghaied into the service of a theory that Brandon finds congenial and that Morris gratefully appropriates. This theory, though, requires subscription to an historical agnosticism more devastating than an exegetical agnosticism. It is one thing to admit uncertainty as to how the Gospels are to be understood, taken at their face value; it is quite another thing, however, to conclude that the Gospels are contrived accounts,

38 *Ibid.*, p. 320, *cf.* pp. 322-23.
39 *Ibid.*, pp. 245, 248, 256, 262.

their facts either so deliberately manufactured and unrecogniza-
bly distorted that without recondite sleuthing and speculating
their minimal residue of "truth" cannot be rediscovered. It is
one thing to sit in a rowboat which, while tossed by the waves, is
tied securely to a wharf; it is quite another thing to sit in a wave-
tossed rowboat loosely tied to a wharf which is itself adrift.

An evangelical declines, then, to accept Brandon's historical
skepticism. He also refuses to take Morris as an exemplar and
handle the Gospels with a caviling subjectivism. That is why he
fails to find support for the view that Jesus was a quasi-Zealot, a
first-century revolutionary, a forerunner of contemporary freedom fighters. He finds, on the contrary, persuasive evidence to
substantiate the view of world-renowned New Testament scholar
Oscar Cullmann. "Jesus was no Zealot," but His "whole ministry was in continuous contact with Zealotism" and "it formed the
background so to speak of His activity." That judgment can be
made even stronger: "For the understanding of the New Testament and the events which led up to the death of Jesus, the Zealot
movement is of extraordinary significance." The evidence indicates that "Jesus had with Him in His innermost circle of disciples Zealots—or at least former Zealots." The evidence indicates further "that He had to come to terms almost daily with
Zealot questions." Would He or would He not adopt "the ideal
of the Zealots, who wanted to resist the Roman State by force of
arms"? Would He or would He not accept their concept of the
Messiah, a revolutionary pretender to the Jewish royal throne?
The evidence, though complex, is unambiguous.[40] As Cullmann
reads the Gospels, Jesus refused to make common cause with
Zealotism.

The complexity of the evidence is shown by the fact that Jesus
"like Barabbas was condemned by the Romans and not by the
Jews, and in fact *as a Zealot*," yet "from the beginning of His
public ministry until its close, Jesus consistently regarded the
Zealot—that is, political—interpretation of the Messiah as a
satanic temptation and consequently combatted it." All the evidence indicates, rather, "that Jesus would fulfill His Messiahship

---

40 Oscar Cullmann, *The State in the New Testament* (New York: Charles
Scribner's Sons, 1956), pp. 49, 11, 12, 17, 20, 28, *cf.* also pp. 14-17; 20-22, 31.

as God's Suffering Servant, not as a triumphant Messiah-King of Jerusalem." [41]

Cullmann's view of Jesus as the pacifist Christ is supported by Hans Windisch, another New Testament authority. "The most important characteristics of His messiahship, speaking negatively, is to be found in His refusal to wage the messianic war." [42]

Hence all the evidence indicates that Morris cannot appeal to Jesus as blessing the use of "guns and sticks" in the name of God. All the evidence, indeed, points the other way. Jesus teaches that "it is wrong to attack the state violently to set up the kingdom of God"; He also teaches that even when a state becomes idolatrous, His church does not have to launch a *holy war*. [43] All the evidence indicates, in short, that Jesus cannot be interpreted fairly as a first-century Camilo Torres. He cannot be drafted as a chaplain for revolutionaries without reducing the Gospels to a nose of wax which is capable of taking whatever shape the whim of its manipulator decides to impose.

At this juncture, however, we need to raise afresh Samuel Dickey's pertinent, far-reaching question: "Although Jesus' programme did not include force, was it any the less revolutionary—in a political as well as religious sense?" Dickey personally thinks that, if anything, it was more radical than the Zealot crusade against Rome.

His course was consciously revolutionary, but he was not a revolutionist. He did not draw the sword against the authority of Jerusalem or of Rome.

---

[41] *Ibid.*, pp. 48, 30, 39. His disciples "had not understood that He had no intention of being a Zealot leader, an earthly Messiah-King, that on the contrary He regarded this very idea as inspired by the devil." *Ibid.*, pp. 40-41. *Cf.* too, Fosdick's remarks: "Rebellious patriots thought Jesus might be the long-sought leader of their revolt. How else can the third temptation of Jesus be explained except in terms of this possibility? ... However the story of this temptation came into our records, the least probable explanation is that it was made up by the later church. The Christ in whom the church believed, by his atoning death and victorious resurrection, had become mankind's Saviour. What motive could possibly have led his followers then to imagine him as tempted to worship the devil—that is, to use satanic means—to win the kingdoms of the world? In Jesus' own lifetime, however, temptation to use bloody insurrection for the kingdom's sake was the most crucial public problem of his people." *Op. cit.*, pp. 192, 193.

[42] Quoted by Fosdick, *op. cit.*, p. 195.

[43] Cullmann, *op. cit.*, pp. 21, 53.

Nevertheless His messianic program included the downfall of both of them and the establishment in their place of a new social order and authority—that of the kingdom of God. He did not, therefore, recognize the authority of either Jerusalem or Rome. He was no "loyal" citizen in the modern sense. For Jewish national liberty He was not concerned. To God and the new order of His kingdom His whole loyalty was given. Other things in comparison were matters of indifference. He might appear a fanatic or a rebel and die as a consequence on the cross—he would be loyal still; through His very suffering God revealed in the Suffering Servant of Isaiah that His kingdom would surely come. [44]

In Dickey's opinion, Jesus occupied "a super-revolutionary position," calling for a transformation which lay a whole dimension beyond politics and economics, little as our Saviour disparaged the hard realities of human existence. The greatest friend of humanity, He was "the most dangerous adversary of ... the established order in this world of violence, falsehood, and base compromise." Any truly "great evangelist," Dickey declares, "is a revolutionary, and the most radical of all. He is the inaccessible source from whence revolutions break through the hard ground, the eternal principle of non-submission of the spirit to Caesar, no matter who he may be—the unjust force." [45] So as the greatest of evangelists, Jesus Christ was the greatest revolutionary. But His revolution was not inaugurated and cannot be implemented by armed violence, whether guns or sticks or atom bombs. It can be implemented only by the power which inaugurated His revolutionary kingdom, the power of suffering love.

[44] Dickey, *op. cit.*, p. 112.

[45] *Ibid.*, pp. 158, 168. Canon B. H. Streeter expresses a similar judgment: "Christ was no iconoclast, no lover of destruction for its own sake. If half that is said of Bolshevism is true, He would not have been a Bolshevist; but He was a revolutionary. ... He saw clearly, that, without drastic change, fulfillment was impossible. His interest was in the creative and constructive; but He knew, and was prepared to pay the price. If, then, I call him a *constructive* revolutionary, I put the emphasis upon the adjective, but with no intent to weaken the meaning of the noun." "Christ the Constructive Revolutionary," *The Spirit*, B. H. Streeter, ed. (New York: The Macmillan Company, 1921), pp. 347-48. More recently, Stephen Neil has resorted to the category of revolution in dealing with the Gospels in their present-day significance; *cf.* his *A Genuine Human Existence: Towards a Christian Psychology* (Garden City, N.Y.: Doubleday & Company, Inc., 1959), pp. 147 ff.

Here, in a single question, is the problem that concerns me, the problem which the events raise for us all: Can a revolt of the violent in the name of a libertarian ideal in a liberal society open the way to the future? Can it help to humanize the authoritarian organizations of a liberal society? Or will it lead, directly or indirectly, either of itself or by the reaction it will bring about, to a repetition of the tragedies of yesterday, even before they have ceased to haunt our minds? Those who want to go beyond liberalism always run the risk of returning to a previous stage.

—*Raymond Aron*

VII. A Just Revolution?

Sane and sensitive people everywhere, whether devout or atheistic, long for a society of order, peace, justice, freedom, and love. But nowhere under the sun does so utopian a society exist. A nation may more or less approximate this ideal state of things, but at its highest and best any national community remains a crude approximation of the utopian ideal. Indeed, as in centuries past, so today human life is often bestially inhuman. Awarded the Nobel Prize for literature in 1957, Albert Camus was a compassionate realist who saw life with penetrating clarity. Mankind, he felt constrained to observe, is in a sad plight:

The most striking feature of the world we live in is that most of its inhabitants—with the exception of pietists of various kinds—are cut off from the future. Life has no validity unless it can project itself toward the future, can ripen and progress. Living against the wall is a dog's life. True—and the men of my generation, those who are going into the factories and the colleges, have lived and are living more and more like dogs.[1]

No wonder, then, that sane and sensible people everywhere are protesting angrily against the discrepancy between the ideal for which they long and the reality which is humanity's lot. No wonder that they struggle to help themselves and one another achieve a better, higher approximation of their utopian dreams. No wonder that revolution fills our twentieth-century horizon. For

[1]Albert Camus, "Neither Victims nor Executioners," *Seeds of Liberation*, Paul Goodman, ed. (New York: George Braziller, Inc., 1964), p. 26.

revolution, as Camus puts it, hopes to effect "a change in political and economic institutions in order to introduce more freedom and justice."[2]

No wonder, either, that some Christians are advocating revolutionary change. They agree with the operational insights of a biblically grounded ethicist like Paul Ramsey, much as many of them may disagree with his proposed policies and specific strategies. Concern for "social charity" and "social justice" is rooted, Ramsey maintains, in "the interior of the ethics of Christian love." It springs from that "supreme compassion" which always seeks to heal the wounds of those "whom by his wounds Christ died to save."[3] Social charity and social justice are concretizations of that *agape,* itself begotten of divine *agape,* which faces "towards a man's existing neighbors and companions in God, seeking to determine what love permits and requires to be now done or not done toward them."[4] And what love permits and requires to be done *now*—Ramsey emphasizes present action—may precipitate conflict and even bloodshed. Though sad and regrettable, so be it! "No authority on earth can withdraw from 'social charity' and 'social justice' their intrinsic and justifiable tendencies to rescue from dereliction and oppression all whom it is possible to rescue."[5] What love permits and requires in its ministry of rescue may likewise involve a revolutionary stance, though Ramsey personally is by no means a protagonist of revolution. He sternly warns, nevertheless, that "at his peril" a Christian fails to "take responsibility for introducing radical changes into the existing world political system."[6]

Of course, the revolutionary stance, taken in response to the demands of social charity and social justice, may motivate nothing more than aggressive political action, a vigorous reformism which seeks to secure change by legal and nonviolent methods. But, as we have seen, an increasing number of sane and sensitive Chris-

[2] *Ibid.,* p. 32.

[3] Paul Ramsey, *The Just War* (New York: Charles Scribner's Sons, 1968), pp. 142, 145.

[4] Paul Ramsey, *War and the Christian Conscience* (Durham, N.C.: Duke University Press, 1961), p. 4.

[5] Ramsey, *The Just War,* pp. 36-37.

[6] *Ibid.,* p. 389.

tians are pressing—or being pressured, they retort—beyond the
limits of legality and nonviolence. They are concluding that the
agape which derives from the "supreme compassion" disclosed
in the Christ-event necessitates literal revolution and all it may
tragically entail:

terrorism, conspiracy, *coup d'état,* general strike, guerrilla warfare,
street fighting, pitched battle, singly or in some combination...the
taking of life, coercion, treachery, lying, destruction, uprooting, the infliction of many kinds of physical and psychological pain and suffering
on opponents and innocents alike. [7]

Literal revolution is both ghastly and costly, yet neighbor-
concern, rooted "in the interior of the ethics of Christian love,"
may not merely condone bloody violence; social charity and social
justice may demand it. Colin Morris is more forthright than most
of his fellow Christians who are moving beyond nonresistance to
the utilization of armed force, but the conclusion which he spells
out is now rather common: "Mercy may *require* revolution—the
use of violence to destroy a system of greater violence which prevents millions from being free men before God." [8]

Needless to remark, this advocacy of revolution on the ground
of neighbor-love has been engendering confusion and controversy
within the Protestant and Catholic churches alike. As Helmut
Gollwitzer exclaims,

Just at this moment, when we...are inclined to regard as mistaken the
traditional approval of Christian participation in the use of military force
and to hoist the flag of pacifism...we hear from our brethren in the
under-developed countries (where the situation is a revolutionary one)
that they consider it incumbent upon them to participate in national and
social revolutionary struggles which involve the use of force. [9]

That message is also being heard from brethren in the West.
Thus, here is the affirmative answer which was given by the
theological study group of the Christian Peace Conference to the
question whether New Testament discipleship allows participa-

[7] George Kateb, *Utopia and Its Enemies* (New York: The Free Press of Glencoe, 1963), p. 24.

[8] Morris, *op. cit.,* p. 140.

[9] Quoted by J. M. Lochman, "Ecumenical Theology of Revolution," *New
Theology No. 6,* p. 113.

tion in violent revolution. It does, as we will note, but only if it is, in fact, an *ultima ratio,* a desperate last resort.

Ultima ratio means:

(a) If violent measures have already been used by the oppressors...; then

(b) if all possible methods of legal criticism and legal actions have been courageously and patiently tried, without success;

(c) if a situation has arisen which (owing to the action or failure to act of the oppressors) is more harmful to human beings than a violent revolution would probably be. [10]

The document issued by the study group "concludes with an important theological explanation":

If Christians support revolution, they derive the right to do so not from the idea of revolution but from the Christian Gospel. In so doing the goals of humanization and justice (which are the goals of revolution) are not made relative. On the contrary, we should understand these goals more deeply, more objectively, more concretely. This means that our participation in revolutionary action must not be motivated by hatred, nor by confidence in force, but solely by sympathy and solidarity with those who suffer...and by the hope of a new, just order, by readiness to forgive. [11]

Obviously, therefore, Christians are wrestling anew with some disturbing problems about which there are widest divergences of judgment. "This is a revolutionary age," William V. O'Brien, professor of government at Georgetown University, warns us. "There will be more revolutions, and the moral issues raised by violent revolution require continuous study and debate. As Christians and as human beings we cannot turn and look away when societies are torn by violent revolution."[12] Instead of looking away we must, whether Protestant or Catholic, evangelical or

10 Quoted in *ibid.,* pp. 114, 115.
11 *Ibid.*
12 William V. O'Brien, *War and/or Survival* (Garden City, N.Y.: Doubleday & Company, Inc., 1969), p. 199.

neoliberal, undertake "a thorough rethinking" of traditional attitudes "on war, deterrence, revolution, and peace." [13]

From the standpoint of Christian morality, then, what are the major issues at stake in violent revolution? Basic to everything else, as one might assume, is the question of violence per se, violence whether licit or otherwise. If, as pacifist critics contend, armed coercion is interdicted, literal revolution can never be a live option for Christians. To single out a distinguished spokesman for nonviolent discipleship, this is the position of French sociologist Jacques Ellul. He holds that to accept "the order of Christ... we must reject violence root and branch.... The Christian faith implies rejection and condemnation of revolutionary violence and the violence of the established powers." [14] In attempting their rebuttal of Ellul's position, however, Christian realists as well as the proponents of revolutionary violence simply point to a melancholy fact. Human life is full of violence, account for it any way one pleases. "All of history," Berger states sadly, "is one endless massacre stretching back to the dawn of mankind. Wherever we are in history, we stand on a mountain of corpses"; and terrible as that thought is, another thought is even more painful: "we are the beneficiaries of all this carnage." [15] Such thoughts may offend our sensibilities, but day after day, inexorably, they thrust themselves to the forefront of consciousness. We live in a fallen world which is full of violence.

It is distressingly true, therefore, that violence characterizes American society as it does all society. A Robert Waelder may rise to the defense of the United States, indignantly denouncing *"the*

13 *Ibid* , p. 274. "The church of Jesus Christ to which by grace I, at least, adhere is a company in which a moral theologian is only an ordinary Christian endeavoring to push out as far as he can the frontier-meaning of the practice of a charitable and rational justice and to draw forth all the actions and abstentions that this requires (and so some times he must say 'may' and 'perhaps' at morally crucial points, without fear lest some 'layman' resolve this opinion into practical certainty, and thus be led to do something that may in reality be objectively wrong). The ordinary Christian layman should also be a moral theologian to the measure that he can, and he should reduce his own remaining subjective incertitudes to the practical certainty required for his own responsible practice." Paul Ramsey, *The Just War*, pp. 364-65.

14 Ellul, *op. cit.*, pp. 129, 145.

15 Berger, *op. cit.*, p. 57.

habit of attributing common human failings to Western civilization in general or to American civilization in particular."

The sins with which Americans are charged by moralists—selfishness, greed, lack of concern for others—are what Christian philosophy calls the *sins of incontinence*. With regard to more severe failings—cruelty, perfidy—the American record compares favorably with the records of other lands; and even with regard to the sins of incontinence, a verdict— if a verdict there has to be—would have to takè into account the long record of American generosity, not equalled anywhere else, and the exceedingly short memory of the American people for iniquities suffered, i.e., their inability to hold a grudge against anybody for any length of time. It is therefore somewhat odd that Western moralists train their guns primarily on those who, while certainly sharing in the flaws of human nature, have, on the whole, sinned less than most others, and have made serious efforts at repairing many of the sins which they have actually committed. [16]

Waelder's exoneration of the United States is, however, too labored and lame. Americans are certainly no worse than other peoples, but it is highly doubtful that they are any better.

Because uncontrolled violence threatens to make human life a Hobbesian "war of everyone against everyone," the organized violence of the state is imperative, a legalized violence which serves to control the violence of anarchy. Luther said it in his usual pungent style.

A man who would venture to govern an entire country of the world with the Gospel would be like a shepherd who should place in one fold wolves, lions, eagles, and sheep together and let them mingle with one another and say, help yourselves, and be good and peaceful among yourselves; the fold is open, there is plenty of food; have no fear of dogs and clubs. The sheep, forsooth, would keep the peace and would allow themselves to be fed and governed in peace, but they would not live long; nor would any beast keep from molesting another. [17]

Adhering to this view, then, mainstream Christianity distinguishes between force and violence, whatever the terminology it employs. Force, the power wielded to make and keep human life truly human, it extols in company with Karl Rahner as one of

16 Robert Waelder, *Progress and Revolution: A Study of the Issues of Our Age* (New York: International Universities Press, Inc., 1967), pp. 315-17.

17 Quoted by Kateb, *op. cit.*, p. 27.

God's gracious gifts.[18] Violence it denounces as the use of power "in such an extensive, indiscriminating, or even unlimited measure and manner that it becomes useless for the rational purposes of politics, which are always limited." Force it praises, in the words of Thomas E. Murray, as "the use of power in such a proportionate measure and in such a discriminating manner as to constitute an apt means for the achievement of legitimate political goals." Hence it deplores, again in Murray's words, "the absurdity of violence," while at the same time it endorses "the rational necessity of force for the purposes of politics."[19] William V. O'Brien, who classifies himself as a Christian realist, offers a kind of anguished testimony on this score: "*Man must accept the reality and necessity of armed coercion as a fact on every level of society. Man must learn how to limit and channel armed coercion insofar as possible in the interests of the community at every level, in order to survive.*" He testifies, too, that he has reached this

18 In his essay "The Theology of Power," Karl Rahner, perhaps the leading Catholic theologian of our time, defines force as the use of physical means "which do not address themselves to the insight and freedom of the other." He lays down four propositions regarding it: (1) "this sort of power ought never to have existed. In the actual order of salvation, as it is and as it was originally willed by God, it stems from sin. It is one of the forms in which guilt manifests itself." (2) "Power, including physical force, is (although stemming from sin, manifesting it and tempting to it) not itself sin but a gift of God, an expression of His power, an element of the reflection of God in the world." (3) "In the actual order of things, its exercise—at least on the whole—is not irrelevant to salvation: it is a process of either *salvation* or *perdition.*" (4) "Only he who strips it of its power, by accepting the weakness of the cross, futility and death as salvation: only he who is ready to fail, even when he fights bravely, confidently and remorselessly, struggling even for power—he alone does not sin when he exercises power. For to use it without faith is to misuse it." Rahner strongly rejects the pacifist position: "The principle of the absolute renunciation of force would not therefore be a Christian principle. It would be a heresy which misunderstood the nature of man, his sinfulness and his existence as the interplay of persons in the *one* space of material being. An order of freedom would be misunderstood, if it were taken to be an order of things in which force was considered reprehensible on principle. A fundamental and universal renunciation of physical force of all kinds is not merely impracticable. It is also immoral, because it would mean renouncing the exercise of human freedom, which takes place in the material realm, and hence it would mean the self-destruction of the subject who is responsible to God." "The Theology of Power," *Theological Investigations,* Vol. 4 (Baltimore, Md.: Helicon Press, 1966), pp. 393, 395-96, 402, 408, 399-400.

19 Quoted by Ramsey, *War and the Christian Conscience,* pp. 277, 302.

opinion only "after years of thought, study, and prayer." He keeps hoping, moreover, "that the normative and/or empirical sciences, or the hand of God, may move men of good will in directions that will change the present system, one characterized by almost unremitting threat or use of force, at every level from the village to the world arena."[20]

Bearing this distinction in mind, mainstream Christianity has taught, Paul Ramsey says, that "the use of power, and possibly the use of force, belongs to the *esse* of politics (its *act of being*) and is inseparable from the *bene esse* of politics (its *proper act of being,* or its act of being *proper* politics)."[21] Persuaded, therefore, that the essence of politics is the wise use of force for the purpose of maintaining order and obtaining justice, mainstream Christianity has sanctioned the sword-bearing and sword-wielding state. This sanction it purports to draw directly from the New Testament. William Lasor, a faculty member at Fuller Theological Seminary, gives contemporary expression to the traditional teaching which is still the majority opinion within Christendom.

The kingdoms of this world are ruled by men. It is the Scriptural teaching that these earthly rulers rule by the will of God, but this does not mean that they are knowingly obedient to the will of God. Rather, they are designated as a "terror to evildoers," a restraining force upon the satanic powers of disorder and lawlessness in this present age (cf. Rom. 13:1-7; I Pet. 2:13, 14; II Thess. 2:1-10). The primary objective of a worldly kingdom is its "national interest," which is defined by its rulers. The method of achieving that objective is force (which does not necessarily, nor even primarily, mean war), Scripturally described as "the sword." ...[22]

A Christian can refuse, of course, to bear and use the sword. But if he does,

He has no Biblical authority to tell the state it must renounce the use of force in order to preserve law, or to demand that the law of the state change to disarm policemen. This would be to take the "sword" from the

20 O'Brien, *op. cit.,* pp. 44, 45.
21 Ramsey, *The Just War,* p. 5.
22 William Sanford Lasor, "Law and Order," *Christianity Today.* January 30, 1970, p. 390.

"magistrate"—and the bearing of the sword by the magistrate is recognized and approved by the Word of God. [23]

Mainstream Christianity, accordingly, has sanctioned the use of force not only against external foes but also internal enemies. Revolutionists, who are violently disrupting order, must, it teaches, be put down with violence. Luther's language was no doubt intemperate, yet the advice he offered to the German nobility when the peasants started to rebel is usually exonerated as a concrete application of the New Testament principle that authorities must preserve security and order: "Dear Gentlemen, hearken here, save there, stab, knock, strangle them at will, and if thou diest, thou art blessed: no better death canst thou ever attain." *Herr Omnes* was Luther's nickname for the rebelling peasants whom he counseled princes to strangle "as you would mad dogs." How else could anarchy be prevented? "The only way to make *Herr Omnes* do what he ought is to constrain him by law and the sword to a semblance of piety as one holds wild beasts by chains and cages." [24] Thus mainstream Christianity has given its benediction to the use of force in the hands of rightful authorities for righteous ends.

We move next to the question of whether force may ever be justly used to oppose the powers-that-be. What about the right of violent revolution? What if the defense of order and the fear of anarchy serve to frustrate justice? What if unrighteousness, technically legal though it may be, is the exorbitant price paid for order and peace? Under such circumstances, may force be used, temporarily disrupting order and peace, to secure a greater measure of justice?

Mainstream Christianity has tended to assign top-priority value to order as the indispensable foundation and framework of justice. So E. Clinton Gardner declares:

In view of the nature of the state as an instrument of the community for the protection of its members and for the harmonizing of their activities, the state may be said to have two main purposes: the provision of *order* and the provision of *justice*. Of these the first is clearly the more funda-

[23] *Ibid.*
[24] Quoted by William Dale Morris, *The Christian Origins of Social Revolt* (London: George Allen & Unwin Ltd., 1949), pp. 74-75.

mental; for order or peace is prerequisite to the achievement of justice. But the ultimate end of the state as a sovereign power is not the achievement of order but the establishment of justice. God does not will that man as a free moral being should live under an order that is based upon coercion alone.[25]

Dubious that a defiance of authority and a disruption of order with all their concomitant evils can ever promote justice, theologians like Luther and Calvin have equivocated on the right to revolution. To be sure, they were applying biblical principles to political and social systems different by far from those of the democratic societies which have evolved in the West; yet they saw little, if any, justification for revolutionary violence. Luther, to consider him first, opposes it. Helmut Thielicke cites passages in which Luther claims that "revolution is always avenged. Even when it succeeds, it has to pay dearly. This in itself shows that revolution is not in accordance with God's will."[26] Luther grants, nevertheless, that in some situations a Christian may disobey his government. He propounds the question, "What if a prince is in the wrong? Are his people bound to follow him then too?" His answer is unhesitating:

If you know for sure that he is wrong, then you should fear God rather than men (Acts 5:29), and you should neither fight nor serve, for you cannot have a good conscience before God. "Oh no," you say, "my lord would force me to do it; he would take away my fief and would not give me my money, pay and wages. Besides, I would be despised and put to shame as a coward, even worse, as a man who did not keep his word and deserted his lord indeed." I answer: you must take that risk, and with God's help let whatever happens, happen.... Since God will have us

25 Quoted by Walter E. Wiest, "Can There Be a Christian Ethic of Violence?" *Perspective*, Fall, 1969, p. 132. Reinhold Niebuhr takes the same view: "Before the rise of democracy, legitimate governments drew their authority from various ideological systems which were identical in their emphasis on justifying the authority of government chiefly by its ability to maintain peace and order, providing the order was not bought at too great a price of justice. Justice is always a secondary, but not a primary, source of authority and prestige. The primary source is the capacity to maintain order, because order is tantamount to existence in a community and chaos means non-existence." Quoted by Wiest, *ibid.*, pp. 132-33.

26 Helmut Thielicke, *Theological Ethics*, vol. 2, *Politics* (Philadelphia: Fortress Press, 1969), p. 341.

leave even father and mother for his sake (Matt. 19:29), we must certainly leave lords for his sake.... If they put you to shame or call you disloyal, it is better for God to call you loyal and honorable than for the world to call you loyal and honorable.[27]

Hence passive disobedience is not simply allowed. It is mandatory, if by obedience the truth of God will otherwise be compromised. But resort to force against legitimate authority is forbidden. A Christian in such a situation fights with no weapon except prayerful endurance. "Suffering! suffering!" Luther admonishes, "Cross! cross! This and nothing else is the Christian law!" Thus Thielicke conjectures that Luther's "concept of authority seems to prevent him from breaking through to the thesis of revolutionary resistance."[28]

But Ramsey thinks that Luther came to believe in the right of princes, though not commoners, to resist the imperial authority by armed force. He quotes Luther's letter to Spengler in which the reformer refutes the charge of inconsistency because he has been counseling vassals of the emperor "to resist him by force." If Ramsey is correct in his interpretation, as he seems to be, then he is also correct in his conclusion.

Luther's final position, therefore, permitted the princes to use armed resistance. "Lawful" resistance was not the same as rebellion or treason. He was instructed in this by the Saxon jurists; and because of a certain ambiguity in the word "lawful," this step taken by Luther was to have decisive importance in the Protestant cultures in the future, leading finally to adoption of legitimate revolution led even by private persons.[29]

However, as for Luther personally, he "always sided with those who condemn rebellion against those who cause it."[30]

As for Calvin, the story is largely the same, although one difference in it produces a more revolutionary sequel. Like Luther, he too inculcated the duty of obedience to legitimate authority. If wrong is perpetrated or commanded, the Christian's sole recourse must be passive resistance in the form of prayerful suffering. But significantly Calvin in his battle against Catholic rulers

27 *Ibid.*, p. 521, n. 3.
28 *Ibid.*, pp. 372, 370.
29 Ramsey, *War and the Christian Conscience*, pp. 119, 120.
30 *Ibid.*

did allow that "lesser magistrates"—members of the nobility, judiciary, and clergy—in contradistinction to "private persons" might resist excessive tyranny.

For, if there be, in the present day, any *magistrates appointed for the protection of the people and the moderation of the power of kings,* such as were, in ancient times, the Ephori, who were a check upon the kings among the Lacedaemonians, or the popular tribunes upon the consuls among the Romans, or the Demarchi upon the senate among the Athenians; *or with power such as perhaps is now possessed by the three estates in every kingdom when they are assembled;* I am so far from prohibiting them in the discharge of their duty, to oppose the violence or cruelty of kings, that I affirm, that if they connive at kings in their oppression of their people, such forbearance involves the most nefarious perfidy, because they fraudulently betray the liberty of the people, of which they know that they have been appointed protectors by the ordinance of God. [31]

Some twenty years later Calvin hedged his permission to lesser magistrates with stringent qualifications: "Better that all the children of God in France should perish than that the Gospel be dishonored by the bloodshed of resistance, unless Princes took action to maintain legal right *and parliament as a whole act with them.* It is not sufficient that a single Prince should lead them." [32]

Despite such stringent qualification, however, Calvin was supplying a rationale for the revolutionary activity of his Puritan heirs: "For only one more small step had to be taken, and not only could any first-class sheriff or justice of the peace lead a revolution, but any heretofore purely private person as well, so long as he acted 'in a magisterial capacity.' "[33] It was a relatively short step from Calvin's position to that of Christopher Goodman, one of the Marian exiles, who in his tractate, "How Superior Powers Ought to Be Obeyed," boldly asserted, "And though it appear at first sight a great disorder, that the people should take unto them the punishment of transgression, yet when the magistrates and other officers cease to do their duty, they are as it were without officers . . . and then God giveth the sword to

31 Ramsey, *ibid.,* pp. 121-22.
32 *Ibid.,* p. 122.
33 *Ibid.,* p. 123.

the people's hand and He Himself is become immediately their head."[34]

But, we must remember, not all theologians by any means have been willing to move from Luther's position or Calvin's to that of Goodman. A Friedrich Julius Stahl was so enamored of legitimacy as to pontificate, "Resistance can never be legitimate under any possible or conceivable circumstances." A Franz Reinhold Von Frank similarly dogmatized that, no matter how unjust a government may have been, in the event of a revolution, a Christian "must always be found on the side of authority, never on the side of those who try to overthrow it to reform it by force." Even a Helmut Thielicke wonders "whether the liabilities which inevitably attend every revolution can ever be justified." At the very best, he declares, "they certainly show that revolution is out of the question except as a last resort, and that any consideration of it must normally begin with the question whether and why this particular case, with its probable ambiguities, is indeed the extreme case."[35]

But as a last resort, the legitimacy of revolution is acknowledged by a rather impressive company of theologians and ethicists. One of them is Thomas Aquinas, whose genius definitively shaped Roman Catholic dogma. He allows that under certain circumstances sedition is not a mortal sin.

A tyrannical government is not just because it is directed not to the common good, but to the private good of the ruler.... Consequently there is no sedition in disturbing a government of this kind, unless indeed the tyrant's rule be disturbed so inordinately, that his subjects suffer greater harm from the subsequent disturbance than from the tyrant's government. Indeed, it is the tyrant rather that is guilty of sedition, since he encourages discord and sedition among his subjects, that he may lord over them more securely; for this is tyranny, being conducive to the private good of the ruler, and to the injury of the multitude.[36]

In our own times, Bishop Eivind Berggrav of Norway, by no means as inhibited and cautious as many other Lutherans, envisions some occasions when a believer, maturely evaluating the

---

34 Quoted by Walzer, *op. cit.,* p. 108.
35 Thielicke, *op. cit.,* pp. 367, 366, 341.
36 Quoted by Ramsey, *War and the Christian Conscience,* p. 116.

edicts of legitimate authority, chooses conscientiously to disobey and defy them.

If the Christian citizen is expected to exercise his political and civic responsibilities, it must be assumed that he has the right and the duty to make decisions for himself and that he is in duty bound to pass judgment upon the lawfulness of the orders which his government issues.... The Christian cannot evade this function on the pretext that he is not responsible for secular affairs.... The hour *may* come when a Christian must ask himself... whether he should not offer active resistance. [37]

Another contemporary, William V. O'Brien, himself a committed Catholic, repristinates the argument of America's Founding Fathers, aligning himself closely to "traditional natural law."

The right of revolution is one of the most fundamental of human rights, ranking with that of self-defense. When a society manifestly fails to provide the rights and necessities for which societies are formed and on the contrary, oppresses its people, they have a right to overthrow that society. [38]

O'Brien's Protestant counterpart, Paul Ramsey, also admits that revolution may be construed as a right, though he reminds us that it took some centuries "before the Christian conscience of the West could give its full approval to military action from below on behalf of a more just order of society."[39] At any rate, Ramsey is ready to grant his approval "to military action from below on behalf of a more just order of society," provided that such action is carefully limited. Luther, he is aware, always sided "against those who make revolution and with those who oppose it." But here Ramsey disassociates himself from Luther: "neither in theory nor in practice is this conclusion to be drawn." So, *contra* Luther, Ramsey sanctions the possible legitimacy of revolution, recognizing that a people may take military as well as political action against an unjust government.

37 Quoted by Thielicke, *op. cit.,* p. 365.

38 O'Brien, *op. cit.,* p. 200. "Revolution, like war, has to be faced as a phenomenon that not only can happen but sometimes ought to happen. It, like war, is a terrible thing. We should study the question as to when it is justified, what the alternatives to it may be, and how it can be mitigated. But violent revolution must be confronted as a rational and often unjust option that sometimes raises questions virtually undistinguishable from those raised by war itself." *Ibid.,* p. 60.

39 Ramsey, *War and the Christian Conscience,* p. 124.

The theory of just revolution provided powerful impetus in the direction of locating in the people themselves the power and right to hold princes and governments politically accountable. Obviously, the justification of revolutionary change in government, by means of violence if need be, surpasses and includes within itself a justification of revolutionary change by political action short of the use of arms. Giving the people on occasion legitimate military initiative at once grants them on more, most, or all occasions legitimate political initiative.[40]

As might be anticipated in view of the revolutionary stance which Shaull deduces from biblical messianism, he sees nothing evil per se in a resort to "military action from below on behalf of a more just society." "The messianic perspective," in his opinion,

creates a sensitivity to the dehumanizing character of violent struggle: at the same time, it opens our eyes to the urgent need for movements that do violence to the old order. In this paradoxical situation we have the freedom to understand our own history, and also to face realistically the options before us in the midst of revolution. We can accept the fact that our nation was born in an act of violence; that the Negro was emancipated and our national unity preserved by means of violence. We are free to admit the possibility that acts of violence may have their place in the struggle of the dispossessed peoples in our urban ghettos and in the underdeveloped world. At the same time, we can concentrate on the type of study and action that will help minimize the necessity of violence and limit its destructiveness in the process of social change. [41]

So messianism enables us to view force realistically instead of sentimentally. It frees us from the fear "that the social order must inevitably fall apart when conflict is allowed to take place. In fact, a type of realism that cannot conceive of peace and stability independently of justice recognizes that, in certain situations, conflict must not only be permitted but also encouraged."[42]

Alves, to mention one more Christian who is not wholly allergic to the use of force, occupies Shaull's revolutionary platform.

40 *Ibid.*, p. 125. "As for theoretical approval or disapproval of revolutionary movements, I *do* mean always to side with the doctrine of justifiable revolution as this was developed out of the just war theory (hedging revolution with the same limits) by Calvinists of the second generation and beyond. I do mean *not* to side always with those who make revolutionary wars and against those who oppose them." Ramsey, *The Just War*, p. 460.

41 Shaull, "Revolution: Heritage and Contemporary Option," pp. 224, 225.

42 *Ibid.*, p. 244.

He, likewise, is thankful that biblical messianism liberates from a sentimental fear of violence and even perceives that force may possibly serve as the instrument of redemptive love.

In order to liberate the oppressed, the lamb must become a lion, the slave must become a warrior. The will to liberation expresses itself as power against those who make liberation impossible. Love for the oppressed is wrath against the oppressors. The process of liberation is thus the judgment on the master. In order to make the slave free, the objective powers and instruments of oppression must be destroyed.... The life of the Messiah, therefore, is a political conflict with the powers of dominion.... The activity of a Messiah, therefore, is like entering a strong man's house in order to plunder his goods. In order to do this, however, the strong man must be tied up first and reduced to impotence (Matt. 12:29).... What looks like the violence of the lion is really the power of counter-violence, that is, power used against those who generate support, and defend the violence of the world of masters and slaves. Violence is power that oppresses and makes man unfree. Counter-violence is power that breaks the old which enslaves, in order to make man free. Violence is power aimed at paralysis. Counter-violence is power aimed at making man free for experimentation.... From the perspective of dialectic, however, since the man who is afraid of the future is unable to liberate himself, love takes shape as an activity that aims at the destruction of the objective and subjective conditions of slavery. This is the dark side of the politics of liberation: the "no," love is power against, wrath against, the oppressors, the *opus alienum Dei*. It is a No, but nevertheless, it remains a work of love, as activity for the liberation of both masters and slaves, because through the destruction of the objective and subjective structures intended to forestall the future they are forced to move towards the future.[43]

All of which means that the repressive power which defuturizes man must be broken—in the name of love, freedom, justice, and God—by the counterviolence of revolution. When circumstances warrant, a Christian ought not scruple to employ this counterviolence. Let Paul Ramsey be summoned as witness: "The pressure of a charitable concern for mankind will be toward the assistance of as many as possible of those who need help where there are means apt to do this, and where we (or we alone) possess

[43] Alves, *op. cit.*, pp. 124-26.

these means."[44] And the means, of course, may be violent. Ramsey's sanction of just war applies equally to just revolution.

We come, then to the complex matter of establishing criteria for a legitimate revolution, the legitimacy of which even a conscientious Christian may be able to endorse. In recent discussion of the tangled issues involved in this complex matter, the probing essay by Richard Neuhaus is notable for its relentless candor. As a Christian "who cares about the ethics of armed revolution" and recoils from "moral nihilism," Neuhaus is aware that "The very term 'just revolution' assumes the possibility of an unjust revolution." He therefore refuses to sidestep a far-reaching question: "What are the circumstances that justify morally the exercise of man's right to revolution?"[45] This single question embraces the three questions which, Raghavan Iyer alleges, insurrection raises:

What is involved in appraising revolutions as good or bad, better or worse?

How do we decide that the act of revolution or the particular revolutionary acts of individuals and groups are right or wrong?

Is one ever obligated to initiate, or participate in, or commit others to, a revolution? How do we assign responsibility for the intentions, acts and consequences of a revolution?[46]

Neuhaus, for one, does not intend to overlook this "annoyingly complicated matter." He suggests that, for want of any more refined apparatus of ethical evaluation, we fall back on the criteria for a just war which have been developed through the centuries, the crystallization of continuous moral reflection and debate. He knows, to be sure, that critics fault this moral theorizing, yet he observes that "the effort to define a just war is important simply because it implicitly rejects crusading fanaticism. It is an acknowledgment that no cause is self-authenticating, self-evidently right. The definition is further important because it supplies the framework, points of reference, by which thoughtful men can

---

[44] Ramsey, *The Just War*, p. 459.
[45] Neuhaus, *op. cit.*, pp. 233, 278, 205, 151.
[46] Raghavan Iyer, "The Ethics of Revolution," *The Center Magazine*, January, 1968, p. 85.

evaluate a course of action."[47] Neuhaus is thinking of critics like
Denis Goulet, who exclaims, "The 'just war' is worthless; it
cannot come to grips with the psychological and political realities
of revolutionary situations."[48] In rebuttal, Neuhaus observes
that "although the just war approach is embattled on many scores,
even its most severe critics admit the continuing relevance of some
of its insights."[49]

Ralph Potter, associate professor of social ethics at Harvard
Divinity School, concurs with Neuhaus. While he freely acknowledges the difficulties and complications in the just-war ethic, he
concludes that "these criteria are rediscovered again and again
by those who have pondered similar questions in earlier
generations."

Everyone who has inquired out of prudence, piety, or pity into the propriety of the use of force has constructed an analogue of "the just war
doctrine." The merit of the version we have inherited rests in its high
level of refinement achieved through continual testing against the entire
range of human concerns and diverse circumstances. The just war doctrine is the precipitate of moral reflection upon political experience in
the West. Its criteria provide an index to the moral economy underlying
the use of force; they specify the type of actions that will eventually entail a high political and moral cost. Of all forms of thinking about the
limits of justifiable use of force, the just war doctrine comes closest to
providing relevant principles that are intelligible, generalizable, and
capable of consistent application.[50]

Ramsey goes so far as to contend that the utility and necessity
of this theory cannot be exaggerated, since in the foreseeable
future violence will apparently be our destiny. "It is of peerless
importance that the justification in these limits, and these limits
as well as the justification, morally regulative of revolutionary

[47] Neuhaus, *op cit.*, p. 163.

[48] Denis Goulet, "The Troubled Conscience of the Revolutionary." *The Center
Magazine,* May, 1969, p. 46.

[49] Neuhaus, *op. cit.*, p. 209.

[50] Ralph B. Potter, *War and Moral Discourse* (Richmond, Va.: John Knox
Press, 1969), pp. 61-62. For other judgments on the utility of the just-war theory
compare O'Brien, *op. cit.*, pp. 17-25; 217 ff.; Ramsey, *War and the Christian
Conscience,* pp. 15-29; Wiest, "Can There Be a Christian Ethic of Violence?"
Perspective, Fall, 1969, pp. 141-54.

movements no less than of wars, gain voice."[51]

There are many statements of just-war criteria available. But, paraphrasing Potter's analysis[52] of the United States intervention in Vietnam, we may assent that a nation resorts to violence ethically provided

(1) There is a justifying cause for such action.

(2) All means of conciliation have been exhausted and no intentions to negotiate are discernible.

(3) The highest lawful authority declares it.

(4) Announcement to begin hostilities is made to the enemy and the reasons for so doing are spelled out.

(5) There is a reasonable hope of victory.

(6) Just intentions motivate the action.

(7) The principle of due proportion—the possible good outweighs the actual evil—is not overlooked.

(8) Just means are scrupulously employed.

Since we shall be following Neuhaus' application of these criteria to the problem of revolutionary violence, suppose we note his statement of the case.

A just war is a war: 1) that is declared by legitimate public authority; 2) that is in response to a real injury that has been suffered; 3) that is undertaken only after all reasonable means of peaceful settlement have been exhausted; 4) in which those prosecuting the war have good intentions; 5) in which damage likely to be incurred by the war will not be disproportionate to the injuries suffered; 6) that employs only legitimate and moral means; 7) in which there is reasonable hope for success.

So stated, these criteria, he admits, "may seem terribly academic"; yet he argues that, if they are "carefully explored," they touch "on almost every aspect of today's revolutionary thought and action."[53] Hence we shall now proceed to discuss these criteria seriatim with Neuhaus as our guide.

The first norm or principle, a "just revolution is a revolution declared by legitimate public authority," has peculiar relevance, Neuhaus avers, and for a very patent reason:

In the present phase of revolutionary consciousness in America, revo-

[51] Ramsey, *The Just War*, p. 461.
[52] Potter, *op. cit.*, pp. 43, 44.
[53] Neuhaus, *op. cit.*, p. 163.

lutionaries frequently declare themselves in favor of chaos. Confusion and chaos, however, are temporary values, necessary to expose the brutal clumsiness of the present regime and to undermine confidence in it. The next revolutionary phase requires positing a credible revolutionary alternative to the regime. This, in turn, requires a clear notion of "legitimate authority" within the revolution itself. In short, "revolution for the hell of it" is only a preliminary to "revolution for a new order." [54]

Notice some of the thorny difficulties which are involved in this criterion. For one thing, it is assumed that the established government has lost its authority and that the loss can be assessed by some calculus other than the visceral reaction of a particular segment of the nation's population. How, for instance, does Carl Davidson of Students for a Democratic Society validate, apart from a pure subjectivism, his sweeping condemnation?

The institutions our resistance has desanctified and delegitimized, as a result of our action against their oppression of others, have lost all authority and hence all respect. As such, they have only raw coercive power. Since they are without legitimacy in our eyes, they are without rights. Insofar as individuals, such as recruiters, continue to remain in association with those institutions, they run the risk of being given the same treatment. ... We can assert the Nuremberg decisions and other past criteria of war crimes as the criteria by which we, in conscience, decide whether or not an institution and individuals associated with that institution have lost their legitimacy and their rights. [55]

But the impossibility of determining when a government has forfeited legitimacy is exactly why Thielicke calls attention to "the dubious character of all revolutionary acts." Granted that a particular system has its defects—peculiarities, Thielicke labels them—who is qualified to "distinguish between tolerable and intolerable peculiarities"? One is driven to speculate "what degree or extreme of peculiarity will have to be reached before a radical or possibly even violent change in rule becomes inevitable." Moreover, before the old government is deposed, barring the advocacy of anarchism, "a new government should already be present, one that plainly possesses the marks of authority." Revolution, in other words, is a "conflict between two authorities."

54 *Ibid.*, pp. 164, 165.
55 Quoted by Neuhaus, *ibid.*, pp. 224-25.

One of these is, of course, the peculiar and impotent authority. The other, though not officially authorized and hence illegal, has moral validation and is prepared to take over as the successor government. A coup initiated without such a potential government at hand necessarily lacks an inner authorization because it is wholly negative. It represents hostility to the state but not improvement of it, and so calls forth anarchical chaos.[56]

But in whose name is the old government ousted and the new government inaugurated? Is it by the authorization of—Neuhaus mentions some of these options—suffering humanity or the people of the Third World or the black minority or Rousseau's ethereal general will which can never be identified with the will of any specific individual or groups "without losing its status as the general will, and which consequently remains a disembodied myth"? Or is it some elitist vanguard, a clairvoyant "three per cent of the population"?[57] Or is it the "democratic educational dictatorship of free men" that Herbert Marcuse espouses? Is it, as Marcuse elaborates his elitist view, the adherents of "small and powerless minorities" which are struggling "against the false consciousness" of our society, "minorities which include 'everyone in the maturity of his faculties' as a human being, everyone who has learned to think rationally and autonomously"? And unfortunately, as is the situation today, "where society has entered the phase of total administration and indoctrination, this would be a small number indeed, and not necessarily that of the elected representatives of the people." Yet for the sake of this "small number"—the elect in Marcuse's socialist version of eschatology—"democratic toleration" cannot be tolerated.

It should be evident by now that the exercise of civil rights by those who don't have them presupposes the withdrawal of civil rights from those who prevent their exercise, and that liberation of the Damned of the Earth presupposes suppression not only of their old but also of their new masters.[58]

Neuhaus, therefore, reaches a pessimistic and negative con-

---

[56] Thielicke, *op. cit.,* pp. 333-34, 343-44.

[57] Neuhaus, *op. cit.,* pp. 170, 171.

[58] Herbert Marcuse, "Repressive Toleration," *A Critique of Pure Tolerance* (Boston: Beacon Press, 1965), pp. 106, 110.

clusion. "How can it be reasonably assured that the revolutionary elite, which by definition is not *of* and *by* the people, will remain *for* the people in a way that does not betray the authority it claims *from* the people?" Since there is no reasonable assurance on this vital point, he is "persuaded that American radicalism cannot meet the first criterion of the just revolution."[59] Is this inability unique to American radicalism? One surmises that it is as intrinsic to revolution as whiteness is to snow.

The second criterion of a just revolution is real injury, a gross, deliberate, systematic perpetration and perpetuation of injustice by a "social order ... corrupt, exploitative, and generally ripe for overthrow."[60] Thus in his habitual hyperbole Colin Morris indicts the West as "a society which needs to be swept away" because of its irremediable evil.[61] Less extreme is Shaull's explanation of the animosity toward the system exhibited by "those young people who are most sensitive to the human situation, and who are prepared to do something about it." He reports that "they have been shocked to find that the order under which they live is almost intolerable."[62]

Neuhaus, however, is not overwhelmed by these charges of dehumanization. He suspects that this criterion is "so vague as to be almost useless." He points out that, for one thing, deprivation is a relative term. It is relative to one's concept of the good life and one's belief as to whether that kind of life is a possibility. He drafts a list of "elementary values," which include "adequate food, shelter, and medical care; freedom from physical terror; freedom of expression; a modicum of participation in those decisions that affect one's daily life." Such a list may not be "very adventuresome," but it is nevertheless, he contends, "a great deal more than millions of Americans have, and it constitutes a fantastic dream for the majority of the world's populations." Yet he also remarks that if we compare the Soviet Union with the United States in the light of his catalogue of values, "we might decide that revolution would be exceedingly just in the Soviet Union but not

59 Neuhaus, *op. cit.,* p. 177.
60 *Ibid.,* p. 184.
61 Colin Morris, *op. cit.,* p. 143.
62 Shaull, "Revolution: Heritage and Contemporary Option," p. 187.

in the United States."[63] Even within our own country, however, Robert Waelder emphasizes, intolerable conditions "can be defined only in relative terms."[64] Poverty for one person may be semiopulence for his neighbor; what some individuals attack as a brutal oppression, others may uncomplainingly accept.

Neuhaus points out, for a second thing, that the poor and powerless have a much higher "revolting level" than those who are better off. What the poor and powerless want is not the over-throw of the system. They want, instead, a larger share of its bourgeois benefits. Violence, as they talk about it, is thus a means of "pressuring the system" to give them more of its products.[65]

Neuhaus points out, for a third thing, that when "injuries suffered" are appealed to as justification for revolutionary vio-lence, it is an *avant-garde* which reaches this verdict, most mem-bers of which have been recruited from a fairly comfortable life where they personally have not suffered the injury they passion-ately denounce. The revolutionary elite, Neuhaus affirms, "is very often the economic and social elite," radicals whose attitude toward the poor and powerless is condescending and romantic. Neuhaus has the suspicion that the radicals are utopians who measure contemporary reality by the yardstick of their own dreams and visions, often overstating the injuries suffered.[66] And unquestionably the visionary insurrectionist is, as Truman

---

63 Neuhaus, *op. cit.*, pp. 186-87. *Cf.* the statement by "a member of the Writer's Union in Prague, made before the Russian occupation of Czechoslovakia: 'Ideally, we want enlightened communism. By that we mean a Communist system that provides constitutional rights, free speech and a free press, a secret ballot in elections in which the voter has a real choice to make, a responsible parliament and a genuine opposition, a passport for everybody, higher living standards, and, gradually, a change for us to become the masters of our own destiny.'" No wonder that Mortimer Adler, after quoting that statement, says, "While many dissident Americans would complain that they do not have all of these things to the fullest degree or complain of their unavailability for everyone in the United States today, they would also have to admit, if their eyes could be opened to statistically sup-ported comparisons, that more individuals enjoy these conditions in the United States, and to a greater degree, than anywhere else in the world." Mortimer J. Adler, *The Time of Our Lives: The Ethics of Common Sense* (New York: Holt, Rinehart & Winston, 1970), p. 336.

64 Waelder, *op. cit.*, p. 220.

65 Neuhaus, *op. cit.*, p. 181.

66 *Ibid.*, pp. 182-83.

|Nelson sympathetically defines him, "A redemptionist ... an optimist."[67] The visionary insurrectionist cries out as Saint-Simon did in 1814 shortly after the French Revolution, "The Golden Age of humanity is not behind us; it lies ahead, in the perfection of the social order."[68] Superfluous to comment, today's society is a shabby caricature of Saint-Simon's vision. While Neuhaus personally is not utopian, he becomes indignant contemplating the United States in the 1970's with millions "denied food, shelter, and medical care that are anywhere near adequate, even, in many cases, to maintain life itself ... terrorized by police, criminals, and a court system indifferent to the poor." In our country, he charges, "freedom of expression is severely limited by vested interests controlling the mass media."[69] So, measured by a utopian yardstick, even the United States is a Lilliputian culture when it might be a Goliath.

But do the defects and deficiencies of the present order lend credence to John Gerassi's invective? The United States is so "closed, oppressive, and violent"—those are his adjectives—that "it must be destroyed."[70] Is his plea for revolution substantiated by the realities of our national situation? Are injustice and oppression so widespread and irremediable as to render violence the sole hope of constructive change? Not according to Paul J. Weber, S.J., who in his appreciative article, "A Theology of Revolution," remarks, "What one must question is the dark despair that sees the present social structures as hopelessly oppressive. To date there has probably never existed a less unjust society than that which exists now—at least in the United States."[71]

Gerassi's plea for revolution is likewise denied by Peter Berger, who from his "intrinsically debunking perspective on society"

67 Nelson, *op. cit.*, p. 118.

68 Quoted by Christopher Hill, *Puritanism and Revolution* (New York: Schocken Books, 1958), p. 53.

69 Neuhaus, *op. cit.*, p. 188.

70 Gerassi, *op. cit.*, pp. 50-51. "No matter how skilled the explanation, it cannot evade the self-evident fact that hundreds of thousands of Americans believe this society needs revolution. That is in itself of momentous political significance, regardless of its alleged dynamics.... Revolutionary consciousness is not a creation *ex nihilo* nor is it immaculately conceived." Neuhaus, *op. cit.*, p. 128.

71 Paul J. Weber, S.J., "A Theology of Revolution," *Worldview*, October, 1968, p. 13.

finds it hard to understand such irrational extremism.

No institution and no society can claim sacredness, necessity, or eternal validity for itself. American society and its institutions are no exception to this. Yet (to use a phrase from theology) "in, with, and under" the institutional forms there may be found human values and human achievements of great worth. It seems to me that the precarious vision of society must include a sense of the precariousness of these values and achievements, especially in a period of rapid and inevitable change. In America today this means *both* a readiness for the changes that ought to come about *and* the will to preserve the valid human accomplishments of the American experience. There are many of these.[72]

Berger also affirms, "Once one looks at American society with eyes that are freed of utopian distortions, it appears as a society with remarkable humane achievements." He affirms something else which is even more important: "It appears as a society with a remarkable capacity to reconstruct itself in response to moral challenge and human needs."[73]

Ernest W. Lefever, who is a member of the Brookings Institute Senior Foreign Policy Studies staff, likewise deplores the revolutionary criticism of our country as being jaundiced and lopsided.

The United States today represents a profound achievement in man's long and tortured quest for free and just political community. By virtually every test, American society is more open and mobile than that of any other state past or present. And because of the remarkable advances of the past three decades, there is no significant national legal or governmental barrier to equality of opportunity for both the competitive and non-competitive minority groups in American society. Prejudice there is, but the law and the moral force of many non-government institutions are on the side of justice.[74]

Is another American revolution, therefore, justified as a "response to real injury suffered"? The answer is no.

Mortimer Adler occupies a position precisely the opposite occupied by Gerassi. Though he recognizes the difficulty of under-

[72] Berger, *op. cit.*, p. 85.

[73] *Ibid.*, p. 59.

[74] Ernest W. Lefever, "Criteria for a Just Revolution," *Ethics, Violence, and Revolution*, Charles C. West, ed. (New York: The Council on Religion and International Affairs, 1969), pp. 55-56.

taking such comparisons, he endeavors to weigh the relevant fac-
tors and then concludes, "I still think it is fair to say that from the
point of view of *providing* the external conditions of a good life
for a larger percentage of its citizens, the United States, is, *on
balance,* as good as, if not better than, any other country in the
world today, and vastly better than any state that ever existed in
the past." Adler even goes so far as to assert this: "If those as
yet unborn in this century could choose the place of their birth,
their choice would be the United States, if it was based solely on
the calculation of the probability that they would be blessed by a
fair modicum of the external conditions required for a good
human life."[75] One rather suspects that Adler is right!

Is another American revolution justified therefore as a "response to real injury suffered"? The answer, admitting to the full
our society's failures, is an unhesitating no.

The third criterion of a just revolution is that no other means
of redress is available; hence violence becomes the last recourse
of people who are suffering real and otherwise irremediable
injury. "The decision for revolution," Neuhaus states, "is made
at the point where it becomes inescapably clear that no amount
of political activism, protest or pressure—legal, or extra-legal—
can make this constitutional order work to the benefit of American
citizens and millions of others who are under the sway of
American power."[76] Has that point been reached? Is it now
inescapably clear that by no other means can a system, allegedly
unjust, inhumane, and thus intolerable, be replaced by one of
superior equity? Is the *status quo* not only unjust, inhumane,
and thus intolerable? Is it also irremediable except by an act of
radical surgery?

Certainly some critics of the Establishment are convinced that
the point of revolutionary no-return has been reached or will
be shortly. If not in the United States, then unquestionably in
Latin American countries violence alone affords a fighting chance
for a life which is at least a little more human. Carl Oglesby
describes the psychology of the man, whether in South or North
America, who is driven to radicalism by the inescapable pressures

75 Adler, *op. cit.*, pp. 219, 335.
76 Neuhaus, *op. cit.*, p. 194.

of his situation.

Rebellion does not take place until it has become compulsory. The rebel is someone who is no longer free to choose even his own docile servitude. He has been driven to the wall. Somebody is even trying to pound him through it. He has been reduced from the slave to the prisoner, from the prisoner to the condemned. ... Except for rebellion, there is nothing. The strange apparent freedom of the rebel, and hence that pride of his which is so enormous when it arrives as to dwarf everything else, a psychic flood which sweeps everything before it, lie in his having finally affirmed the only life that is available to him: "*the rebel is someone who has accepted death.*" ... In desperation and despair, driven to accept death, the rebel is the dehumanized human being who has no choice—except violence.[77]

Under such circumstances, what other recourse is available? "The rebel is the man for whom it has been decreed that there is only one way out."[78] Violence is indeed his last resort.

Much more ambivalently, Shaull explores and explains the justification of violent insurrection as the *ultima ratio* advocated by younger radicals in the U.S., the New Leftists who insist that they are being forced beyond protest to revolution. Existence in our bourgeois society, they have discovered, is empty and meaningless. They feel that our world "is a complete mess, a world which in their eyes preceding generations have botched up." Gradually they are becoming estranged from the Establishment, completely so, and there are, tragically, no reconciling agents who can help overcome their deep and bitter estrangement. "Those institutions that could perform this mediating task—family, school, church, *et al.*—have by and large failed to do so. In some instances, they seem to exist in order to preserve the old forms." The Establishment from which these young Americans are estranged is more than a meaningless mess. It is an interlocking network of reactionary forces.

What makes the present situation so revolutionary among the younger generation is their discovery that when they begin to work for change at any specific point, they are confronted by a total system—a complex of attitudes, institutions, relations, and power alignments—which blocks

[77] Oglesby, *op. cit.*, pp. 153, 156.
[78] *Ibid.*

fundamental changes in society. ... Since the traditional means of redress and reform fail to work, what option remains but violence?[79]

Shaull hopes, nevertheless, that violence may be unnecessary. Guerrilla warfare, he realizes, "has under some circumstances proved effective." But perhaps a revolutionary strategy, analogous to it, can be practiced without bloodshed and terror. "Guerrilla warfare need not be restricted to its military expression. At this stage in the development of technological society, *its political equivalent* may offer a valuable instrument for bringing about changes in our major institutions."

What, however, if this nonviolent equivalent of guerrilla warfare fails? What if the Establishment, ideologically blind, "motivated by a legitimate concern for stability and order, grows more and more reactionary"? "The end result of this ideological blindness is our failure to see that such stress upon stability may make an explosive situation more unstable, and that this way of dealing with violence can make a violent solution more probable." In that case, fortified by the biblical insight that "stability and order take shape *on the other side of change,*" a Christian is free to decide that a social structure in its rigidity is blocking change and that "its destruction may be necessary." Agitation and action for the new order "of necessity implies a 'violation' of the old ... violence can be an important element in blocking change and in bringing it about."[80]

Neuhaus is even more ambivalent than Shaull as to whether or not violent revolution is now a regrettable *ultima ratio* in our own nation. He dismisses as "patent nonsense" the New Leftist criticism that there is "nothing good in America." He alludes to "the long list of improvements" which one can draw up to show that remarkable progress and humanization have occurred in the past two hundred years. But he then proceeds to examine the agencies which might be hoped to spearhead deep and rapid change—American education, religion, politics as well as our judiciary system—concluding that all these "have been tried and found wanting." Hence some radicals, he tells us, no longer

---

[79] Shaull, "Revolution: Heritage and Contemporary Option," pp. 188, 198, 190.

[80] *Ibid.*, pp. 223, 224.

pin their hopes on reform. They are already "in the business of making revolution." Yet Neuhaus discloses his own ambivalence as well as his commendable objectivity when he indicates the excruciating circularity of the revolutionary contention that our society lacks "the capacity for radical change."

Reform is out because the society is irreformable, but only efforts at reform reveal the irreformability of the society. The *a priori* assumption that revolution is the only way is both unpersuasive in recruiting for the revolutionary movement and, for the revolutionary leader, a commitment built on sand; in the storm of struggle it will shift and erode, resulting in the collapse of the movement's plausibility.[81]

A political scientist and ethicist like Ernest Lefever is neither ambivalent nor pessimistic concerning our country's capacity for effective change. As he sees it,

America has perhaps the most sensitive and responsive political system ever created. The will of a decisive majority can be forged quickly into effective law and policy. When the public mandate is not as clear, we have ample institutions, processes, and habits to move slowly in response to changes of the general will. Minority views are quickly registered by the political system.[82]

Unequivocally, therefore, he confronts and answers the question which troubles "the morally concerned observer":

Will the prospect for freedom and justice be helped or hurt by the continuation of the status quo, by peaceful reform, or by the introduction of revolutionary violence? Continuous adaptation and change are needed in America in the interests of a more perfect union, but there is no need for revolution. All worthy objectives (insofar as the government can contribute toward them) can be achieved peacefully, legally, and even quickly if there is a sufficient popular support for them.[83]

The issue at stake here can be brought to sharp focus by setting the opinion of Carl Oglesby in juxtaposition with that of Mortimer Adler. Speaking for the radical humanist, Oglesby spurns the policy of reform, which essentially is a continuation of the *status quo*: "We shall accept this dismal house of bondage and

[81] Neuhaus, *op. cit.*, pp. 194, 195, 201, 202, 203.

[82] Lefever, *op. cit.*, pp. 56, 59.

[83] *Ibid.*

try to redecorate it."[84] The policy of the radical humanist, rather, is to tear it down or burn it up. Adler, on the contrary, is unconvinced that our society, while not in "blooming health," is suffering from an "incurable disease." Thus with no reference to Oglesby he waxes metaphorical:

One can ask, "Is it so bad a house that the only thing to do is to tear it down or gut it, and start from the ground up?" Or one can ask, "With all its defects, is it nevertheless good enough to remodel, improve, and redecorate?" The present state of the U.S.A. should inspire us to ask the second of these questions. And we should answer it by saying that,the United States, with all its defects, is good enough to deserve our trying to improve it by carrying forward the peaceful revolution, reform by due process of law, that has been the course—more than that, the genius—of our development from the beginning. Recourse to violence is justified only when civil or legal measures are not available. [85]

And adequate measures of redress and reform, Adler assures us, are still available. Berger echoes that conviction.

I still find it hard to understand how people, who after all are literate and thus not condemned to a view of the world limited to their own experience, can seriously come to the conclusion that American society is so hopelessly rotten that the anguish and the dubious outcome of revolution are morally preferable to even the *status quo*, let alone to the improvements of the *status quo* that are realistically possible [86]

The fourth criterion of a just revolution is right intention. Those participating in it must have right objectives in view and be rightly motivated in battling to attain them. This principle means, as Neuhaus defines it, the pursuit of "humanizing and democratizing goals."[87]

84 Oglesby, *op. cit.*, p. 164.

85 Mortimer Adler, *op. cit.*, p. 221. Significant is the joint statement made by Berger and Neuhaus at the very conclusion of *Movement and Revolution*. Talking about supporting efforts for deep-seated change, they write: "*One presses in the confidence that these efforts will confirm his belief in the reformability of American Society. The other engages in the same efforts, confident that frustrated reformism will strengthen the revolutionary struggle that will then be necessary, but open to the possibility, however improbable, that successful reform will preclude the necessity of revolution.*" p. 240.

86 Berger, *op. cit.*, p. 58.

87 Neuhaus, *op. cit.*, p. 205.

The imprecision of this criterion is apparent from O'Brien's analysis of right intention in the waging of war. Among its components he singles out these three:

(a) The just party must continue the war only so long as it is necessary to obtain the just goals for which it was initiated. Once a war is pressed beyond that point in pursuit of unjust or insufficiently grave goals it becomes unjust.

(b) Nothing must be done to imperil the ultimate object of every just war, namely, the establishment of a just and lasting peace. Thus if the conduct of the war is needlessly brutal or the peace terms patently unfair, sentiments of hatred and desire for revenge may be encouraged in the defeated nation.

(c) Finally, an initially just war must not be permitted to become the occasion for indulgence in unjust and uncharitable attitudes and practices, of the kind that tend to be unleashed in warfare. [88]

One gathers, accordingly, that right intention requires not only right goals but also right sentiments, motives, attitudes, and practices. An imprecise principle, indeed, which allows free play for subjectivism and actually provides no external norms! [89]

Neuhaus endeavors to minimize its subjectivism by arguing

[88] William V. O'Brien, *Nuclear War, Deterrence and Morality* (Westminster, Md.: Newman Press, 1967), pp. 24, 25. In the same book, p. 77, O'Brien says, "Hatred begets more hatred. This natural psychological phenomenon must be overcome by Christians and all men of good will. No matter what the provocation, defense and deterrence policies must be conceived and carried out in a spirit of charity. No amount of injustice in the attitudes and behaviour of actual or potential opponents can justify a departure on the part of national decision-makers and citizens from the requirement of right intention in a just war."

[89] *Cf.* Ramsey's discussion of Robert W. Tucker's argument "that motives and the subjective states of the agents are too various and variable to be of much help in determining the meaning of just conduct or of prudent conduct in politics and in military strategy." Ramsey, *The Just War*, pp. 398-99. For the life of him, Tucker cannot grasp the difference between knowing what is going to happen as the result of an act and intending that the result happen. One may sharply differentiate, as Ramsey does, between clear foresight and pure intention. One may not want to kill some people; one may not directly intend to kill them; but one may, nevertheless, with clean hands and a pure heart, engage in military action knowing that those unintended targets are certainly going to be killed! No doubt military commanders always have right intentions in mind. Who but God can know that their intentions were otherwise?

that right intention must not be mistaken for fanatical devotion
to a cause. It is "more a matter of objectives than it is of purity
of heart. It is more a political than a psychological reality." Yet
he does not deny that "the intention, the deed, and the motivation
are interdependent. If they are not in harmony, "the revolution
suffers a plausibility collapse."[90]

May one assume, therefore, that no revolution is justified
unless its participants are totally exempt from vengeance, anger,
hate, sadism, ambition, and a desire to rise above boredom and
meaninglessness? Obviously not! Revolutionists, however
devoted, are still "human, all too human." Their motives, like
those of conservatives, are a bewildering mixture. Some vocal
apostles of violence, in the United States at any rate, may be in-
dulging in mere talk which is, as Berger debunks it, "self-
indulgence and unseriousness. It is not so much motivated by
sympathy with black people in slums and yellow people in rice
paddies as by boredom with Connecticut. In this boredom the
talk of revolution offers a vicarious identification with adventure,
strength and moral purity."[91] Moreover, where the advocacy of
violence is sincere, it may be propelled by the dynamics of hateful-
ness and vengeance. Morris says this bluntly: "Most of the men
who make revolution in our day will not do so because they have
convictions about God, man, society, or anything else, but out
of a terrible anger and a deadly despair." Hence he urges "a
down-to-earth theology of revolution" to investigate "the role
of a healthy hate in nerving men to do what any normal understanding of love would never allow."[92]

On the other side of the world, Stokely Carmichael has been
sanctifying vengeful violence by appeal to the dictum of Che
Guevara: "Hatred as an element of the struggle, relentless hatred
of the enemy that impels us over and beyond the natural limita-
tions of men, and transforms us into effective, violent, selected and
cold killing machines."[93] No doubt this is an understandable

[90] Neuhaus, *op. cit.*, p. 205.

[91] Berger, *op. cit.*, p. 60.

[92] Colin Morris, *op. cit.*, pp. 145-46.

[93] Stokely Carmichael, "Black Power," *To Free a Generation: The Dialectics
of Liberation.* David Cooper, ed. (London: Collier Books, 1969), p. 162. John
Gerassi quotes a similar Che Guevara sentiment, *op. cit.*, p. 89.

emotion when people have been suffering from gross and grinding injustice, but does it qualify as right intention?

A revolutionist who has become an effective, violent, selected, and cold killing machine probably has little concern for right intention. He has purity of heart only in the sense that he is a singleminded fanatic who subsumes all other values to that of his cause. Years ago in their "Revolutionary Catechism" two Russian anarchists, Mikhael Bakunin and Sergei Nechaev, depicted the ideal insurrectionist.

The revolutionary is a lost man; he has no interests of his own, no cause of his own, no feelings, no habits, no belongings; he does not even have a name. Everything in him is absorbed by a single, exclusive interest, a single thought, a single passion—the revolution.

In the very depths of his being, not just in words but in deed, he has broken every tie with the civil order, with the educated world and all its laws, conventions, and generally accepted conditions, and with the ethics of this world. He will be an implacable enemy of this world, and if he continues to live in it, that will only be so as to destroy it more effectively.

The revolutionary despises all doctrinairism. He has rejected the science of the world, leaving it to the next generation; he knows only one science, that of destruction.

He despises public opinion; he despises and hates the existing social ethic in all its demands and expressions; for him, everything that allows the triumph of the revolution is moral, and everything that stands in its way is immoral.

The revolutionary is a lost man; with no pity for the State and for the privileged and educated world in general, he must himself expect no pity. Every day he must be prepared for death. He must be prepared to bear torture.

Hard with himself, he must be hard towards others. All the tender feelings of family life, of friendship, love, gratitude and even honour must be stifled in him by a single cold passion for the revolutionary cause. For him there is only one pleasure, one consolation, one reward, and one satisfaction—the success of the revolution. Day and night he must have one single thought, one single purpose: merciless destruction. With this aim in view, tirelessly and in cold blood, he must always be prepared to die and to kill with his own hands anyone who stands in the way of achieving it.

The character of the true revolutionary has no place for any romanticism, sentimentality, enthusiasm or seduction. Nor has it any place for private hatred or revenge. The revolutionary passion which in him becomes a daily, hourly passion must be combined with cold calculation. Always and everywhere he must become not what his own personal inclination would have him become, but what the general interest of the revolution demands.[94]

For the ideal insurrectionist, then, revolution is a Moloch whose service is self-justifying; no other motive is needed.

It is the possibility of moral nihilism latent in revolution which prompts Berger to indict idealists, no matter what their political orientation, who sacrifice compassion for the sake of some future Utopia. Though they pay lip service to humanitarianism, they are inhumane. So he cautions with respect to dedicated activists of all varieties:

Only believe those whose motives are compassionate and whose programs stand the test of rational inquiry. ... When it comes to revolutionaries, only trust the sad ones. The enthusiastic ones are the oppressors of tomorrow—*or else they are only kidding.* ... The thirst for domination, the intoxication with a "redeeming" system, the dark thrust of madness—these are motives that are hard to control over a period of time.[95]

Goals as well as motives, however, must be taken into account as we appraise the legitimacy of a revolution. What are its objectives other than the undermining of the *status quo*? What social order does it plan and purpose to substitute for the moribund Establishment that now exists? Does it aspire after improvement as well as change? Admonishing would-be revolutionaries from within a theological framework, Luther once indulged in some wise negativism. "It is easy to change a government, but it is difficult to get one that is better, and the danger is that you will not. Why? Because it is not in our will or power, but only in the will and the hand of God."[96]

Mindful of this issue, Shaull is concerned that he and his radical confreres hammer out "an ideology of revolution," a kind of

---

94 Quoted by Raghavan Iyer, *op. cit.,* pp. 86, 87. Even when one allows for rhetorical exaggeration, the portrait is that of a moral nihilist who does not give a snap of his fingers for right intention.

95 Berger, *op. cit.,* p. 19.

96 Quoted by Thielicke, *op. cit.,* p. 341.

social-political philosophy which, by providing a theoretical orientation, will enable them "to define goals and work for change." He is keenly cognizant that such an undertaking represents "a formidable task." But for the sake of the cause it is imperative that a guiding ideology be formulated, a fusion of theory and strategy. "We have no right to urge people to become revolutionaries unless we can give some concrete indication of how the goals of revolution are to be reached. Otherwise, we share responsibility for their frustration and despair, as well as the results of it, if they abandon the struggle or are led to act irresponsibly."[97]

Morris, though, is skeptical about any too definite a formulation of goals. "Revolution begins as a blind thrust for freedom, not as a crusade to change the world. A man suffocating to death in an airless cellar does not plan the rest of his life before kicking down the door."[98] In other words, destroy the present order and out of its ashes, phoenixlike, something new and, *ex hypothesi,* better must arise.

This is Oglesby's approach as well. Overthrow the Establishment, and by a process of social parthenogenesis a new and better mode of existence will be born.

The rebel is an incorrigible absolutist who has replaced all "problems" with the one grand claim that the entire system is in error, all "solutions" with the single irreducible demand that change shall be total, all diagnoses of disease with one final certificate of death. To him, total change means only that those who now have all power shall no longer have any, and that those who now have none—the people, the victimized—shall have all.[99]

How could he express more succinctly the negative thrust of subversion, together with its lack of any concrete program, than he does in these crisp words?

The rebel fights for something that will not be like *this.* He cannot answer the question about the future because that is not his question. It is not the future that is victimizing him. It is the present. It is not an

97 Shaull, "Revolution: Heritage and Contemporary Option," pp. 215, 212, 209, 236.
98 Colin Morris, *op. cit.,* p. 147.
99 Oglesby, *op. cit.,* pp. 146, 147.

anticipated Utopia which moves him to risk his life. .... His motivating vision of change is at root a vision of something absent—not of something that *will* be there, but of something that will be there *no longer*. His good future world is elementally described by its empty spaces: a missing landlord, a missing mine owner, a missing sheriff. Who or what will replace landlords, owner, sheriff? Never mind, says the revolutionary, glancing over his shoulder. Something better. If he is thereupon warned that this undefined "something" may turn out to make things worse than ever, his response is a plain one: "Then we should have to continue the revolution." The fundamental revolutionary motive is not to construct a Paradise but to destroy an Inferno. [100]

But Shaull is worried over the outcome of revolutionary destruction. How can a closer approximation of Utopia emerge unless the destroyers intend to be builders, carrying at least a few tentative ideas in their minds? Oh, confessedly, he realizes that nobody as yet "has a clear blueprint for the future." Yet Shaull is likewise sure that "to build a new society requires a 'new beginning.' We must develop new ideas and perspectives on life by the cultivation of creative imagination." A revolutionary need not "rely on a total world-view for security," neither can he wait "until all the evidence is in" or until he has figured out an inclusive "scheme of things to guarantee the results of his efforts." At this stage of history, the "revolutionary vision of a new society may still be somewhat blurred," but, it is hoped, "the diagram of a new society is gradually taking shape, one in which certain specific elements can already be distinguished." And towering beyond all these is "the ultimate goal of authentic messianism ... human fulfillment." [101]

Herbert Marcuse, the patriarch among revolutionary gurus, has a vision of human fulfillment in a liberated Utopian society, and he is not in the least reluctant to project his vision "in concrete terms."

We are not concerned here with private sensitivity and sensibility, but with sensitivity and sensibility, creative imagination and play, becoming forces of transformation. As such they would guide, for example, the total reconstruction of our cities and of the countryside; the restoration

100 *Ibid.*
101 Shaull, *op. cit.*, pp. 216, 217, 192, 229.

of nature after the elimination of the violence and destruction of capitalist industrialization; the creation of internal and external space for
privacy, individual autonomy, tranquility; the elimination of noise, of
captive audiences, of enforced togetherness, of pollution, of ugliness.
These are not—and I cannot emphasize this strongly enough—snobbish
and romantic demands. Biologists today have emphasized that these are
organic needs for the human organism, and that their arrest, their perversion and destruction by capitalist society, actually mutilates the
human organism, not only in a figurative way but in a very real and
literal sense. I believe that it is only in such a universe that man can be
truly free and truly human relationships between free beings can be
established. I believe that the idea of such a universe guided also Marx's
concept of socialism, and that these aesthetic needs and goals must from
the beginning be present in the reconstruction of society, and not only
at the end or in the far future.[102]

These, then, are the goals; this, then, is the vision; here, then,
we have spread before us the diagram of the new society. This,
ostensibly, is what the revolutionary intends. We must not forget, however, that these goals, this vision, this diagram, this
intention has no majority endorsement, no official sanction.
Rather, as Neuhaus indicates regarding the amorphous New
Leftists, "It is difficult to find a common vision, a specific idea
of the new order, that holds the movement together." Yet this
very lack of a doctrinaire ideology may prove a virtue, allowing
for flexibility and growth, preventing "a deceptive self-righteous-
ness that can only end in suspicion and disillusionment, tolerating as any movement of broad appeal" must do "all the ambiguities that mark the human condition itself."[103]

The fifth criterion, which Neuhaus treats only briefly, is this:
the damage likely to be inflicted by the revolution "will not be
disproportionate to the injury suffered." As Neuhaus states it
more fully in another passage, "one weighs the probable damage
caused by the revolution against the real injury that provokes
the revolution. If the probable damage is greater than the real

---

[102]Herbert Marcuse, "Liberation from the Affluent Society," *To Free a Generation: The Dialectics of Liberation,* David Cooper, ed. (New York: Collier
Books, 1968), pp. 185-86.

[103]Neuhaus, *op. cit.,* pp. 124, 208.

injury, the revolution is unjust."[104]

The elusive and imprecise nature of this criterion—indeed, the elusive and imprecise nature of all the proposed criteria of a just war or revolution—must be freely admitted. Regardless of how farsighted they are, human beings cannot predict the future because they cannot control it. There is always the possibility of surprise, accident, caprice, or the absurdly irrational, to say nothing of judgments which are sincerely mistaken. And when ethical values are taken into account, the imponderables of good and evil, man's most painstaking calculus becomes a precarious balancing of probabilities. Risk is unavoidable, a measure of faith indispensable; error and failure are sometimes inevitable.

When so explosive and complex a phenomenon as revolution is being appraised pragmatically and morally, the most extreme care is called for. The cost, to quote Kateb again, is astronomically exorbitant—"terrorism, conspiracy, *coup d'état*, general strike, guerrilla warfare, street fighting, pitched battle, singly or in some combination ... the taking of life, coercion, treachery, lying, destructing, uprooting, the infliction of many kinds of physical and psychological pain and suffering on opponents and innocents alike." It is, Kateb writes, against this frightful cost that "moral absolutism, revised utilitarianism, and common sense rebel." Furthermore, he says, "It is, of course, the Russian experience—revolution and its aftermath—that has promoted a great deal of thought in recent times on the moral and practical cost of revolutionary and radical reformist activity."[105]

In fact, D. W. Brogan has devoted an entire book to this subject, *The Price of Revolution*. Realistically he remarks concern-

---

[104] *Ibid.*, pp. 163, 210. Ramsey calls this criterion "the principle of proportionality," and suggests that everything "Reinhold Niebuhr ever said about politics and war falls under this principle. ... Nations, statesmen, and citizens are acting responsibly when they choose and vigorously support policies and decisions which are likely to secure the lesser evil (or the greater good) among their mixed consequences." Ramsey, *The Just War*, p. 429. O'Brien endorses the same principle. "Much as a just war must give promise of probable good results exceeding probable evil, a violent revolution should be undertaken only when good—even if only very distant and problematical—seems likely to be proportionate to the foreseeable evil resulting from a violent revolution." O'Brien, *War and/or Survival*, p. 200; *cf.* p. 203.

[105] Kateb, *op. cit.*, pp. 24-25.

ing the situation in France under Louis XVI, "There are in politics no necessarily good solutions; there may be only a choice of evils, and of great evils, and the Revolution may have been the lesser of the evils." One may rejoice that, in the revolutionary era which ensued on the heels of regicide in Paris, "so much lumber was swept away." Yes, he exclaims, "So much lumber was swept away with such general approval (most of it was not put back) that it is not easy to count the cost. But there was a cost." He then engages in a cost-analysis.

No one can compute how many millions of soldiers' lives were lost in twenty years of war, lost by bullets, by disease, by starvation, by cold. The main burden fell on France herself, for she alone was never neutral; she alone had armies in Moscow and Madrid at the same time. The French peasant, freed from the tithe and the gabelle in its most odious form, from the *taille* and from futile servitudes, probably gained by the revolution; he thought then that he did; he thinks so still. But the price is paid by unending draft on his sons that no king had ever dared to make. ... The wars were costly to an incompetent treasury, but did not seriously affect domestic development or seriously diminish French human or economic resources. The victories, the glories, the conquests of the Revolution and the Empire were paid for with two million lives, directly lost and with unknown and incalculable economic losses that may have kept France at least a generation behind in its economic progress, a handicap that she never overcame.[106]

Thus, he concludes, "It is the French Revolution, not the American that puts the question of the price of Revolution, the certainty that there will be a high price, the uncertainty that the price will buy the goods ordered."[107]

Paul Ramsey also emphasizes the necessity of counting the cost. He does so in a sermon by that title which is based on Christ's teaching in Luke's Gospel, chapter 14, verses 28 through 33, where a man planning to build a tower and a king deliberating on resistance to invasion both illustrate the need of counting the cost. Ramsey interprets the passage as significantly illuminating the nature of "political wisdom."

It is largely a matter of correctly counting the costs in relation to the

10 Brogan, *op. cit.*, pp. 17-18, 5.
107 *Ibid.*

goods to be obtained. This is, in fact, a principal word that through all the centuries Christians have addressed to the world, and to themselves and to their offices as magistrate or citizen. (This word is called the *principle of proportion*.) In projecting any policy or putting forth any action that has multiple consequences—some good, some tragically and unavoidably evil or destructive—one should look to see that the good likely to be achieved or the evil prevented is worth the cost, that it is greater than any evil that also will follow.[108]

Applicable to war, this principle is applicable likewise to revolution. Will greater good or greater evil probably follow the resort to armed force? Imprecise and agonizing though the practice of such calculus may be, freighted with uncertainty as it is, we must recognize that it is the essence of political sagacity and governmental responsibility.

We cannot trammel public policy with the platitude that any peace is better than any war, or that de-escalation always leads to lesser evil than a higher level of violence, or that negotiation should be carried on upon the premise that negotiation need never fail. Decision as to whether very great evil must be chosen in order to prevent still greater evil, or as to whether a higher level of violence for possibly a shorter time may not be better than a lower level of counter-insurgency warfare for a longer time, or decision as to whether *this* is an opportune moment for negotiations, or not—these are precisely the decisions that must come from "taking political counsel" amid the claims and actions that have come upon us in this age.[109]

Can less be said, then, in justifying revolution? Or what else is required in a resort to armed force from below other than a reasonable expectation that evil will be lessened and good increased?

This is the juncture, however, at which humanitarians like Peter Berger and Albert Camus part company with the apostles of revolutionary violence. Berger is afraid that they will not be "painstakingly miserly in calculating the human costs of their political programs"; neither, he suspects, will they suffer overwhelming anguish if "these costs, out of real or imagined necessity, are high."[110] As for Camus, he fears that the champions

108Ramsey, *The Just War*, pp. 524, 527.
109*Ibid.*
110Berger, *op. cit.*, p. 18.

of absolute Utopia, as he terms the militant revolutionists, are quite cheerfully ready to pay any price for the possible fulfillment of their dreams instead of being contented with a relative Utopia; the militant revolutionists, he is afraid, face with equanimity the possibility of a cataclysm which will cost us ten times "the thirty million fresh corpses of recent wars."[111]

In short, to let Neuhaus crystallize the debate over this criterion, "we must compare the high price of revolution with the high price of not having a revolution."[112] Having made this comparison, we may elect with Camus "to choose a more modest and less costly Utopia"[113] than a new order which will entail evil and suffering outrageously disproportioned to any good it achieves.

The sixth criterion for a just revolution which Neuhaus proposes is that of right means. Affirming, as he does, that in certain situations armed insurrection is necessary and permissible, he admits its ethical difficulties.

Those who engage in and support such conflict must wrestle with the agonizing questions of what are "the limits of permissibility," if any. The guidelines are few and contradictory. This much is certain: talk about revolution is credible only when men stop speaking about revolution in general and address themselves to particular revolutions, including the "moral means" by which they are pursued.[114]

Agonizingly aware that revolution is a brutal business, he declines to be a glib apologist for methods which are a compound of horror and barbarism. He knows that the insurrectionist must be "prepared to act in specifics against all his most humane and compassionate instincts in order to achieve the higher good of the revolution." He must be prepared, consequently, "to exploit friendships, betray personal trust, to tell lies ... to utilize

---

[111]Camus, *op. cit.*, p. 34.

[112]Neuhaus, *op. cit.*, p. 214.

[113]Camus, *op. cit.*, p 32.

[114]Neuhaus, *op. cit.*, p. 227. That the problem of "moral means" weighs heavily upon Neuhaus is apparent from his repeated references to it; *cf. ibid.*, pp. 158, 159, 213, 217, 221. "There are other unavoidable dilemmas to be resolved. A moment's reflection on, for example, the bombing of stores and restaurants crowded with men, women, and children raises questions worthy of a thought beforehand." *Ibid.*, p. 226.

torture, the most degrading and dehumanizing violation of
humanity." To isolate a specific, the revolutionist must be prepared to assist in destroying the very people who are "effectively
concerned about society's problems and might have some chance
of limited success" in solving them without revolution. "The
best and the *worst*—that is, those who make reform credible and
those who are most obviously corrupt—are brought before isolated communities and ceremoniously executed, sometimes with
mutilation, and frequently with their families." And Neuhaus is
remorselessly unambiguous. "Second phase armed revolution
in the United States at present requires the effective elimination
of persons such as Galbraith, McGovern, McCarthy, Randolph,
Harrington, Goodwin, Chavez, and, if someone had not already
seen to it, Martin Luther King." Thus the insurrectionist must
be prepared to have his conscience contradicted and changed.
"Training for armed revolution requires a reeducation of some
of the most fundamental human instincts around which our no-
tions of morality revolve. ... The revolution, not conscience, is
the guiding point of reference for behavior. In questions of war
and personal loyalty, conscience must conform to revolutionary
reality."[115] Only by such a reeducation, apparently, can a
painful dilemma be resolved: is it right for the sake of humanity
to be ruthlessly inhumane? Neuhaus, of course, is not a sophisti-
cal propagandist for a revolutionary morality which inverts and
subverts traditional ethics. He insists, on the contrary, that these
perplexities and paradoxes be thought through with unflinching
realism. He acknowledges that the ignoble means which subversion requires for its success may frustrate its noble ends, ruling
it out as an option for humane people, although their own humanity is being degraded by inhumane oppression. Humane people may decide to suffer inhumane oppression instead of imitating
the contemptible inhumanity of their oppressors.

   The cruciality of this issue—are the means legitimate because
humane?—is brought out by Ramsey in his appraisal of insurgency and counterinsurgency.

Unless one knows something about the discriminations to be made and
the limits to be acknowledged along the way toward achieving victory

115*Ibid.*, pp. 158, 217, 221, 222.

for a greater justice, he has already *in mente* unleashed unrestrained violence in the means and methods of revolutionary war—*particularly* if the cause is just.116

Unrestrained violence in the means and methods of warfare, Ramsey argues, is simply murder, whether carried out by a government's army or a guerrilla band. He dogmatically equates indiscriminate violence and murder no matter how urgent the strategic necessities. Noncombatants must never be directly and intentionally killed; the sole purpose of armed force is to incapacitate those belligerents who by their armed force are furthering or maintaining gross injustice. "Directly attacking non-combatants or destroying the structures of civil society as a means of victory ... is the meaning of murder, which is never just even in war." Hence Ramsey, standing within the classical Christian tradition of morality, brands any act of war as gravely wrong if

its primary trust and purpose is to kill the innocent: that is murder, which no good end can justify. ... Murder is never ordinate; but unfortunately a good deal of killing may be. Direct attacks upon a civil population can never be justified; but unfortunately—in this world to date —the great many incidental deaths and extensive collateral damage to civil societies may still be knowingly done lest worse befall.117

The distinction between murder and killing, whether in war or revolution, may seem to be invisibly fine and hopelessly tenuous. Yet Ramsey insists that it is really humanity's frail dike against the flood tides of irrational barbarism.

The principle forbidding indiscriminate warfare pertains to the nature of warfare itself and its own proper laws—so long as this human action remains, by the skin of its teeth, a rational activity at all, so long as war is even conceivably a proper extension of national policy, so long as war barely remains an affair in which a human being at all above the level of the beasts of the field can justifiably participate, or (to go higher and yet

116 Ramsey, *The Just War*, p. 463.

117 *Ibid*, pp. 429, 431. *Cf.* Ramsey's statements in *War and the Christian Conscience*, pp. 43-45, 51, 54. Going back to the founders of just-war theory, Augustine and Aquinas, Ramsey argues that killing in self-defense should be the indirect and unintended effect of using counterforce against an attacker. Subjectively and primarily, counterforce aims to prevent injustice by resisting and merely incapacitating the attacker. The killing of an attacker is secondary and objective, a somewhat regrettable side effect!

lower for a comparison) so long as engagement in war has not been reduced merely to an exercise of technical reason and efficiency.[118]

This distinction is accepted by Neuhaus as absolutely basic if the human community is to exist. Whenever society forces a person to take the life of a person who is either innocent or noncombatant, it is ordering murder. Erase this distinction, grounded in respect for humanity, and the foundation of community is threatened.

Every society has felt it necessary, however, to distinguish between killing and killing. We distinguish among murder, manslaughter, assassination, and killing in war, for instances. We distinguish between willful and accidental killing. The deliberate and socially legitimated killing in some societies, such as in infanticide, head hunting, the killing of very old people, and cannibalism, would be classified as murders in ours. ... In short, the very existence of a human community requires severe sanctions for the doing of murder.[119]

Killing, then, can be distinguished from murder only when right authority legitimizes it and when that authority prevents killing from degenerating into unprincipled, indiscriminate, barbaric slaughter.

This is Berger's strong insistence, too. In the cases of both war and revolution, he writes, "the deepest motive for thinking about questions of justice is the abhorrence of killing."[120]

O'Brien, another moralist who is concerned to keep killing from degenerating into unprincipled, indiscriminate, and barbaric slaughter, expresses grave doubts, though, that the traditional principle of noncombatant immunity can realistically be applied in any way except as a counsel of prudence. His ground for skepticism concerning *jus in bello* is quite simply this:

In *all* present forms of warfare—so-called conventional, subconventional, guerrilla or irregular—literal application of the rule against intentional, direct attack on non-combatants (even if one could form a satisfactory definition for true non-combatants in modern war) would make moral

118 Ramsey, *The Just War*, p. 164, *cf. ibid.*, pp. 146, 415. For other of Ramsey's statements on the morality of armed force, *cf. ibid.*, pp. 260, 267, 275, 309, 350, 429, 431, 433.

119 Neuhaus, *op. cit.*, p. 150.

120 Berger, *op. cit.*, p. 54.

engagement in warfare virtually impossible.[121]

Elaborating his argument, O'Brien lists seven reasons against accepting the principle of noncombatant immunity from direct intentional attack. Two of them are relevant here. The first of these O'Brien expresses thus:

Efforts to solve the problem by designating virtually all of the enemy's population as participants in the war effort and hence not non-combatants will continue to be in vain. No matter what criteria are used, a considerable number of the enemy population are non-combatants and they will inevitably fall victim to the fate of the rest in major nuclear war. [122]

The other of these reasons he states at greater length:

Efforts to solve the dilemma by justifying "unintended, indirect" attacks of non-combatants under the principle of double effect have been un-satisfactory and will become more so. When a belligerent unleashes many large nuclear weapons, even though they mav be directed at military targets, the inevitable result will be death, injury, and contamination for large numbers of non-combatants. ... The author has neither the desire nor the competence to evaluate the validity and usefulness of the principle of double effect generally. But he does contend that in the con-text of modern war and deterrence, it does not furnish a tool of norma-tive analysis that is morally, rationally, and psychologically satisfactory. It simply does not ring true. ... Given the state of military technology, strategy and tactics, modern war is characterized at every level by the military necessity of taking measures that will inevitably involve death and injury to non-combatants no matter what the "intention" of the belligerents. [123]

The difficulty, if not the impossibility, of appealing to the principle of noncombatant immunity, which according to Ramsey forms the heart of the traditional *jus in bello* theory, is com-pounded by the very nature of insurgency. It is armed violence, to be sure, but scarcely armed violence between the military forces of two warring nations. "It is almost out of the question

[121]O'Brien, *Nuclear War, Deterrence and Morality*, pp. 31, 82-83. Notice O'Brien's further reason for rejecting noncombatant immunity: "acceptance of this as an absolute principle derived from theology guides one logically into a pacifist position with regard to modern war." *War and/or Survival*, p. 266.

[122] *Ibid.*
[123]*Ibid.*

for a modern revolutionary force, even at a very primitive and badly run state, to aspire to an open, 'fair' trial by combat with the incumbent regime. This is substantially the case whether the revolution occurs in Vietnam or Nigeria or Detroit."[124]

What means, then, are used in a resort to armed force from below and how moral are these techniques and tactics? To follow O'Brien's concise exposition, there are three principal tried and proved "means of violent revolution."

1. *Terror*—destroying the structure and substance of the society by sheer terror; making life unlivable for a substantial majority of the population, the government, and all essential co-operating elements of society.

2. *Destruction of progressive elements*—destruction or obstruction of every individual, program, or institution which seems to respond to the needs of the society and, therefore, to impel the claims of the revolutionaries that progress within the existing system is impossible and that progress will only come after the system is overthrown.

3. *Successful manipulation of "attentisme"*—coercing and persuading the uncommitted or faltering majority of the population, those who in Edgar Furniss' studies of French counter-insurgency he calls *"attentistes,"* those who are watching and waiting to see who is going to prevail ultimately, that the rebels will outlast and succeed incumbent regime.[125]

O'Brien, whose exposition has been appropriated almost verbatim by Neuhaus,[126] comments that "acts of terrorism, coldly calculated for symbolic effect," are first perpetrated only occasionally; but as the revolution moves into high gear, these acts are accelerated and expanded in order "to shake confidence in the existing order." He says what we have already been told by Neuhaus:

A persistent campaign to kill, kidnap, intimidate, or discredit any individual or institution which reflects real and effective concern for the society's problems and indicates some prospect for success in meeting them. When circumstances permit, two types of individuals, the *best* and the *worst*, in the governmental hierarchy are dragged before isolated communities and executed ceremoniously and hideously, often with

124 O'Brien, *War and/or Survival*, p. 203.
125 O'Brien, *War and/or Survival*, p. 203.
126 *Cf.* Neuhaus, *op. cit.*, pp. 216-29.

their families.[127]

Torture, also, is a species of violence which O'Brien analyzes, trying with a clinical detachment to assess its morality. He raises questions which shock and disturb our sensibilities.

1. Authority: What, if any responsible authority, orders acts of torture?
2. Torturers: Who inflicts torture, what is the relation between the treatment of the tortured persons and the intentions and policies of the responsible authority ordering such acts?
3. Victim: Is the victim a suspected or even a known criminal under the rules of law? Is he a person whose status insures possession of significant information? Or is the victim a comparatively anonymous person who has been rounded up more or less indiscriminately?
4. Means: What are the means, physical and psychological, that are used? Can we distinguish means that are intrinsically immoral, *mala in se*, from those which may be disproportionate and wrong in a particular context but permissible in other situations, from those that, however regrettable, may not appear excessive even as general operating procedure *if* torture, however defined, is ever legally and morally permissible?
5. Effects: What are the physical and psychological effects of the form of torture used? How lasting are these effects? How can the element of the subjective reaction on the part of the victim or, for that matter, of the victim's race or ethnic group be evaluated?[128]

Torture, in his opinion, may be ethically permissible, "if it is carried out by order of responsible authority by torturers acting in accordance with the intentions of that authority with respect to information, capacity to act, or other capability which it is certain or highly likely the victim possesses and which is of critical military importance by means which are as limited and barely sufficient as possible and which do not leave inadmissible lasting physical and psychological effects." This is O'Brien's summation of the moral rationale for the employment of torture, despite its agreed proscription:

A moral case can be made for the proportionality of good resulting from torture for outweighing the evil done to the victim. If international law is what is stated in the conventions, all torture is illegal. If international law is what states and revolutionary forces are doing on a near universal

127 O'Brien, *War and/or Survival*, p. 188.
128 *Ibid.*

basis without, apparently, great feelings of guilt, a legal-moral case can be made for torture as an exceptional measure when it involves a high degree of suffering and is a fairly routine measure if it is limited to "roughing up" and intimidating prisoners in interrogation in ways that will not have lasting effects. [129]

A Christian, therefore, contemplating not only endorsement of but participation in revolutionary violence must work out self-satisfactory solutions to some excruciating problems.

To be specific, does the Christian honestly believe that the principle of noncombatant immunity will be honored except by almost total disregard? See how even today's most articulate and intransigent proponent of the just-war morality, Paul Ramsey, bends this principle to fit the emerging pattern of armed violence. In his 1961 volume, *War and the Christian Conscience*, he adamantly refused to budge from the position that only military forces were to be the objects of intentional attack. "A wider circle of direct violence," he concluded, is incompatible "with the dictates of love or mercy, or a love-informed justice, or even simple justice." He said further, "Counter-forces warfare—the modern term for the just conduct of war—is the only kind of warfare in which just or merciful men can ever engage without a direct violation of those moral norms in terms of which they know they are ultimately judged." [130] But in his 1968 volume, *The Just War*, Ramsey himself has started to equivocate. Suppose an insurrectionist like Mao Tse-tung enlists practically an entire population in support of insurgency. Suppose, as Mao has graphically pictured the situation, "the people are like water and the soldiers like the fish who inhabit it. With the common people of the whole country mobilized, we shall create a vast sea of humanity and drown the enemy in it." Then, Ramsey argues, since "the insurgents themselves have enlarged the target, it is legitimate for the counterinsurgents to attack," abandoning the principle of discrimination for that of proportionality.

Since in the nature of insurgency the line between combatant and non-combatant runs right through a great number of the able-bodied people

129*Ibid.*, pp. 227-28, 232.

130Ramsey, *War and the Christian Conscience*, p. 306.

in a given area, male and female, above, say, ten years of age, and since anyone may cross over the line in either direction by the hour, it is not the business of any moralist to tell the soldiers and military commanders who are attempting to mount an effective counter-insurgency operation that this cannot be done in a morally acceptable way because under these circumstances they have no legitimate military target. ... When war is planned and carried out by an opponent on the principle that the guerrilla lives among the people like a fish in water, we may be justified in accepting the destruction of an entire school of fish (and the unavoidable and foreknown destruction of a great many people intermingled with them) incidental to the elimination of the guerrillas, provided only that the elimination of the school of fish is important enough to the whole course of the war, the winning of which is judged to be the lesser evil (or greater good). [131]

Walter E. Wiest's criticism of this modified *jus in bello* theory seems, therefore, to be well taken.

Ramsey has said that we can legitimately ask how many deaths might be justified by a just war, but not how many murders. Now he is telling us that murders are justifiable homicides if someone has arranged it so that murder is the only resort left to us. At the very least, Ramsey is now saying in effect that the rules of the ethical game hold only if both sides obey them, and the opponent does not clutter up the legitimate targets on his own soil with noncombatants. If he allows us only indiscriminate targets, then he has established a new set of rules and we are free to play the game his way. Whatever may be said for such a move, it certainly does strange things to the original notion of "inherently wrong."[132]

So if even Ramsey equivocates on this principle, it requires a Christian of extraordinary faith to hope that under the exigencies of revolution military targets will be kept justly limited. O'Brien, always the realist, entertains no such hope. "Across the board, if you insist on noncombatant immunity you insist on pacifism and non-violence, a perfectly rational and perhaps more moral position which I am unable to take."[133]

To mention another specific, does the Christian honestly believe that the humane principles he advocates—and as a Christian he must hypothetically do so—are likely to get any serious con-

131 Ramsey, *The Just War*, pp. 435-36.
132 Walter E. Wiest, *op. cit.*, pp. 148-49.
133 O'Brien, *War and/or Survival*, p. 249, *cf.* p. 256.

sideration by his more hard-bitten, less conscience-troubled comrades-in-arms? Does he honestly believe that pleas for discrimination and restraint, based presumably on a just-war morality, are going to be heeded in the throes of desperate struggle? Does he honestly believe that the moderates will be able to control the extremists in the face of massive counterinsurgency? O'Brien stresses this point hard.

If you are optimistic you will hope that courage and skill in combat will obviate the need for the dirtier means of revolutionary war, that the positive elements in your revolutionary program *will* win the hearts and minds of enough people so that your revolution will succeed with a minimum of evil-doing. Then you will hope that bad elements in the revolutionary movement can be handled and that reasonable and efficient men will take over the government. But in a real violent revolution, one involving fundamental change, not merely replacement of personnel or changes within the prevailing system, is it not the moderate, the liberal, who usually loses out and the radical or charismatic demagogue who usually ends up on top? It need not always be so, but these are some of the problems that Christian and other well-intentioned enthusiasts for revolutionary change will have to ponder. [134]

If, to quote Neuhaus, "in the revolution there is no substitute for success," what are the probabilities that military necessity will dictate the abandonment of scruples? Will conscience become a casualty of rationalizing expediency? Neuhaus tells about one American deserter who left the country because his conscience would not permit him to kill in the war against the Viet Cong. But in exile he had been learning that the dictates of personal ethics are relatively unimportant. So, speaking for his fellow deserters as well as for himself, he declared,

Now I see my motivation was screwed up. I thought you just had to follow your conscience. But political analysis is more important than conscience. It worked out O K in this case because our [the deserters'] feeling turned out to be right about the war and everything. ... But now I might do a lot of things that are against what I used to call my conscience, if it would help the [desertion] movement. [135]

In the thick of revolution one may likewise do a great many things

134 *Ibid.*, pp. 204, 205.
135 Quoted in Neuhaus, *op. cit.*, p. 223.

against conscience if those things are apt to help the cause.

Does the Christian honestly believe, moreover, that the nature of insurgency has changed since the time of Thucydides two thousand years ago?

When troubles had once begun in the cities, those who followed carried the revolutionary spirit further and further, and determined to outdo the report of all who had preceded them by the ingenuity of the enterprises and the atrocity of their revenges. The meaning of words had no longer the same relation to things, but was changed by them as they thought proper. Reckless daring was held to be loyal courage; prudent delay was the excuse of the cowards; moderation was the disguise of unmanly weakness; to know everything was to do nothing. Frantic energy was the true quality of a man. A conspirator who wanted to be safe was a recreant in disguise. The lover of violence was always trusted, and his opponent suspected. He who succeeded in a plot was deemed knowing, but a still greater master in craft was he who detected one. On the other hand, he who had plotted from the first to have nothing to do with plots was a breaker up of parties and a poltroon who was afraid of the enemy. In a word, he who could outstrip another in a bad action was applauded, and so was he who encouraged to evil one who had no idea of it. . . . The tie of party was stronger than the tie of blood, because a partisan was more ready to dare without asking why. **136**

If a Christian naïvely believes that violence tends to decelerate, he had better ponder Ellul's sociological analysis of a phenomenon which like a forest fire grows as it destroys. Ellul states five laws of violence which are, with slight rephrasing, (1) continuity ("once you start using violence, you cannot get away from it"), (2) reciprocity ("violence imprisons its practitioners in a circle that cannot be broken by human means"), (3) similarity ("it is impossible to distinguish between justified and unjustified violence, between violence that liberates and violence that enslaves"), (4) inequity ("whenever a violent movement has seized power, it has made violence the law of power. . . . No government established by violence has given the people liberty or justice—only a show of liberty [for those who supported the movement] and a show of justice [which consists in plundering the erstwhile 'haves']"), (5) hypocrisy ("the man who uses violence always

---

136 Quoted by Crane Brinton, *The Anatomy of Revolution* (New York: Vintage House, 1965), pp. 257, 258.

tries to justify both it and himself. .... In acting violently he is so unsure of himself that he has to have an ideological construct that will put him at ease intellectually and morally").[137] Hence all violence, but revolutionary violence especially, tends to behave like cancer, increasing its malignancy as it spreads and spreads.

To take still another specific, does the Christian honestly believe that he can virtually guarantee a revolution without atrocities and reprisals? A Rap Brown cries out, "For every Huey Newton, there must be two dead racist cops, and for every Black death, there must be a Dien Bien Phu!"[138] Yet O'Brien denounces the "pernicious institution of reprisals."

Few rights are more solidly established in the law of nations than the right of reprisal, and few principles have done so much to gloss over immoral behaviour with an aura of legality. ... This exceptional right applies to all the laws of war. It is supposed to serve two purposes: it provides a sanction for the law and it tends to restore the balance upset when one belligerent uses illegal means. Obviously, this kind of "legality" is ridiculous.[139]

And when any pretense of legality is thrown to the winds, will reprisals become the order of the day?

To mention one more specific, does the Christian honestly believe that torture can be all but eliminated or, if practiced, be carried out with minimal brutality and maximal humanity? Sensitive individuals are shaken when, for instance, Ivan Illich, director of the Center for Intercultural Documentation in Cuernavaca, Mexico, reports that the Brazilian government is resorting to a policy of torture as a repressive measure.

I lived under Hitler as a Jew. The cruelty in Brazil, however, is something entirely new—to put an entire people, anyone at any moment under the threat of torture. What is new is the picking up of people *at random*, having them go through unspeakable torture and then *releasing*

---

[137]Ellul, *op. cit.*, pp. 95-116. In the early stages of the French Revolution Edmund Burke warned prophetically, "Criminal means once tolerated are soon preferred. ... Justifying perfidy and murder for public benefit, public benefit would soon become the pretext and perfidy and murder the end. ... By hating vices too much, they [the revolutionaries] come to love men too little." Quoted by Kateb, *op. cit.*, pp. 47-48.

[138]Quoted by Neuhaus, *op. cit.*, p. 109.

[139]Quoted by Ramsey, *The Just War*, p. 246.

them. The Brazilian officials do not hide them. The Nazis and Stalinists made their victims disappear. The Brazilian torturers release people because this is an effective way of subduing a whole population. The exercise of violence cannot go further.[140]

There is no need of repeating the ghastly details which have been widely publicized, though by no means widely enough. But in a revolutionary situation, as Fanon's famous *The Wretched of the Earth* gruesomely testifies, the provocation to use any kind of torture is greatly increased. With his customary directness O'Brien minces no words, though he is talking about a use of torture which professes to remain within certain humane boundaries.

Friends of the New Left, please note, before the euphoria developing for a "theology of revolution" gets utterly out of hand, Christian advocates of violent revolution had better face the issue of torture and who is going to do it. It is reported that drafted seminarians in the French army in Algeria, when ordered to serve as interrogaters, worked the "electros," which tortured through electrical shocks, "gently." Will the priest-guerrillas of Latin America find "gentle" means of torturing their enemies to obtain the information which may be the difference between survival and annihilation by the counterinsurgents? Or will they take a walk and say some prayers while a tough leftist rebel does the job?[141]

Indeed, then, a Christian advocate of violence had better face the issue of torture and who is going to do it. He ought to reread that scene from Shaw's *Saint Joan* in which the English chaplain, who has been loudly demanding Joan's death, cries out piteously after he has watched her horrible martyrdom, "I meant no harm. I did not know what it would be like. . . . It is so easy to talk when you don't know. You madden yourself with words. . . . But when it is brought home to you: when you see the thing you have done, when it is blinding your eyes, stifling your nostrils, tearing your heart, then, then—."[142]

140Quoted in Robert H. Bolton, "Brazilian Torture: Specifically New, Specifically Terrible," *The Christian Century*, April 1, 1970, p. 387. *Cf.* the pamphlet "Terror in Brazil: A Dossier," released by the American Committee for Information on Brazil with headquarters in New York City.

141O'Brien, *War and/or Survival*, pp. 230, 231. Fanon, a psychiatrist by profession, cites a number of cases which reveal repulsively the horror and inhumanity of torture. The lasting emotional effects on the tortured are described objectively. *Op. cit.*, pp. 90-93, 253-93.

142Quoted in Judith N. Shklar, *After Utopia: The Decline of Political Faith* (Princeton, N. J.: Princeton University Press, 1957), p. 95.

To take a final specific, does the Christian honestly believe that revolutionary violence can be practiced without inducing emotions and attitudes which negate the prospect of brotherhood and humanization, let alone compassion and love? Ellul argues that violence and hatred are inseparable, quoting Rap Brown's statement, "Hate has a role to play. I am full of hatred, and so are the other blacks. Hate, like violence, is necessary for our revolution."[143] Hate—the "terrible anger" and "deadly despair" Colin Morris mentions—is no doubt understandable when people have been the victims of injustice. Morris blazes out against the oppressive Establishment which produces an unjust situation: "Love, compassion, and forgiveness have no place in the animal world, and that is where the majority of mankind lives." Consequently, to transform that animal world into a more human world, the gentle feelings of love, compassion, and forgiveness—chains forged by the astute apologists of repression and reaction—must be ruthlessly chiseled off. "One of the themes of a down-to-earth theology of the revolution might be the role of healthy hate in nerving men to do what any normal understanding of love could never allow. But it will take a theologian with a strong stomach to write that sort of thing."[144]

Has this strange inversion of love ever been more powerfully stated than by Arthur Koestler in his novel, *Darkness at Noon,* as he portrays a dedicated revolutionist?

He reads Machiavelli, Ignatius of Loyola, Marx and Hegel; he is cold and merciful to mankind, out of a kind of mathematical mercifulness. He is damned always to do that which is most repugnant to him: to become a slaughterer in order to abolish slaughtering, to sacrifice lambs so that no more lambs may be slaughtered, to whip people with knouts so that they may learn not to let themselves be whipped, to strip himself of every scruple in the name of a higher scrupulousness, and to challenge the hatred of mankind because of his love for it—an abstract and geometric love.[145]

[143]Quoted in Ellul, *op. cit.*, p. 104.
[144]O'Brien, *op. cit.*, p. 145-47.
[145]Arthur Koestler, *Darkness at Noon* (New York: The Modern Library, 1941), pp. 149-50.

In short, on behalf of the humanization which the revolutionary theologians espouse, brutal dehumanization must be practiced, reluctantly no doubt, but with a stoical dedication, nevertheless. Men must be reduced to the level of things, subhuman entities. But, as Vernard Eller indignantly objects, "What insult is it to the other man, what damage to my personal relationship to him and to God, what affront to that God Who has given His only Son that both I and my enemies might become true persons, when I deliberately suspend my Christian understanding in order to consider men as mere things.[146]

The Christian, therefore, is under obligation, morally and spiritually alike, to engage in some hard thinking. Does he honestly believe that the means which revolution inescapably entails will justify the ends it may achieve? Will violence produce peace, torture produce justice, hate produce love, reprisal produce reconciliation, suppression produce freedom, inhumanity produce humanization? In forgetfulness of the old axiom that the result cannot be greater than the cause, does he honestly believe this? Then he is either a man of mountain-moving faith or a man of pathetic credulity. At any rate, he certainly needs to do more than glance casually at Jean Lasserre's confession of doubt regarding the noble ends which ignoble means will hypothetically produce:

We do not believe that peace can come out of violence, that justice can issue from generalized criminality, that respect for man can emerge from contemptuousness. Hatred and crime result neither in justice nor in reconciliation, but in bitterness, cowardice, vice and crime. ... All these attitudes are in no way propitious for the creation of a just and humane society. ... [Those who hold that] have bent the knee to bloody idols. And since they are swept along by the internal logic of violence, their struggle soon ceases to be a means of attaining justice and becomes an end in itself. Ultimately, the cruelest and most clamorous among them take over—the toughest, not the most just. And the revolution is aborted under the dictatorship of a new tyrant How can you defend and build man when you begin by suppressing and destroying men?[147]

But some Christians apparently do little more than glance at

146Vernard Eller, *The Promise: Ethics in the Kingdom of God* (Garden City, N. Y.: Doubleday & Company, Inc., 1970), p. 131.
147Quoted by Ellul, *op. cit.*, pp. 102-03.

these strictures and dismiss them. Thus while Neuhaus manfully grapples with these agonizing issues, Shaull ignores them. He nowhere discusses in depth the means-ends problem. He is vague and sanguinary about violence, much as it contradicts the very elements which he takes to be central in God's humanizing activity—forgiveness, freedom, justice, and reconciliation. No wonder Ellul comments, "His doctrine is idealistic, theologically negligible, and all but totally unrealistic." [148] And when revolution is being advocated, wide-eyed realism is imperative. Without it, one may vainly lament as the English chaplain does in Shaw's *Saint Joan.*

The seventh criterion which Neuhaus proposes for a just revolution is success. Every other criterion may be met, and thus the right to use insurrectionary violence may be established, but, he writes, "if there is not 'reasonable hope of success' it would be unjust to exercise that right." [149] Hence something more is in view here than simply a fighting chance that the subversives will be able to overthrow the old regime and replace it with their own government. In addition—and far more significantly—the prospect of a less oppressive and less inequitable society ought to be at least a possibility. Unless the odds favor the emergence of a greater good, the resort to means which are in themselves evil becomes morally indefensible. If, however, by revolution the evil of society is reduced in the long run, the resort to evil means may then lose some of its reprehensible quality. If, on the contrary, the evil of society becomes worse, the resort to evil means loses whatever dubious morality it may have claimed. That is why Dr. G. B. Caird says, "Whatever we may think of the argument that the end justifies the means, one thing at least is clear: that a means which is not in itself good cannot be justified by the end unless it achieves the end." [150] Several things, accordingly, must not be overlooked by the revolutionist who is ethically oriented.

For one thing, violence from below involves the considerable risk of failure until "a society is ripe for dissolution." According

[148]*Ibid.*, p. 56.

[149]Neuhaus, *op. cit.*, p. 228.

[150]Quoted by John Campsie, *Objection to Murder: The Conscience of the Unilateralist* (Toronto: McClelland & Stewart, Ltd., 1967), p. 118.

to Morris, who lays down this dictum, and according to common sense as well, where ripeness does not obtain, "overwhelming fire power, modest reform or judicious bribery will nullify it." Morris therefore cautions radicals against essaying insurrection in a country like the United States, "unless the rottenness of the West's foundations will no longer bear the weight of material affluence soured by spiritual arrogance."[151] Incidentally, in their joint statement at the conclusion of *Movement and Revolution,* Berger and Neuhaus declare: "We agree that, whether or not an armed revolution is necessary, the United States is not ripe for it."[152]

If a revolution is essayed prematurely and precipitously, it can provoke a crushing reaction which will intensify rather than diminish evil. So Thomas Merton envisions the dire consequences which might follow if in desperation American blacks were to launch a civil war:

A victorious Negro revolution is out of the question unless the country is crippled by some disaster (such as nuclear war or catastrophic collapse of the economy). The most likely thing is that extreme provocation by irrational violence may create such disorder and such panic in the country that a new order based on force (a police state) may have to be established. In that event, the possibility of extremists on the white side taking over and ruling by irrational and arbitrary violence is very likely. Even "prison camps" for Negroes and then for other unacceptables are not beyond the bounds of possibility.[153]

How difficult it is, though, to gauge when any country is ripe for successful revolution!

For a second thing, violence from below involves the considerable risk of anarchy succeeded by tyranny. This is the melancholy pattern of almost every revolution in history with the notable exception of the American War of Independence. Precisely for this reason, John Bennett counsels urgently that one refrain from insurrection unless he sees "near at hand the possibility of establishing a new and better order"; barring that possibility, however,

---

[151] Colin Morris, *op. cit.*, pp. 150, 151.

[152] Berger and Neuhaus, *Movement and Revolution,* p. 239.

[153] Thomas Merton, *Faith and Violence: Christian Teaching and Christian Practice* (Notre Dame, Ind.: University of Notre Dame Press, 1968), p. 176.

one must reckon on "the risk of long, continued anarchy, which may result in an even worse tyranny."[154]

Even if a new government is successfully set up, however, it may succumb to dictatorship. Think of how Lenin and his Bolsheviks sabotaged the Kerensky government. This is the danger that haunts Neuhaus.

Of course, there is no guaranteed leadership formula to prevent the perversion of the revolution. But before the revolutionary pledges his "life, fortune and sacred honor" to the cause he will want to be reasonably confident that the revolution itself will not be delegitimized by inter-meshing conflict and corruption.[155]

And Neuhaus has cause for apprehension. A sharp-minded Frenchman, Bertrand Jouvenal, describes the revolutionary phenomenon and its strange devolution.

Before the rapids, there was the rule of a Charles I, a Louis XVI, a Nicholas II. After them, that of a Cromwell, a Napoleon, a Stalin. Such are the masters to whom the people that rose against Stuart or Bourbon or Romanov "tyranny" find themselves subjected next. The phenomenon is as startling as the usual interpretation of it is misconceived. How sad, it is said, that the revolution strayed from its natural course, that the anti-social extravagances of liberty called for a constraining force to discipline them, that these extravagances caused so widespread a ruin that there had to be a man to reconstruct! If this or that mistake had been avoided! Ingenuity is freely expanded in unearthing the exact moment at which licentiousness set in, in isolating the act that made the revolution sin, in naming the criminal. *O pectora caeca!* What a misunderstanding is here of the revolutionary phenomenon! The Cromwells and Stalins are no fortuitous consequence, no accidental happening, of the revolutionary tempest. Rather they are its predestined goal, towards which the entire upheaval was moving inevitably; the cycle began with the *downfall of an inadequate Power* only to close with a *consolidation of a more absolute Power.*[156]

For a third thing, violence from below involves the considerable risk of setting up a government, dictatorial or otherwise, which stumbles along improvising, experimenting, exacting a frightful

154 Quoted by Ramsey, *The Just War*, p. 12, n. 5.
155 Neuhaus, *op. cit.*, p. 173.
156 Quoted by Waelder, *op. cit.*, pp. 260-61.

toll in suffering in order finally to secure minimal or minus benefits. Usually revolutionists, as we have previously observed, offer no blueprint for an improved order; glittering slogans and propagandistic shibboleths are the stock-in-trade they sell their fellow travelers. They are serenely confident that a miracle which is the political equivalent of resurrection will occur; thus even a militarily successful revolution becomes the prelude to a time of chaos and travail, a period when a whole people undergoes surgery without anesthesia. Koestler has probed this matter in *Darkness at Noon*, which George Kateb properly eulogizes as "one of the master works of political ethics in the twentieth century." [157] Ivanov, a Communist functionary, exonerates the Bolshevik dictatorship for its vivisection politics, its trial and error tactics, its laboratory approach to the reconstruction of society. Revulsion against experiment he derides as "rather naïve."

Every year several million people are killed quite pointlessly by epidemics and natural catastrophes. And we should shrink from sacrificing a few hundred thousand for the most promising experiment in history? Not to mention the legions of those who die of undernourishment and tuberculosis, in coal and quicksilver mines, rice fields and cotton plantations. No one takes any notice of them; nobody asks why or what for; but if here we shoot a few thousand objectively harmful people, the humanitarians all over the world foam at the mouth. Yes, we liquidated the parasitic part of the peasantry and let it die of starvation. It was a surgical operation which had to be done once and for all; but in the good old days before the Revolution just as many died in any dry year—only senselessly and pointlessly. The victims of the Yellow River floods in China amount sometimes to hundreds of thousands. Nature is generous in her senseless experiments on mankind. Why should mankind not have the right to experiment on itself? [158]

The opposite position is powerfully set forth by Rubashov, a broken party leader who is facing death for ideological error. "What a mess we have made of our golden age!" he sighs, as he attacks the perverted logic which does not shrink from the consequences of its principle that the present generation is merely manure to enrich the future stages of history. Yes, he concedes

[157]Kateb, *op. cit.*, p. 37.

[158]Koestler, *op. cit.*

with indignant eloquence, we are logically consequent!

So consequent, that in the interests of the just distribution of land we let die of starvation about five million farmers and their families in one year. So consequent were we in the liberation of human beings from the shackles of industrial exploitation that we sent about ten million people to do forced labor in the Arctic regions or the jungles of the East, under conditions similar to those of antique galley slaves. So consequent that, to settle a difference of opinion, we know only one argument: death, whether it is a matter of submarines, manure, or the Party line to be followed in Indo-China. ... We whip the groaning masses of the country toward a theoretical future happiness, which only we can see. For the energies of this generation are exhausted; they were spent in the Revolution; this generation is bled white and there is nothing left of it but a moaning, numbed, apathetic lump of sacrificial flesh. ... I see the flayed body of this generation; but I see no trace of the new skin. We all thought one could treat history like one experiments in physics. The difference is that in physics one can repeat the experiment a thousand times, but in history only once. [159]

Dispassionately evaluated, then, by the yardstick of its consequences, is revolution likely to be successful? At the end of his very praiseworthy study, *The Anatomy of Revolution*, Crane Brinton draws up a balance sheet and finds as one of his four major conclusions "that in general many things men do, many human habits, sentiments, dispositions, cannot be changed at all rapidly, that the attempt made by the extremists to change them by law, terror and exhortation fails, that convalescence brings them back not greatly altered." [160]

Brogan is just as skeptical concerning the success of revolution.

The impatience of the young is not an excuse for the abandonment of responsibility by their elders who have noticed how quickly the rosy dawn turns into a hang-over period. For behind the idea of revolution as a normal remedy, as a beneficent panacea instead of as a last desperate operation, is a refusal to learn with what difficulty the not very high standards of order, liberty, decency, to which we still cling, have been attained and how easily they can be lost. It is presumably unnecessary to stress the point that they are less likely to survive an atomic war-cum-revolution than either a plain revolution or a plain war. ... What this

159*Ibid.*
1603rinton, *op. cit.*, p. 262.

world needs is a long period of time to adjust itself, even if that means postponing some attractive solutions till the world can afford to digest them. It means, too, an acceptance of the fact that there is no quick and easy and cheap way to Utopia and that all salesmen of such quick and easy and cheap ways are deceiving themselves or their customers or both.[161]

Camus' measured judgment can serve, therefore, as a summation of all we have been saying with respect to a just revolution.

Whatever the desired end, however lofty and necessary, whatever happiness or justice or liberty—the means employed to attain it represent so enormous a risk and are so disproportionate to the slender hopes of success, that, in all sober objectivity, we must refuse to run this risk.[162]

[161]Brogan, *op. cit.*, p. 268.
[162]Camus, *op. cit.*, p. 36.

God is just as concerned about deprived people today as He was when Israel was in bondage in Egypt. One of the proofs that Jesus gave to John was that "the poor have the gospel preached to them." The people who opposed Christ were those made confortable by the establishment. Jesus' support came from "dropouts," people who gave up solid jobs as fishermen and tax collectors to follow a fanatic. And with His help, they turned the world upside down.

We need men today who will drop out of their comfortable jobs to start a revolution, men who like Moses will leave Pharaoh's palace to lead a downtrodden minority to a promised land. Universities are the main source of such revolutionary leadership. Young people are not as bound as their elders by political and religious tradition, by clichés and stereotypes. Students haven't had time to develop calluses which make them insensitive to the needs of the poor. Their minds don't spring shut like steel traps at the mention of change, interracial marriage, social justice, revolution. . . .

If there is a student who like Moses will try to relate God's unchanging message to this revolutionary age, then he faces the greatest and most challenging task that can be entrusted to man. He must do his job well or the church will wither and society will come under a new and hideous dictatorship or anarchy.

—John and Fred Alexander

VIII. Revolutionary Christianity

Thus far we have been cross-examining the theology of revolution from a moral perspective, indicating the grave difficulties and contradictions it encounters in its advocacy of change by violence if change without violence proves either too improbable or too slow. Now, shifting ground, we shall seek to appraise this radical reinterpretation of Christianity purely as a theology; for, we must not forget, it claims to be a theology, and thus it ultimately stands or falls as judged from a theological perspective.

Before we launch into this evaluation, however, it is essential that we have a clear understanding of the traditional interpretation which the theology of revolution repudiates, that view of Christianity which mainstream orthodoxy, Protestant and Catholic alike, has consistently espoused, that revelationally derived faith to which evangelicals still tenaciously adhere. A succinct sketch of orthodoxy is imperative precisely because Shaull and other theologians who occupy a revolutionary platform are pronouncing traditional Christianity, if not quite dead, at any rate hopelessly moribund. Theologically, in Shaull's opinion, we have reached a state of "bankruptcy" which requires that as Christians we be willing "to allow dead theological systems to be buried, to stand before the world empty-handed, and to expect a theological resurrection." Today's revolutionary situation demands "the reworking of our whole theological heritage, the development of new paradigms, and the exploration of elements of the tradition which have been largely ignored or forced underground."[1]

[1]Richard Shaull, "The Christian in the Vortex of Revolution," *Projections: Shaping an American Theology for the Future,* Thomas F. O'Meara and Donald M. Weisser, eds. (Garden City, N.Y.: Doubleday & Company, Inc., 1970), pp. 59, 56, 69.

But before arranging for a funeral, one ought to be sure that there is a corpse; and perhaps the death of Christian orthodoxy, like Mark Twain's mistakenly reported demise, has been grossly exaggerated. What, then, is the traditional faith which Shaull regards as a dead system that ought to be interred?

It is, as Jacques Ellul unequivocally states it, "Christianity accepted in its revealed totality—accepted absolutely, intransigently, without cultural or philosophical or any other kind of accommodation or adaptation."[2] As such, it is a Christ-centered faith which, while necessarily aware of man's horizontal relationships ("thou shalt love thy neighbor as thyself"), assigns all-controlling importance to man's vertical relationship ("thou shalt love the Lord thy God with all thy heart, and with all thy soul, and with all thy mind"). Unlike the theology of revolution, it doggedly resists reduction to a horizontalism in which God becomes experientially and theoretically an impersonal transcendence, a symbol with which fellowship is about as possible as communion with the formula $E = mc^2$. In keeping with the New Testament, orthodoxy teaches that the vertical relationship governs the horizontal relationship for which it supplies design and dynamic.

Orthodoxy also teaches that man, created by God, has in sinful disobedience become fatally maladjusted to his Creator, apart, of course, from the Creator's own redemptive activity. Orthodoxy, therefore, sees man as the proud insurrectionist and defiant rebel "who has not learned to be content with his lot"—which Harvey Cox denounces as a seriously "misleading view of sin." It disagrees flatly with Cox that sin is fundamentally sloth, indolence, laziness, acedia, a cowardly apathy—the "self-doubt, hesitancy, and dependency" exhibited by Adam and Eve as they listened to the snake. Orthodoxy does not shrivel transgression to political indifferentism, "a fear of involvement" which furnishes a rationalization "for not assuming one's share in the responsible use of power in the world."[3] Orthodoxy does not construe sin as something negative and passive, man's failure to fulfill the role of

2Ellul, *op. cit.*, p. 145.

3Harvey Cox, *On Not Leaving It to the Snake* (New York: The Macmillan Company, 1967), pp. x-xvii.

cocreator in bringing about a happier future on earth. It construes sin, rather, as something positive and active, man's revolt against God in order to enthrone himself, autonomously setting his own laws and limits. Orthodoxy holds, as Paul Minear does, that by deliberately abandoning the sovereignty of God—not just irresponsibly letting some snake tell him what to do—man has put himself under a frustrating tyranny.

Man is a creature whose existence is defined by his dependence upon God. When he ... defies this status ... he has cut himself off from the only Giver of life. His pseudo-existence, his new "world," is the world where death has become a tyrant, ruling all those who have forfeited their true humanity. This prison of illusion and vanity can be breached only by a new act of God "who gives life to the dead and calls into existence the things that do not exist."[4]

By rebelling against God, man has thus been plunged into dehumanization and has alienated himself from true fulfillment.

So orthodoxy holds, still further, that it is only "God's act in Christ which restores man to his true humanity."[5] Hence orthodoxy in keeping with the New Testament likewise teaches a Christ-centered forgiveness, a reconciliation to God by an incredibly gracious and costly atonement. It proclaims that the cross is measurelessly more than a sign of God's unchanging attitude toward man. It frontally disputes John Macquarrie's deductions from Jesus' parable of the prodigal son. He writes that the prodigal

finds the father willing to receive him, though there is no special machinery to make possible a reconciliation. ... The father, in turn, does not need to be placated. This parable stresses the unchanging character of God's attitude and work, which is always one of reconciliation. It is necessary indeed that some particular historical event should bring to light in a signal way "the mystery hidden for ages and generations," but no historical event changes God's attitude, or makes him from a wrathful God into a gracious God, or allows his reconciling work to get started— such thoughts are utterly to be rejected.[6]

[4]Quoted by Donald G. Miller, "God Reconciles and Makes Free," *Reconciliation in Today's World,* Allen O. Miller, ed. (Grand Rapids, Mich.: William B. Eerdmans Publishing Co., 1969), p. 24.
[5]*Ibid.*, p. 22.
[6]Quoted in *ibid.*, p. 19.

But this reading of the parable—and of the entire New Testament—orthodoxy faults as a lamentable misreading. It protests, in the words of P. T. Forsyth, that the parable of the prodigal son emphasizes a single point, the "centrality, the completeness, the unreservedness, the freeness, fulness, wholeheartedness of God's grace," but it says nothing about "the *method* of its actions."[7] And that method, orthodoxy teaches, was the atoning cross. Atonement, then, which procures the possibility of sin's forgiveness, this, on the orthodox reading of the New Testament, is the very heart of the Gospel. James Denney affirms this traditional Christ-centered, cross-centered faith, this gospel of the sacrifice made by the holy God to provide human rebels with the possibility of forgiveness: "A finished work of Christ and an objective atonement ... are synonymous terms; ... unless we can preach a finished work of Christ in relation to sin, a ... reconciliation or peace which has been achieved independently of us, ... we have no real gospel for sinful men at all."[8]

Again, in keeping with the New Testament, orthodoxy teaches a Christ-centered freedom without which true humanization is a delusive dream. Much as it respects the aspirations of what Alves styles messianic humanism, orthodoxy follows Donald G. Miller in charging that this one-dimensional humanism is a rival faith which believes its "goals may be ultimately achieved by forces generated purely within man." Thus it is actually the quintessence of "rebellion against and alienation from God," and precisely this "is man's slavery." Pointedly therefore Miller demands, "How can that which has produced man's slavery set him free from that slavery? ... To define freedom as man's true humanity in political, sociological, or economic terms, then, is a contradiction, according to the New Testament."

Consequently, when biblically loyal, the Church announces "the truth that men are bound by an enslavement that they can never conquer; that however desirable freedom from the oppression of external circumstance is, such freedom can never take the place of that freedom from sin which is *God's act in Christ*." So Miller, as a spokesman for orthodoxy, brings a crucial theological issue to focus.

7Quoted in *ibid.*, p. 20.
8Quoted in *ibid.*, p. 19.

While advocates of "revolutionary theology" do battle with the forces of evil entrenched in the social order, can the Church abdicate its function of reminding them that all power tends toward corruption, and that unless we offer them an inner freedom from thralldom to the powers of darkness through the liberating work of Jesus Christ, the exorcising of the demons they seek to cast out could open the way for more demons to enter, leaving the last state worse than the first?[9]

Yet again, in keeping with the New Testament, orthodoxy teaches a Christ-oriented fellowship, a new community of love and hope entered by faith in the atoning cross. This societal aspect of the traditional faith has been expressed concisely by John Mackay:

The "new men in Christ" are members of a fellowship, a community of faith called the church, a unique association created by Christ through the Holy Spirit. This historic community was born in dramatic form at Pentecost. From its inception the church gave expression to its universal character, across all linguistic boundaries. It expressed also the reality and practical implications of loving God and one another. It was hailed by the apostles and early Christians as the "New Israel," the "Israel of God," the "fellowship of the Spirit."[10]

This community of self-confessed, Christ-forgiven sinners, whatever its structural form, is, as Calvin said, "the instrument of God's glory." Mackay indicates, accordingly, some of its distinctive characteristics: "Obedience, action, truth that inspires goodness, fellowship that is fulfilled in service, community that takes to the road—all are constituent elements of what it means to belong to the church, which is Christ's body."[11]

Besides these things, orthodoxy teaches, in keeping with the New Testament, a Christ-centered future, a future which embraces a world to come as well as the time-and-space world of the here and now. Without losing sight of its mandate to do God's will on earth as that will is done in heaven, orthodoxy hopes for heaven beyond earth. Sensitive to the anesthetizing dangers of otherworldliness, it nevertheless maintains that the Christian is only a colonist in this world. So sophisticated a sociologist as Jacques Ellul has no hesitancy in declaring, in sharp disavowal

[9]*Ibid.*, pp. 24, 26, 28.

[10]John A. Mackay, *Christian Reality & Appearance* (Richmond, Va.: John Knox Press, 1969), p. 26; *cf.* p. 67.

[11]*Ibid.*, p. 28.

of the current emphasis on a one-dimensional faith, that *"the Christian belongs to two Cities."*

Living in this world, he belongs to another: like a man of one nation who resides in another nation. A Chinese residing in France thinks in his own terms, in his own tradition; he has his own criterion of judgment and of action; he is really a stranger and a foreigner: he is also a citizen of another state, and his loyalty is given to this state, and not to the country in which he is living. It is the same with the Christian, he is the citizen of another kingdom, and it is thence that he derives his way of thinking, judging and feeling. His heart and his thought are elsewhere. ... He may be in this world, it is true, but all his "ties" are elsewhere; all his ties of thought, truth, and fidelity depend on his Lord, and he owes no allegiance to the world.[12]

And orthodoxy fails to perceive why a Christian's allegiance to heaven prevents him from being vitally and effectively concerned about earth. It takes the opposite position, maintaining with Canon H. S. Holland, that

The sense of the imminent end of all things, far from tending to disorder or eviscerate the demands of the moral law or the steadfastness of self-control or the urgency of present conduct or the vitality of living interests, actually emphasizes and intensifies these demands. The motives intertwine and the appeals coincide.[13]

Himself not a protagonist of orthodoxy, Ernst Troeltsch sympathetically analyzes the genius of a biblical otherworldliness which does not lose its this-worldly relevance.

The idea of the future Kingdom of God, which is nothing less than faith in the final realization of the Absolute (in whatever way we may conceive this realization), does not, as short-sighted opponents imagine, render this world and life in this world meaningless and empty; on the contrary, it stimulates human energies, making the soul strong through its various stages of experience in the certainty of an ultimate, absolute meaning and aim for human labour. Thus it raises the soul above the world without denying the world. ... All social utopias, then, become superfluous; over and over again experience teaches that the ideal cannot be fully realized; but this does not mean that the seeker for truth and justice need lose heart and fall back into skepticism, a temptation to which serious and

12Jacques Ellul, *The Presence of the Kingdom* (Philadelphia: The Westminster Press, 1951), pp. 45-47.
13Quoted by Ray C. Petry, *Christian Eschatology and Social Thought* (New York: Abingdon Press, 1956), p. 19.

truth-loving souls are prone, and the effects of which are very manifest among the finest spirits of the present day. The life beyond this world is, in very deed, the inspiration of the life that now is.[14]

Not only that, but orthodoxy, just as it expects a nonsymbolic heaven with Christ, expects the nonsymbolic return of Christ, a divine denouement which will finish and fulfill history and which will be no less a reality than the incarnation. So discussing the "promise of the glorious return of Jesus Christ, the Parousia," Ellul asserts:

The Christian is essentially a man who lives in expectation. This expectation is directed toward the return of the Lord which accompanies the end of time, the judgment, and proclaims the kingdom of God. Thus one who knows that he has been saved by Christ is not a man jealously and timidly attached to a past, however glorious it may be ... But he is a man of the future, not of a temporal and logical future, but of the *eschaton*, of the coming break with this present world.[15]

Orthodoxy, therefore, in keeping with the New Testament, teaches that the believer has a Christ-centered function. As an agent of the reconciling God, the coming kingdom, and the life beyond, the Christian is charged with a unique mission which he alone can discharge. Merely because a movement like that of revolution is *au courant*, the Christian is not to jump enthusiastically on this newest bandwagon. There, indeed, may be compelling reasons for him to withhold from it his endorsement and help.

He has a part to play in this world which no one else can possibly fulfill. He is not asked to look at the various movements which men have started, choose those which seem "good," and then support them. He is not asked to give his blessing to any particular human enterprise, nor to support the decisions of man. He is charged with a mission of which the natural man can have no idea; yet in reality this mission is decisive for the actions of men.[16]

Ellul then brings out the unique dimension of the Christian's task:

God has not sent him into the world for any other purpose than to fulfill this function. But this specific function cannot be compared with other human ends; it cannot be understood by the "natural man"; yet the significance of all other functions depends upon it. This function is

[14]Quoted by Petry, *ibid.*, pp. 16, 17.
[15]Ellul, *The Presence of the Kingdom*, p. 49.
[16]*Ibid.*, pp. 8, 9, 11-12.

defined by the Scriptures in three ways:
1) You are the salt of the earth.
2) You are the light of the world.
3) I send you forth as sheep in the midst of wolves.[17]

Ellul, together with orthodoxy, therefore ringingly concludes:

Here Jesus Christ confronts us with the specific function of the Christian—and there can be no other. Things cannot be otherwise; the Christian has no choice, and if he does not accept this function, he does not fulfill the part assigned to him. He then betrays both Jesus Christ and the world. Of course he can always immerse himself in good works, and pour out his energy in religious or social activities, but all this will have no meaning unless he is fulfilling the only mission with which he has been charged by Jesus Christ, which is first of all to be *a sign*.[18]

Hastily and imperfectly sketched, such is Christianity as orthodoxy teaches it, a redemptive faith which the theology of revolution dismisses as not only archaic but also moribund. It is this faith which—in the hands of daring surgeons like Lehmann, Shaull, Alves, Morris, Cox, Novak, Neuhaus—has been undergoing a whole series of operations. The worn-out Gospel, they claim, will be made fit for the rigors of guerrilla service by these grafts, transplants, and resectionings. Are these surgeons, though, misguided experimenters who will transform their patient into a cadaver rather than a rejuvenated freedom fighter?

An evangelical, moving *con amore* within the framework of orthodoxy which he takes to be the biblical framework as well, is hard put to interact objectively with the theology of revolution. He appreciates the social passion of its advocates, their sensitivity, courage, insight, and commitment, their insistence on the futility of Christian theory divorced from Christian praxis, their desire to make a traditional faith legitimately relevant. Yet he wonders by what strange process they have been able to extrapolate their concepts and conclusions from the New Testament. Consequently, he challenges this metamorphosis of the Gospel on three counts.

First, as an evangelical appraises it, this theology seems to be an abject capitulation to the *Zeitgeist* of the twentieth century. It

17 *Ibid.*
18 *Ibid.*

is not drawn from the thought world of the Bible but from the contemporary milieu instead. It is an alien ideology imposed upon the New Testament rather than a faithful interpretation of the Gospel. It is a surrender to the very temptation against which J. M. Lochman warned in the 1966 WCC Geneva Conference on Church and Society, "the notorious danger" of so adapting Christianity to its changing environment that the adaptation becomes accommodation and in the end capitulation, a case of the salt's losing its savor.

One look at the history of the church shows that fact. Consider the extent to which Christianity in the feudal age became feudalized—even to the most subtle problems of theology! And in the bourgeois epoch Christianity became simply—bourgeois! Why, then, in a socialist epoch should a "socialist Christianity" not come into being? Why do people only then, as so frequently happens, get frightened and sound the alarm? Yet it is, and remains, a temptation.[19]

Lochman explains that the Word of God must certainly be applied prophetically to emerging events and issues, but he fears that all too often it "is made a relative entity with which other historical entities are associated. The Word of God loses its sovereignty, it is made to conform."[20]

Ellul, too, is keenly aware of this danger. The Church, trying to be relevant, may degenerate into "a sociological movement ... another secular movement." When it forgets its distinctive message and mission, "it has ceased to be a 'leaven' in the life of the world. ... It is no longer the salt of the earth, or the light of the world. ... It no longer represents the power of the action of God in the world."[21] Hence he urges that the Church, though involved in the complexities and problems of every age, refuse to pursue that relevance which is really compromise with the world, a compromise which tends toward capitulation to the *Zeitgeist.* "The Church ought not to justify itself, or to justify the world's solution, but it ought to find its own way, given it by God, which it alone can follow. It is only on this condition that the Church will cease to be a sociological movement, and be present in the

19 J. M. Lochman, "The Church in a Socialist Society," *The Church amid Revolution*, Harvey Cox, ed., pp. 50, 51.
20 *Ibid.*
21 Ellul, *The Presence of the Kingdom*, p. 151.

world with the effectiveness given by the Holy Spirit."[22]

This, then, is what impresses an evangelical about the theology of revolution: it seems to be a surrender to the dominating ideology of our day, the administration of baptism to a movement which is completely secular. "Fifty years ago, it would never have occurred to Christians to favor such movements. But, it is fair to say, the dominating ideology everywhere is the socializing, anticolonialist ideology, and 'advanced' Christians fall in line and march along on the road to violence."[23]

Ellul's charge, then, sticks fast: "All today's preachers of violence seem unable to grasp the fact that they are conformists."[24] As radicals, they may scorn the culture bondage of conservatism, but they also are in bondage, the captives of a revolutionary *Zeitgeist* which they ought prophetically to transcend.

Consider, illustratively, the concept of humanization which is central to this theology. Is it uniquely biblical or is it only secular notion rephrased in Christian terminology? David Willis is not overly tart in his judgment:

The criteria used to distinguish between humanization and dehumanization are frequently drawn simply from whatever sociological and psychological parlance happens to be fashionable at any given time, although in theory anyone is justified in drawing ambitiously from the secular well inasmuch as the water there is christologically sweetened.[25]

Consider, in addition, its implicit view of human nature, a view which it does not systematically explicate. Is it distinctively Christian? Ramsey declines to so identify it.

What has happened in the "what God is doing" school of Christian ethics is—in the absence of the full range of Christian perspectives upon politics—an identification of human freedom (and man's moral decisions) with man's *consciousness* of his determination. This is to try to give Christian coloration to the Hegelian-Marxist understanding of man.[26]

22 *Ibid.*, p. 152.
23 Ellul, *Violence*, p. 66.
24 *Ibid.*, p. 136.
25 David Willis, "Reconciliation and Stewardship," *Reconciliation and Today's World*, p. 62.
26 Ramsey, *The Just War*, p. 463.

Consider, moreover, Lehmann's concept, which is the backbone of revolutionary theology, what God is doing in the world to make and keep human life truly human. "This," Ramsey comments, "is the position that seems to be in the ascendancy in much 'ecumenical' Christian ethics today and in many seminaries where young men must be given a quick word and an obviously relevant word to speak in this generation." But is this word uniquely Christian and, for that matter, even relevant? Not in Ramsey's opinion:

The trouble is that the word is entirely too relevant to be profound, or to contain any proper guidance for Christian decision and action. This is in fact a new parochialism, and an exceedingly narrow and dangerous one at that. What God is doing in the world is not identified with Jesus Christ—political reflection proceeding then upon this basis, in this light, and in the darkness cast by the shadow of this light upon human existence. Instead, what God is doing in the world is said to be making revolutions. Doubtless, any theism would say these do not occur without God's doing; but a Christian theological ethics should have more to say than that upon this subject, and it should not yield the primacy to other categories of analysis in telling what Christians should do in revolutionary times.[27]

Thus, to quote Alan Austin's rather biting observation, the kind of theology Paul Lehmann advocates may cause the queen of the sciences to become a "whore, losing her own integrity." [28] And in losing her integrity, Christianity will at the same time lose her relevance. So the evangelical, who sees the revolutionary theologians throwing out the baby with the bath-water, pleads that they listen to Vernard Eller:

If the New Testament makes anything clear it is that the Gospel operates out of a perspective different enough from that of the world that inevitably one will be somewhat irrelevant to the other. Let us beware, then, of the popular cry that the church must become relevant. Once "relevant" (in this sense) and it is no longer the church; it has forsaken its unique perspective to become simply a part (even if, perhaps, a "better" part) of the world.[29]

27*Ibid.*, p. 462.
28Austin, *The Revolutionary Imperative*, p. 58.

29Eller, *op. cit.*, p. 216. An evangelical sincerely wishes that Paul Lehmann and other revolutionary theologians would remember Lehmann's own comment:

How ironical if the revolutionists prove to be the captives of our twentieth-century *Zeitgeist*!

Second, as an evangelical appraises it, this theology seems to be a flat, denuded, one-dimensional reductionism which, enamored of the *Zeitgeist*, is willing to sacrifice its specifically Christian content. In order to make the old faith relevant to the contemporary situation, revolutionary theology hits upon the idea of God as politician carrying out His own politics in history. This idea, then, becomes a Procrustean bed, with Christianity stretched or amputated to fit it. Ellul minces no words: "This theology is not really a theology but an ideology ... based not on the Revelation but altogether on philosophical considerations." Its purpose, he declares, "is to justify a certain kind of behavior on the part of Christians in relation to society—a kind of behavior that is dictated by conformism to the modern world." Indeed, he suspects that it "amounts to a justification of the behavior of pretend-Christians."[30] That harsh verdict is merited. One reads this theology and is distressed by its high-handed hermeneutic, an arbitrary exegesis which like the old methods of allegorism and typology discovers in Scripture symbolical meanings patently foreign to the intention of its writers.

Here is a reductionism which diminishes Christianity to a modern ideology. After all, Lehmann assures us, "when theology talks about incarnation" or atonement or anything, "it means only one thing"—God's "breaking in and through to make and to extend the territory of humanization."[31] Here is a reductionism that an evangelical adjudges, frankly, a *reductio ad absurdum*. By this hermeneutical strategy, which reduces all theological talk to essentially the same thing, faith means in Herbert W. Richardson's reconceptualization, "the commitment of man to oppose

---

"The concern for relevance on its own terms is misleading; it is what always makes Christians fall flat on their faces—because they are out of character. They are not supposed to be relevant; they are supposed to be Christian, which is to *be* involved in the very center of the dynamics of revolution (much like the eye of a hurricane)." "The Shape of Theology for a World in Revolution," p. 61. An evangelical, as we shall see, is a revolution*ary*, but not a revolution*ist* as Lehmann and his fellow theologians understand revolution.

30Ellul, *Violence*, pp. 77-79.

31Lehmann, "The Shape of Theology for a World in Revolution," p. 68.

the separation of man from man. It is a commitment to struggle against attacks on the common good, against racialism and segregation, and against the fragmentation of man's intellectual and spiritual life."[32] By this hermeneutical strategy which reduces all theological talk to essentially the same thing, the task of seminary education becomes, as one anonymous churchman has suggested, the "grooming of a sort of sociological task force,"[33] dedicated to humanitarian activities which will promote humanization. Why not if, regardless of what theology may be talking about, it is always saying one and the selfsame thing?

Christianity, then, is reduced to a concern for the space-time world with any dimension of reality beyond this world virtually canceled out. Thus Lehmann's concept of God as politician at work to make and keep human life truly human in the world causes an evangelical to engage in some quizzical reflection. In the world! What does that phrase insinuate? Is God's redemptive activity confined exclusively to the here and now? Does Lehmann view the then and there as a quite trifling addendum to man's present existence? Perhaps that phrase reduces theology to a more or less sanctified sociology. Perhaps it is telling us that the significance of Christianity lies in its power to improve man's space-time experience with any divine-human relationship serving as a means to the end of better human relationships. Perhaps that phrase implies the radical shift which Thomas W. Ogletree perceives in a martyred theologian of tremendous profundity and originality.

Bonhoeffer forces us to recognize that the patterns of thought which attend simply to "private matters" such as death, guilt, and meaninglessness involve a flight from the realities of the world. As such they are little more than contemporary versions of the old pietistic concern for individual salvation in the world to come. In contrast, our present task is to bring to awareness the processes by which the fundamental issues of Christian existence confront us in the midst of the social and political struggles of contemporary life.[34]

---

[32]Quoted by Kenneth Hamilton, "Reconciliation and New Humanity," *Recconciliation and Today's World*, p. 39.

[33]Miller, *op. cit.*, p. 23.

[34]Thomas W. Ogletree, "The Shifting Focus of Theological Reflection," *New Theology No. 6*, p. 57.

Admittedly, salvation has been all too often construed as atomistic, privatistic, individualistic, and almost wholly postmundane. Admittedly, Johannes Metz has ample reason for urging that such a lopsided conception of salvation be "overcome through the working out of a theology which we have characterized with the phrase 'political' theology."[35] But what when politics swallows up dogmatics and dogmatics becomes merely a set of symbols to serve as a catalyst for politics? Or what when Philippe Maury's epigram "Politics Is the Language of Evangelism" establishes a new equation? What when evangelism becomes exclusively a political affair? What when Harvey Cox, advising us "to speak in a secular fashion of God," offers a graphic illustration?

It may be that the opportunity given us by God to speak His word comes when we are found in the struggle for social justice now going on in our world. Someone asks: What are you doing anyway on this picket line? What are you getting out of it? Why is it your fight? What are you doing here in Asia or Africa helping Asians or Africans to some kind of dignity, some kind of freedom? Why is it your interest? This may be our God-given opportunity to say the word however reticently and stumblingly. The blunt question "what the hell are you doing here?" may be the way in which twentieth century man asks "what must I do to be saved?"[36]

But this really has a hollow ring. For Cox elsewhere suggests that participation in the struggle for social justice can be a word which needs no explanatory God-words; the act itself can be God's word. To speak in a secular fashion about God may thus turn out to mean that "we shall stop talking about 'God' for a while, take a

---

[35] Johannes B. Metz, "Creative Hope," *New Theology No. 5*, p. 139. *Cf.* Moltmann's remarks: "After the humanistic ethic of hope in the nineteenth century and its impotence in the catastrophes of the twentieth century, many in Europe and America developed an ethic of faith. That was justified, but it appears to me that today we should develop a *new ethic of the hope of faith*. Together with Joh. B. Metz, I call it *political theology* in order to make clear that ethics is not an appendix to dogmatics and also that it is not a consequence of faith, but that faith itself has a messianic context in which it becomes meaningful and that theology itself stands in a political dimension in which it becomes relevant." *Religion, Revolution, and the Future*, p. 218.

[36] Cox, *God's Revolution and Man's Responsibility*, p. 75.

moratorium on speech until a new name appears."[37]

Reflecting on the totally this-worldly emphasis of the revolutionary theology, an evangelical recalls the scene from Dostoevski in which the devil is describing to Ivan Karamazov the future earth without God and morality: "Men will then unite to extract from life all possible joys, but in the world only. The human spirit will rise with a gigantic pride and thus mankind will be deified."[38] Note the devil's specification, "in the world only." An evangelical may be forgiven if he wonders whether the revolutionary theology does not have in mind this same specification.

It strikes an evangelical, furthermore, that this theology reduces Christianity to an anthropocentrism which retains God as merely a superannuated partner in the historical enterprise. This theology, very curiously, impresses an evangelical as a deism *revividus*. God is acknowledged, but He sits on the sidelines while man plays the game by himself. So Cox almost arrogantly announces that "there are no powers anywhere which are not essentially tameable and ultimately humanizable"[39]—and the context makes it plain that man is to do the taming and humanizing. Apparently God is not desperately needed. Apparently, too, the New Testament stress on enabling grace can now be demythologized by technological man. Apparently, as a matter of fact, it is

[37] Cox, *The Secular City*, p. 266. Lehmann has a similar view of evangelism. "When a believer and an unbeliever are met on the level of their common involvement with the issue of the possibility and the integrity of their humanity, and when by reason of this involvement the question 'what shall I do to be what I am?' however it might be formulated, can no longer be suppressed, then the integrative power and the possibility of the Christian gospel are exposed. The New Testament offers no evidence for putting the question 'are you saved?' *That* is simply not a biblical question. However, the question 'what shall I do to be saved?' *is* a biblical question. It appears also in the form 'what shall I do to inherit eternal life?' The question means, in short, 'what shall I do *to be what I am?*' The lawyer trying to justify himself, the Macedonian jailer who found himself on the threshold of unemployment, put the question of authentic life on the level of an inescapable confrontation with a claim upon them to move in the direction of self-fulfilling self-surrender. It is only out of this kind of authentic human situation that the question of belief and unbelief, the religious question, has integrity." *Ethics in a Christian Context*, p. 155.

[38] Quoted by Jules Chaix-Ruy, *The Superman from Nietzsche to Teilhard de Chardin* (Notre Dame, Ind.: University of Notre Dame Press, 1968), p. 100.

[39] Cox, *The Secular City*, p. 129.

all up to the revolutionists. Don Helder Camara exclaims concerning the struggle for humanization: "We shall win by creating widespread good will for our cause; or we shall lose all, and then *nothing can be saved.*"[40] Nothing can be saved! That is certainly a drastic reduction and contradiction of New Testament salvation. An evangelical, therefore, is apprehensive lest the anthropocentrism of the revolutionary theology become the titanism of a Nikos Kazantzakis: "It is not God who will save us; it is we who will save God, by battling, by creating, and transmuting matter into spirit."[41] No bridge can ever be built over the abyss between that position and the Bible, and the revolutionary theology has its face turned toward that position.

Third, as an evangelical appraises it, this theology is a rationalization for an absolutized ideology. Evidently one of its deepest motives is the justification of radical change in the structures of society. *A priori* revolution is assigned supreme value; everything else is subordinated to that end and forced to subserve it. An evangelical is not overly surprised to find Colin Morris avowing indiscriminately, "God is the inspiration of every strategy which breaks down the old to make way for the new. He is behind *all* the revolutions of our time."[42] But an evangelical is somewhat surprised to have Lehmann make as sweeping an avowal: "The Messianic transfiguration is the theme of the Christian story of God's humanization of man through revolutionary social change in whatever form it takes."[43] That leaves little room for a distinctively Christian critique of revolutionary theology. In whatever it takes, revolution is to be baptized and blessed as a divine activity, seemingly with no questions asked. This process of absolutizing the relative was once known as idolatry.

To be sure, Lehmann alludes to authentic revolution, intimating that some revolutions may be inauthentic. Yet even so enthusiastic a fellow radical as Alan Austin is unimpressed by his distinction. "Does the faith also give criteria for judging a revolution *inauthentic,*" he asks, "or is Lehmann hedging?" Since Lehmann

40Quoted by Ellul, *Violence*, p. 149.
41Quoted by Chaix-Ruy, *op. cit.*, p. 123.
42Colin Morris, *op. cit.*, p. 142.
43Lehmann, "The Shape of Theology for a World in Revolution," p. 70.

contends that "the Christian style of participation in revolution is theological imagination," Austin fairly inquires, "Might not a sense of inauthenticity be more likely a lapse of our imagination than a wrong turn in history?"[44] Lehmann, alas, is hoist with his own petard. For the fact is that this theology leaves the Christian without any helpful criteria which will enable him to determine where in any revolutionary movement God is *not* at work. Since this theology merely nods to the Holy Spirit and treats Scripture hermeneutically as a nose of wax, it forces man—why not in view of human autonomy and sufficiency?—to play the score by ear. Cox likes the way Archie Hargraves illustrates "the work of God in the world, where Jesus Christ is present." He compares it "to a 'floating crap game' and the church to a confirmed gambler whose 'major compulsion upon arising each day is to know where the action is' so he can run there and 'dig it.'" Cox also likes Thomas Weisner's statement of the Church's responsibility as it follows Christ wherever He may lead or choose to appear.

The way of the church as related to the fact that the Kyrios himself is on his way in the world ... [and] the church has no choice but to follow him who precedes. Consequently obedience and witness to the Kyrios require the discernment of the opening which he provides, and the willingness to step into this opening.[45]

But how does the Church discern an opening which Christ Himself is providing? How does an individual do that? What criteria furnish guidance as to where God's action rather than a demonic counterfeit of divine activity is happening? Regrettably no helpful criteria are provided. The ambiguity and subjectivism of this position emerge in the problem of integration. Assuredly people of both the black and white races who are concerned about humanization can discern that wherever desegregation is proceeding "with all deliberate speed" God must be at work breaking down one of the barriers that separate human beings and creating a face-to-face fraternity. But Joseph Hough points out that "some Negro leaders are pressing for continuing separation from their side as part of an over-all strategy to mobilize Negro power, and many of them view integration as irrelevant." Hough explains

[44]Austin, *op cit.*, p. 71.
[45]Cox, *The Secular City*, pp. 125, 126.

that these leaders feel separation is essential "to solve the very difficult problem of Negro identity."

It takes no special insight to see that mutuality and openness between Negroes and whites have long been complicated by the Negro's own self-image. ... Negroes have widely adopted the negative stereotypes about them as their own understanding of their group. Therefore it has been and still is difficult for many Negroes to think of themselves as equal partners in a relationship with whites. ... Face-to-face contacts with whites too often serve as reminders of an old identity that is inhuman, and before true mutuality can become a possibility between the masses of Negroes and whites in America, the problem of identity must first be solved.[46]

What, therefore, is Hough's conclusion with respect to discerning the place where Christ is breaking through?

In light of the problem of identity, then, it appears that Lehmann could no longer argue with confidence that a policy of desegregation is a "sign of God's humanizing action in the world." If one takes seriously the new Negro pluralism, desegregation understood as broadening interracial contacts may at best be irrelevant, and may even be dehumanizing[47]

If desegregation of all things is not necessarily a step toward humanization, how can one be sure that any piece of social activism is a sign of Christ's liberating work? Richardson lists among "the institutions and movements of our time which are ... special instruments of redemptive power ... the United Nations, the Peace Corps, the work of priests, federal mediators, and ecumenism." In his eyes, "these are the institutions where God is working today." In his eyes: for Richardson admits that "only the *fides reconciliens* will have the eyes to see." To which Kenneth Hamilton witheringly retorts:

Such a judgment seems to me extraordinarily naïve. All the institutions and movements Richardson mentions are excellent ones, which men of goodwill should welcome and support. And one could add others; motherhood, for example, and parent-teacher associations! But to say that these institutions are where God is working, and to suggest (even indirectly) that He is not working also in places where reconciling work

[46]Joseph C. Hough, Jr., *Black Power and White Protestants: A Christian Response to the New Negro Pluralism* (New York: Oxford University Press, 1968), p. 144.

[47]*Ibid.*, p. 145.

is not being carried on obviously and expressly, is to deify and sacralize aspects of our corporate cultural existence in themselves ambiguous and full of potentiality for both good and evil. It is to be full of impartiality and to foster a blurred vision in the area where faith should be critical and clear-eyed. And it is to declare whole areas of the world to be in the power of the devil, areas where, indeed, God may be working with power, showing his mercy and his judgment while we, believing we have the eyes to see, are staring resolutely in the opposite direction.[48]

Since no helpful criteria for the discernment of the divine action are provided by revolutionary theologians, they tend to absolutize their ideology, using a reconceptualized Christianity as a justifying rationalization for their cause. To them, accordingly, it seems to be a matter of indifference whether or not a man consciously accepts the Gospel, provided only he is unconsciously doing God's will as a revolutionary. The French Franciscan Father Maillard, who is director of *Frères du Monde*, advises Christians to join the insurrectionary movement not as believers but simply as human beings, keeping silent about their faith. Bluntly he avers, "The Christian as such does not interest me. I care only about the man who shows his concern for his brothers on a global level: If he truly wants to save mankind, we shall solve the problem of means together." Hence in Ellul's opinion revolution has become Maillard's absolute. "True men participate in revolution, and revolution begets the hope of a liberated humanity. So revolution is the only way a man, as a man, can take. Revolution has all the marks of an absolute value; it needs no motivation."[49] If revolution is elevated to the level of an absolute, then personal faith in the Gospel no longer really matters. One can argue that the declared atheist is an anonymous and unconscious member of the Church precisely because he also declares his dedication to the revolutionary cause.

As for Christian values, they likewise can be given up. Non-Christian means can be sanctioned if they promise to achieve revolutionary goals. The faith itself can be forfeited if only one is loyal to the revolution. That is what Father Maillard unequivocally says. To him the cause is more important than the Gospel:

[48] Hamilton, *op. cit.*, pp. 39, 40.
[49] Ellul, *Violence*, pp. 57-59.

"If I noticed that my faith separated me however little from other men and diminished my revolutionary violence, I would not hesitate to sacrifice my faith."[50] That is what missionary Colin Morris likewise says:

I frankly doubt that the Christian faith *as we have learned it* can accommodate the revolutionary who really means business. But then I don't believe that the Christian faith as we have learned it can open a way into the future either. The revolutionary is probably the truly tragic figure of our time, risking the loss of salvation that his brethren may be saved and have wholeness of life. Yet it is surely true that the manifold acts of our lives have no value unless the total act of living can be justified. And it is necessary for at least one of the things we do in living to have absolute value. The Christian who becomes a revolutionary takes the risk that in a world locked up in the past, the blow which opens the way to the future may count as the "one thing needful" about which Jesus taught. He steps beyond any traditional understanding of Jesus into a spiritual and ethical No Man's Land in the hope that the future is where God is.[51]

Note, incidentally, that Morris absolutizes revolution: it is necessary for at least one of the things we do in living to have absolute value.

This, more guardedly, is what Shaull also says with respect to his own reconceptualizing of Christianity. "Whenever such an approach to theology has been suggested, the fear has been expressed that it will inevitably lead to a new humanism." Shaull grants that "this risk is certainly present." But we must take the risk, he insists, we must make the wager, and "only the future will show whether this wager about the relevance and vitality of theology is justified"—the revolutionary theology, of course. And the risk, bear in mind, is that of ending in a dechristianized humanism.[52]

One must, of course, follow the truth as he sees it regardless of risk. But an evangelical is saddened by what he considers a sellout to the *Zeitgeist*. His sadness is compounded because he thinks the sellout is as futile as it is needless. Non-Christian revolutionaries are utterly disinterested in the hermeneutical legerdemain performed by radical theologians to show the relevance of the Gospel.

50 Quoted in *ibid.*, p. 59.
51 Colin Morris, *op. cit.*, p. 157.
52 Shaull, "The Christian in the Vortex of Revolution," pp. 61, 69.

Typical of their reaction is Steve Weisman's forthright article, "New Left Man Meets the Dead God," in which he dismisses Christ as irrelevant. Discussing the issues of political organization, he comments, "Radical theology would do well to find better revolutionary figures than Jesus. ... Black Power militants and Frantz Fanon probably have better things to say on these sticky problems than either the Biblical or the Dostoevskian Jesus." He also remarks, *contra* Harvey Cox, "Neither Jesus nor the Christian sources can provide much of a guide to questions of political strategy." Indeed, he dismisses *The Secular City* as

a *tour de force* of Christian sources, theories, and analogies, interspersed with urbanity and social science. Unfortunately, he seems to think that he can slip social revolution into the thinking of his Christian readers without their noticing the change. Thus the reader senses the same inauthenticity as an effort to present "Communism as Twentieth Century Americanism" or to wrap the New Left in the American Flag.[53]

No doubt the New Testament and its Jesus are understandably irrelevant from the perspective of a revolutionary whose concept is purely social and political. But if a spiritual revolution is needed, as it is, Jesus the Saviour and Lord of self-confessed sinners will prove supremely relevant. And it may be that a spiritual revolution, which is genuinely New Testament, will have transforming effects socially and politically.

But at this juncture it is time to acknowledge frankly that the radicals who have been criticized in the foregoing pages may serve to disturb, rebuke, and challenge Christians of a traditional orientation. They may compel those of us who as evangelicals too facilely equate piety and peace-loving patriotism to engage in a searching reappraisal of our own discipleship. For who can blame cynical skeptics, inside as well as outside the church, if they question the revolutionary nature of our faith? The dominant religion of the Western world, at least since the time of Constantine, Christianity has usually been aligned cheek by jowl with the Establishment in a throne-and-altar *entente* or in the role of sanctifying the *status quo*—e.g., intoning hymnologically "God Bless America"! Christianity may be inherently radical, but its radi-

[53]Steve Weisman, *op. cit.*, pp. 40-43, 27.

calism has been safely defused. Instead of being political dynamite, it has most of the time served as, at best, a cultural fertilizer.

This is not to deny that Christianity has again and again upset
society, transforming *mores* and *institutions*. This is not to forget,
either, if we turn our attention to American evangelicalism, what
Timothy Smith has documented in his enlightening work,
Revivalism and Social Reform. In the years before the Civil War,
the fervid preaching of the need for life-changing regeneration,
together with the possibility of Christlike sanctification, began to
produce a pietism which was intensely concerned with public
evils. "The quest of personal holiness became in some ways a kind
of plain man's transcendentalism, which geared ancient creeds to
the drive shaft of social reform. Far from disdaining earthly
affairs, the evangelist played a key role in the widespread attack
upon slavery, poverty and greed." Smith states further that

The rapid growth of concern with purely social issues such as poverty,
working men's rights, the liquor traffic, slum housing, and racial bitterness is the chief feature distinguishing American religion after 1865
from that of the first half of the 19th century. Such matters in some cases
supplanted entirely the earlier preoccupation with salvation from personal sin and life hereafter. Seminaries reorganized their programs to
stress sociology. Institutional churches and social settlement work became prominent in the cities. Crusades for the rights of oppressed groups
of all sorts absorbed the energies of hundreds of clergymen. The vanguard
of the movement went far beyond the earlier Christian emphasis on
almsgiving to a search for the causes of human suffering and a campaign
to reconstruct social and economic relations upon a Christian pattern.[54]

While, then, Christianity's far-reaching effects upon society
must not be forgotten, an evangelical cannot deny that, historically, his faith has been complacent, compliant, and compro-
mising, an uncritical ally of whatever authority might happen to
be in power. Thus an evangelical repentantly concurs with
Reinhold Niebuhr's critique of the ethics generally derived from
orthodox theology. That ethics has included, as Ellul summarizes
Niebuhr,

an authoritative code which bypasses the problems of modern man, a

---

[54]Quoted by Melvin Gingerich, *The Christian and Revolution* (Scottdale, Pa.:
Herald Press, 1968), pp. 169, 170.

break between the imperative and the real, irrelevant precepts, a premature identification of a canonical moral code with the transcendent will of God, elimination of the tension between present grace and eschatological promise, suppression of the reality of human history in favor of eternity, acceptance of an authoritarian order for fear of anarchy caused by sin, complacency toward wicked historical forms on the ground that all is ultimately sinful, suppression of the positive aspect of the commandment of love, on the ground that since it cannot be realized its only function is to reveal evil, sin, man's incapacity, etc.

"All these criticisms," Ellul says, "are just and formidable." [55] They are. Hence it is extremely difficult to present Christianity, at least Protestant orthodoxy in general or American evangelicalism in particular, as a revolutionary force in our own day. The opposite is much too much the case.

For one thing, orthodoxy has traditionally preached and practiced a *conservative* version of Christianity. Perhaps its theological conservatism has made it politically conservative as well, though there is reason to challenge the theory that the believer in religious authority is usually a personality type disposed to obey any authority unquestioningly. But leaving psychological theorizing aside, the history of the Christian Church is a history of opposition to change. This allergic attitude toward innovation of any kind, Charles P. Lutz surmises, may be grounded in a misunderstanding of the divine immutability.

When the newer theologians tell us that God is in fact responsible for the turbulence, that He is stirring things up, that He is the center of the action which would change our values and our institutions, the faithful Christian tends to be incredulous. For he has been given an image of a God set *against* change, of a God who is the great Stabilizer, the One who changes not. And certainly if God does not change, He must be as uncomfortable with change as are we. He is therefore on the side of those who would maintain the status quo, or who would even return us to an earlier, better time. [56]

And Lutz cites as an example of "the innocent way in which such images are buttressed," the well-known and often-sung hymn:

[55] Jacques Ellul, *To Will and To Do* (Philadelphia: Pilgrim Press, 1969), pp. 299-300.
[56] Charles P. Lutz, "Middle America: Theologically Formed," *The Christian Century*, March 18, 1970, p. 324.

> In heavenly love abiding
> No change my heart shall fear;
> And safe is such confiding,
> For nothing changes here.[57]

Whether or not Lutz's surmise is correct, Christianity as a rule has been in favor of preventing the yeast of change from producing any heady fermentation. It stands, Rolland Smith asserts, on the side of quietism and detachment.

The churches embody a code of *mores* for proper, private, and passive behaviour. The poor are preached patience, and the rich are asked to offer paternal charity. Saul Alinsky's use of power is labelled "sub-Christian." Stokely Carmichael is "anti-Christian." Father Groppi and Pastor King are deviants tolerated by the churches, but less and less as they become more and more revolutionary. The churches have little to do officially with the Viet Nam protest, with Students for a Democratic Society, with Black Power. The more a university is influenced by a church, the more it seems to avoid student or faculty rebellions against government or administration policies.[58]

Whatever judgment an evangelical may pronounce on the issues and individuals Smith mentions, he cannot gainsay that his faith has played and still plays a conservative role in society. Interpreted moralistically, it has served to keep people, white and black alike, in their places, resigned to inequities. It has often been an opiate, inducing passivity toward the present by inducing dreams of "pie in the sky, by and by." Consider, typically, Hannah More, the nineteenth-century English author whose devotional writings continue to enjoy popularity in some evangelical circles. She and her sister established Sunday Schools and Women's Benefit Clubs among the poverty-stricken workers of the Mendip villages. In 1801 addressing a Shipham audience on the scarcity of food, Hannah counseled her listeners to be thankfully resigned to their lot.

Let me remind you that probably that very scarcity had been permitted by an all-wise and gracious Providence to unite all ranks of people together, to show the poor how immediately they are dependent upon

[57] *Ibid.*
[58] Smith, *op. cit.*, p. 136.

the rich, and to show both rich and poor that they are all dependent on Himself. It has also enabled you to see more clearly the advantages you derive from the government and constitution of this country—to observe the benefits flowing from the distinction of rank and fortune, which have enabled the high so liberally to assist the low: for I leave you to judge what would have been the state of the poor of this country in this long distressing scarcity had it not been for your superiors. ... We trust the poor, in general, especially those that are well instructed, have received what has been done for them as a matter of favor, not of right—if so, the same kindness will, I doubt not, always be extended to them whenever it shall please God so to afflict the land.[59]

Miss More's interpretation of Christianity, the antithesis of that propounded by today's theology of revolution, was also propounded by a far more illustrious evangelical of the nineteenth century, William Wilberforce. He also affirmed that grateful acceptance of the existing order, even periodic famine, is the revealed will of God. In his widely circulated *Practical View of the System of Christianity,* Wilberforce reminds the inferior orders

that their more lowly path has been assigned to them by the hand of God; that it is their part faithfully to discharge its duties, and contentedly to bear its inconvenience; that the present state of things is very short; that the objects about which worldly men conflict so eagerly are not worth the contest; that the peace of mind, which Religion offers indiscriminately to all ranks, affords more true satisfaction than all the expensive pleasures which are beyond the poor man's reach; that in this view the poor have the advantage; that, if their superiors enjoyed more abundant comforts, they are also exposed to many temptations from which the inferior classes are happily exempted; that "having food and raiment, they should therewith be content," since their situation in life, with all its evils is better than they have deserved at the hand of God; finally, that all human distinctions will soon be done away, and the true followers of Christ will all, as children of the same Father, be alike admitted to the possession of the same heavenly inheritance.[60]

It is this interpretation of Christianity which has earned the scorn and hatred of secular radicals. With Marx, they have fulminated that "the criticism of religion is the beginning of all

59 Quoted by William Dale Morris, *op. cit.,* pp. 156-157.
60 Quoted by William Dale Morris, *loc. cit.*

criticism." How, they have demanded, can social evils be eliminated if orthodoxy claims that to agitate for change is to disobey
God's will?

For a second thing, evangelicalism has traditionally preached
and practiced an otherworldly version of Christianity. We have
observed previously that in contrast to the revolutionary theology
with its onesided this-worldliness, orthodoxy is in fact otherworldly. But if loyal to the New Testament, Christianity cannot
be as lopsidedly otherworldly as evangelicalism has generally
been. If loyally biblical, evangelicalism cannot disdain the present world as a mere vestibule to eternity. If loyally biblical, it
must recognize, rather, that this world has goods and values
which are good and valuable in their own right. It must therefore
hold out hope *in* this world and *for* this world as well as *beyond*
this world. Instead of inculcating an indifference toward this
world and detachment from it, a biblically loyal evangelicalism
must inculcate a concern for this world and the service of this
world. A biblically loyal evangelicalism, consequently, must con-
cur with Bonhoeffer: "The Christian hope sends a man back to
his life on earth in a wholly new way which is even more sharply
defined than it is in the Old Testament."[61] A biblically loyal
evangelicalism must inculcate profound care for what takes place
here and now because, in the words of Valentine Foy, its Gospel
affirms

that God Himself cares about what happens on this earth. Jehovah God
was portrayed by the prophets as being concerned about such things as
military alliances, the selling of debtors into slavery, the plundering of
the poor by the rich, the cheating of the buyer by the seller, and the oppression of the weak by the strong. The God of the Bible, the God Christians know through personal faith in Jesus Christ, is no abstract First
Cause or Prime Mover or Great Somewhere who can be placated by a
bit of discreet crying in the chapel. He is a personal God who is very
deeply and very definitely concerned about military alliances, racial
segregation, the unconscionable profits of the drug industry, the indefensible price fixing that honeycombs big business, and the criminal
corruption that persists in organized labor. He is concerned about tax
evasion, padded expense accounts, the exploitation of violence as enter-

61 Quoted by Braaten, *The Future of God,* p. 53.

tainment, the toleration of senseless killings in the boxing ring, family fragmentation, and the unsolved problems of the aging. He is concerned about the unemployment which has been almost 6% of our labor force in recent years (the U.S. lost more time in one recent year from unemployment than we lost in the past thirty-five years from strikes) and the one hundred billion dollars a year (or about 8% of its gross annual product) which the world now spends on weapons. He is concerned about the hideous inanities preached as a sorry substitute for the Christian Gospel, the infuriatingly bland and crashingly dull church programs calculated to produce an attitude of profane indifference, the immensely absurd spectacle of loving the souls of Negroes in Africa and hating their guts in America, and all the other moral flotsam and spiritual jetsam that could be orchestrated into this melancholy tune.[62]

For a third thing, evangelicalism has traditionally preached and practiced an *individualistic* version of Christianity. Its mistaken position has been that of no less an eminent Roman Catholic than Monsignor Ronald Knox: "The Christian virtue of hope has nothing whatever to do with the world's future. ... [Hope] in the theological sense is concerned only with the salvation of the individual believer and the means which will help him obtain it."[63] The evangelical defense of that position has been based on "the fact, true enough in itself," to quote Roger Mehl, "that the gospel is addressed to the individual." But evangelicalism has drawn wrong deductions from that fact.

It holds that the church's sole task is to preach the good news of man's reconciliation with God. The gospel has only one meaning: It proclaims that in Jesus Christ we have peace with God, that our sins are forgiven and that by resting in Christ we have the certainty of salvation and of eternal life. All the rest, including political and social action, is vain agitation.[64]

Thus it has concentrated entirely on changing individuals, refusing quite universally to undertake the task of changing institutions. Quite universally, moreover, it has treated individuals as if they were disincarnate atoms moving privatistically in

62Quoted by Gingerich, *op. cit.*, p. 183.

63Quoted by Shklar, *op. cit.*, p. 178.

64Roger Mehl, "The Basis of Christian Social Ethics," *Christian Social Ethics in a Changing World*, John C. Bennett, ed. (New York: Association Press, 1966), pp. 47-48.

a spiritual vacuum where the massive evils of unemployment, racism, inflation, poor housing, political corruption, and bad sewage are nonexistent. So to refer again to Hannah More and her equally indefatigable sister Martha, they were, J. L. and Barbara Hammond acknowledge in their definitive study, *The Town Labourer, 1760-1832,*

benevolent women who put themselves to great trouble and discomfort out of pity for these villages, and yet from the beginning to the end of *Mendip Annals* (in which they describe their "charitable labours") there is not a single reflection on the persons or systems responsible for these conditions. It never seems to have crossed the minds of these philanthropists that it was desirable that men and women should have decent wages, or decent homes, or that there was something wrong with the arrangements of a society that left the mass of people in this plight.[65]

Sometimes, no doubt, evangelicalism has concentrated exclusively on individual salvation for fear of dirtying its hands with the sordid dilemmas of public life and thus losing its own purity. More frequently, however, it has simply failed to grasp the full significance of faith in Jesus Christ. This, at any rate, is how Emilio Castro inclines to account for its privatism: evangelicalism has failed to grasp that personal salvation necessitates social action.

Conversion means that we become aware of a relationship with Jesus Christ, and this means, in time, relationship with our neighbor. It means becoming part of the discipleship of those who serve. These two elements—relation with Jesus Christ and relation with my neighbor— can be distinguished, but they cannot be separated. ... The lack of a correct relationship with one's neighbor is authentic proof of the absence of the correct relation with God. Conversion understood as a personal advantage does not exist. It is always understood as a call to form part of the movement of God's ministry of love to the world.[66]

In other words, evangelicalism has managed to overlook the New Testament teaching that "to draw near to Christ is to be placed in a position of service to your neighbor. It is to have a changed

---

[65] Quoted by William Dale Morris, *op. cit.*, p. 155.
[66] Emilio Castro, "Conversion and Social Transformation," *The Church amid Revolution*, pp. 96, 93.

attitude toward society. To enter into discipleship means to follow Him who identified Himself with the need."[67] But the
neighbor cannot be effectively served in today's society unless
institutions are changed. In modern society if travelers on some
Jericho Road are to be served effectively, a lighting system is
called for, a police force is needed, and entrenched corruption
at City Hall becomes a legitimate target of Christian opposition
if it interferes with the functioning of lights and policemen.

Nor is that all. Evangelicalism's very concern for personal
conversion demands political action with a view to affecting and
altering structures. "The gospel," Castro reasons, "requires
certain historical conditions if it is to reach people: freedom of
conscience, peace, communications. If we are to assure the conditions of orderly life and make the proclamation of the Gospel
possible, we must enter into the social struggle."[68] But traditionally, despite the fairly obvious implications of the Gospel,
evangelicalism has been almost exclusively individualistic in its
concept of Christian mission. To paraphrase Gerald O'Collins, it
has amiably accepted large-scale evils because its attention has
been confined to sexual problems and the niceties of person-to-
person encounter.[69]

In the fourth place, evangelicalism has traditionally preached
and practiced a *bourgeois* version of Christianity. At its inception,
to be sure, the Church was a proletarian movement. Paul, accordingly, could write to the Corinthian church, "Consider your
call, brethren; not many of you were wise according to worldly
standards, not many were powerful, not many were of noble
birth; but God chose what is foolish in the world to shame the
wise, God chose what is weak in the world to shame the strong,
God chose what is low and despised in the world, even things
that are not, to bring to nothing things that are, so that no human
being might boast in the presence of God." (I Corinthians 1:26-
27) But gradually the Church became established; and, after the
rise of Protestantism and capitalism, it was more and more identified with that segment of the population in our Western world

[67] *Ibid.*
[68] *Ibid.*, p. 107.
[69] *Cf.* Gerald O'Collins, *op. cit.*, p. 149.

loosely characterized as the middle class. Increasingly a bourgeois religion, it canonized the virtues of decency, respectability, legality, industry, propriety, and prosperity. In the United States, for example, being a church member was synonymous with being a good neighbor and a good American. To be a WASP was *qua* WASP to be a Christian.

Gradually, therefore, evangelicalism lost its relationship with the proletariat, except as it carried on witness and philanthropy among the poor. It lost sight of its oneness with "the wretched of the earth," those who, according to the New Testament, ought to be the primary and particular concern of the Nazarene's followers. Evangelicalism forgot what its Lord explicitly instructed it to remember. It forgot a responsibility which Karl Barth has thrown into sharp relief.

The Church is to witness to the fact that the Son of Man came to seek and to save the lost. And this implies that—casting all false impartiality aside—the Church must concentrate first on the lower and lowest levels of human society. The poor, the socially and economically weak and threatened, will always be the object of its primary and particular concern, and it will insist on the state's special responsibility for these weaker members of society.[70]

Evangelicalism forgot a New Testament demand which Ellul powerfully enunciates: "The place of the Nazarene's followers is not with the oppressor but with the oppressed, not with the mighty but the weak, not with the overfed but with the hungry, not with the free but the enslaved, not with the opulent but the poverty-stricken, not with the well but the sick, not with the successful but the defeated, not with the comfortable majority but with the miserable minorities, not with the bourgeois but with the proletariat."

Where man is exploited, crushed, degraded by man, the Christian can neither avoid involvement by escape into the realm of spiritual values, nor side by default with the dominating party (as he has done so often in the course of history). Necessarily, in virtue of the calling to which Christ has called him, in virtue of the Lord's example, in virtue of the order of love, he is on the side of the little people, the poor. His place in the world is there—the only place the way of love leads to. Even if he does not

70 Quoted by Hough, *op. cit.*, p. 165.

deliberately choose this place, he is there, because his communion with Jesus Christ is communion with the Poor One who knew total poverty, total injustice, total violence. But when the Christian consciously keeps faith with his Lord, he is led to the least of these, the brethren of the Lord, and to the Lord Himself (Matt. 25:40 ff.).[71]

Forgetting this demand of discipleship, however, evangelicalism has lost its true identity and become the captive of a bourgeois culture.

For a fifth thing, evangelicalism traditionally has preached and practiced an *acquiescent* version of Christianity. Summoned to a prophetic ministry, commissioned to speak against society as well as to it when there are evils which scream to high heaven for denunciation, enlisted to do battle on behalf of freedom and justice in the name of love, evangelicalism has signally failed to fulfill its calling. It has not only counseled that the *status quo*, despite its inequities, be maintained; it has not only sanctioned whatever course of action a government has elected to pursue. It has not only, William Stringfellow charges, "generally followed and endorsed prevailing public policy." For instance,

Apart from a tiny minority of pacifists and a few other individuals ... the churches have been pathetically servile to the nation on the issues of war and peace. In World War II, in the Korean conflict, and in the debate about the morality of nuclear war (admitting, of course, significant individual exceptions) the churches and church people for the most part dutifully bless the cause of the nation with the dignity of allegiance that ought to be given only to God.[72]

Not only that. Evangelicalism has also fought to prevent change. It has sometimes been in the vanguard of reaction preventing innovation and reform. Its antirevolutionary stance— which may, we must not forget, be fully justified in specific cases—can be seen in this 1819 address adopted at the Conference of Methodist Ministers in Bristol, England, during a period of unemployment, hunger, inflation, and unrest:

As many of you to whom this measure of national suffering has been appointed reside in places where attempts are making by "unreasonable and wicked men," to render the privations of the poor the instruments

[71] Ellul, *Violence*, pp. 134-35.
[72] Quoted by Gingerich, *op. cit.*, p. 177.

of their own designs against the peace and the government of our beloved country, we are affectionately anxious to guard all of you against being led astray from your civil and religious duties by their dangerous artifices. Remember you are Christians, and called by your profession to exemplify the power and influence of religion by your patience and suffering, and by *"living peacefully with all men."* Remember that you belong to a Religious Society which has, from the beginning, explicitly recognized this high and essential part of Christian duty, to *"fear God and honour the King;* to *submit to magistrates for conscience's sake, and not to speak evil of dignities."* You are surrounded with persons to whom these duties are objects of contempt and ridicule; show your regard for them because they are the doctrines of your Saviour. Abhor those publications in which they are assailed, along with every other doctrine of your holy religion; and judge of the spirit and objects of those who would deceive you into political parties and associations, by the vices of their lies, and the infidel malignity of their words and writings. *"Who can bring a clean thing out of an unclean?"* [73]

Taking such a stance, evangelicalism has by and large sided with the haves against the have-nots, deploring any resort to radical means and measures for redress of grievances.

Conservative, otherworldly, individualistic, bourgeois, even reactionary—this is the indictment its critics level against evangelicalism. With Ernst Käsemann, himself a distinguished New Testament scholar, these critics denounce Christians because "through their silence, their mistaken respect for the authorities, their pious short-sightedness and narrow-mindedness, they have in the main given way to the tyrants, supported the exploiters, and belonged to the privileged." With Käsemann, once more, these critics aver that "to keep clear of revolutionaries in order to help maintain the *status quo* is at least as discreditable as it is to rush into the arms of revolution." [74] To attempt a dispassionate evaluation of the possible exaggerations and errors in this sweeping indictment would prove useless. Substantially, however, it is irrefutable. An evangelical, therefore, ought not waste time in nitpicking with these critics. Accepting their brief of Christian failures as a pride-shattering word of judgment, he ought, instead, to take any insights thus painfully gained and apply

73 Quoted by William Dale Morris, *op. cit.*, pp. 161-62.
74 Ernst Käsemann, *op. cit.*, pp. 135, 136.

them to his present situation.

Joining, then, in Ellul's confession "that the Churches have failed to play their revolutionary part" and that "too often they have been immersed in the lowest form of politics, or in a 'spirituality' which has lost touch with ordinary life," how can the evangelical show "that his real position is revolutionary"?[75] How can he show that Bernard Häring's claim is not an empty boast: "Rightly understood, Christianity is a force promoting peace and a revolution"? How can he validate Häring's further claim that "the Christian is really the all-out revolutionary, the one who knows no rest or repose"?[76] How can he convince the skeptics that Archpriest Vitalij Borovoy of the Russian Orthodox Church is not guilty of fantastic exaggeration when he says: "Christianity is by its very nature revolutionary; and the new life required by Christian social ethics is more radical, more profoundly revolutionary, more novel than any other social system or doctrine which has grown up outside Christianity."[77]

The evangelical can do this, it is to be hoped, by showing, first, that the Christian revolution is more profound in its diagnosis of society's sickness and its prescription for the healing of that sickness than the secular revolution. He can do this, secondly, by showing that the Christian revolution is also more radical in its demand and dynamic. He can do this, in the third place, by showing that he personally embodies its radicalism, a flesh-and-blood homogenization of theory and practice.

Christianity does indeed call for revolution; but its revolution, while insisting on the need for vast changes politically and economically, moves nevertheless in a dimension which is different and deeper. It takes with inexpressible seriousness the concluding statement in Novak's book, *A Theology for Radical Politics*: "The revolution is in the human spirit or not at all."[78] In this dimension, then, the dimension of the human spirit, that Christianity contends a revolution must occur. A person's relationship to God must be revolutionized, transforming in turn all his other

[75] Ellul, *The Presence of the Kingdom*, p. 58.

[76] Bernard Häring, *A Theology of Protest* (New York: Farrar, Straus, & Giroux, 1970), pp. 5-6.

[77] Quoted by Lochman, *op. cit.*, p. 108.

[78] Novak, *op. cit.*, p. 128.

relationships. It is this revolution which Häring describes for us:

Christ demands of his disciples a new way of thinking, or renewal of the
mind, a reorientation toward new purposes and ideals. The newness is
so great that it cannot emerge from man alone; it must emanate from
God's grace. By this grace and the preaching of conversion, a man sure
of himself becomes profoundly shaken. The goal of total renewal, however, is never complete in this life. ... In faith Christ is accepted not only
as the Saviour of the soul and the hope of resurrection; he is the redeemer
of the whole man and all his relationships, and Redeemer of the world.
Therefore the redeemed man cannot remain indifferent to inequities in
the world or unconcerned about the inhuman conditions of his fellow
man. [79]

The theological term for this reorienting experience is conversion. But conversion, as Häring brings out, is more than a subjective matter, a change of opinion together with some new
emotional attitudes. When a person undergoes a revolutionary
encounter with Jesus Christ in the dimension of the spirit, he becomes a catalyst of revolution; for "there can be no genuine renewal of heart and mind without concern for social reform.
Conversely, there can be no healthy and effective attempt to
reform conditions without constant conversion of mind and
attitudes." [80] Hence Ellul does not put the case too strongly: If a
person "really lives by the power of Christ, if, by hope, he makes
the coming of the kingdom actual, 'that person, regardless of any
appearance to the contrary,' is a true revolutionary." [81]

The Christian revolution, therefore, moves in a deeper dimension and a different dimension, too. The Christian revolution
eschews a self-defeating resort to violence; it is a spiritual revolution, a revolution not by the sword but by the cross. "Armed with
a new vision of revolution," Douglas writes, the first disciples of
Jesus "went on to initiate thousands in the Christian revolution
with the sign of the cross." [82] This new revolution, this different
revolution which takes the cross as its sign, is a revolution of

[79] Häring, *op. cit.*, p. 5.
[80] *Ibid.*, p. 6.
[81] Ellul, *The Presence of the Kingdom*, p. 51.
[82] James W. Douglas, *The Non-Violent Cross: A Theology of Revolution and
Peace* (New York: The Macmillan Company, 1968), p. 187.

love—a love, Douglas reminds us, which sees and suffers and shares and serves and sacrifices, a love which acts, remembering that God, because He loved the world, did His own God-sized act in Jesus Christ.

Revolution begins in the revolutionary himself by his response to the present world, creating through the crisis of vision and shared agony the kind of power which rises anew to meet a torn world with the word of love and the act of transformation. The revolutionary has no other choice in love than to seek with his whole being a new heaven and a new earth. Anything less is an infidelity to the suffering family of man and to his own vision born of crisis. His commitment is to man made whole again and to a community restored to visible love. What begins as a recognition of massive injustice must grow into a commitment to global love. Thus the man of conscience faces the world today as a revolutionary seized by the crisis of injustice, and thus he prepares to act in it.[83]

A revolution of love! To a secular revolutionist, the Christian revolution seems the nadir of impotent idealism. And throughout much of the Church's history it has been little more than that—an impotent idealism. So we must clarify the significance of that insufferably abused word "love." Thomas Merton, then, deserves focused attention as he makes this attempt from a Christian perspective:

A theology of love cannot afford to be sentimental. It cannot afford to preach edifying generalities about charity, while identifying "peace" with mere established power and legalized violence against the oppressed. A theology of love cannot be allowed merely to serve the interests of the rich and powerful, justifying their wars, their violence and their wrongs, while exhorting the poor and underprivileged to practice patience, meekness, longsuffering, and to solve their problems, if at all, non-violently.

The theology of love must seek to deal realistically with the evil and injustice in the world, and not merely to compromise with them. Such a theology will have to take note of the ambiguous realities of politics, without embracing the speciousness of a "realism" that merely justifies force in the service of established power. Theology does not exist merely to appease the already too untroubled conscience of the powerful and the established. A theology of love might also conceivably turn out to be a theology of revolution. In any case, it is a theology of *resistance*, a refusal

[83] *Ibid.*, p. 8.

of the evil that reduces a brother to homicidal desperation.[84]

This revolutionary love, this love which is born in the depths of the human spirit by a love which has a cross as its source and sign, is a tough love. It is all that Häring declares it to be, not an impotent idealism, but "the strongest power," a power stronger than the power of "police clubs or machine guns ... concentration camps or atom bombs ... the spoken and written word, a power of ideas, a power of peaceful alliances, a power of community which comes from common and freely acquired convictions." Yes, stronger than all of these is the power of love, that love which "mobilizes, epitomizes, and musters all energies, that love which triumphs even in defeat."[85]

The rhetoric is impressive indeed; but what about the reality of this power in face of the ugly, brutal, and unloving facts of life? How can an evangelical refute the criticism that in practice the Christian revolution is an impotent idealism grounded in an antiradical individualism? Perhaps, to take the second of these strictures first, the individualism of the Christian revolution is actually an effective strategy by which foci of revolution are established on the analogy of a behind-the-enemy-lines attack by paratroopers. Perhaps, as Ellul perceptively points out, the breaking down of dehumanizing structures ("technical, economic, bureaucratic, and also mental") and the creation of new humanizing forms ("political, moral, religious, aesthetic") require Kierkegaard's "single one" as their *fons et origo*:

In both cases we can only start with the individual; that is to say, the present movement is so radical that it is only by going back to the root—which is always the individual human being—that it will be possible to mend matters. ... When I speak of the individual as the source of hope I mean the individual who does not lend himself to society's gain, who disputes what we accept as self-evident (for example, the consuming society), who finds an autonomous style of life, who questions even the movement of the society. This individual must make a radical diagnosis of the situation, must live in ever renewed tension with the forces of society.[86]

84 Merton, *op. cit.*, pp. 8, 9.
85 Häring, *op. cit.*, p. 8.
86 Jacques Ellul, "Between Chaos and Paralysis," *Christian Century* June 5, 1968, pp. 748-50.

Having explained the necessity for radical subjectivity, Ellul proceeds to express some of his own radical convictions which are the antithesis of what commonly passes for radicalism today.

What then do I mean when I say that our hope lies in starting from the individual—from total subjectivity? This: that in politics, for example, it is no longer at the level of economic or social democracy that we must fight (a point at which we have stopped in Europe), but at the level of the citizen's *virtue,* his powers of criticism, his "participation-contestation." What is needed is the creation of a new style of life, and this cannot be accomplished save by starting with the individual's discovery of himself. Every individual must become the creator of his own life—and that is an undertaking which will require a terrible effort; for not only will he have to oppose the forces of conformity but (at least in many cases) he will have to carry on his trade or profession or fulfill other obligations at the same time. . . . I think that the difficulty of doing this is so great, the effort required so unending, that it is not possible save as one can lean on something other than one's self. I am convinced that Christians are absolutely the only ones who can attempt it—but here too on the condition that they start from zero. . . . Yet as I see it only the Christian faith (and no other belief or revolutionary stimulus) gives man sufficient hope to prompt him to embark on the undertaking I have described. If we are to question our society in so radical a fashion, we must adopt a point of view essentially different from that society's—one that we cannot arrive at by starting from our human wisdom. It is precisely because it speaks of a Wholly Other that the revelation provides us with a point of view and a point of departure that are essentially different.[87]

A Christian who thus becomes a revolutionary will serve as a revolutionary catalyst in the Church; and by the multiplication of revolutionized Christians, the Church will become a revolutionary catalyst in society; and if society is sufficiently revolutionized, a revolution of violence will no more be needed than a windmill in a world of atomic energy.

With one criticism of his unique perspective on revolution thus deflated, the evangelical turns to the second objection. How does the rhetoric of Christian love become an effective reality? How, dynamically, can it be put into practice? What hope is there that the Church will give up its posture of foot-dragging reaction

[87] *Ibid.*

and adopt a stance of revolutionary love? Candidly, there is little hope unless Christians who have been sleeping through a revolution are providentially roused from their somnambulism by the convulsions of a world in agony. It may be that God in His gracious sovereignty will use the agitation and anguish of the twentieth century to wake up at least a segment of His Church. It may be that Christians will hear themselves joltingly addressed as, in Christopher Fry's *A Sleep of Prisoners*, one of the four soldiers locked up in a ruined church addresses his apathetic comrades:

> The human heart can go to the lengths of God.
> Dark and cold we may be, but this
> Is no winter now. The frozen misery
> Of centuries breaks, cracks, begins to move,
> The thunder is the thunder of the floes,
> The thaw, the flood, the upstart Spring.
> Thank God our time is now when wrong
> Comes up to face us everywhere,
> Never to leave us till we take
> The longest stride of soul men ever took.
> Affairs are now soul size.
> The enterprise
> Is exploration into God.
> Where are you going? It takes
> So many thousand years to wake,
> Will you wake for pity's sake. . . . [88]

And Christians, jolted wide-awake, may be driven to pray as they begin to feel the pain and pressure of their times. This, Ellul hopes, will be the experience of those Christians

who are no longer "revolutionary" in their outlook ... because they have lost their spiritual vitality. The remedy is in their own hands; they must turn to God, and ask Him to give them the power of His Holy Spirit; they must pray for this continually, asking God to guide them and to give them strength to act as He wills in the life of this world—that they might be His instruments for the changes men so sorely need.[89]

[88] New York: Oxford University Press, 1951.
[89] Ellul, *The Presence of the Kingdom*, p. 59.

Driven to pray, Christians may begin to experience for the first time the power of the Holy Spirit, "power of a kind that is certainly beyond human power." Christians, Ellul believes on the authority of the New Testament, "through their prayer incarnated in action" will discover that "they can bring into play the power which will not fail us if we are serious in the battle of faith. It is the power of the Holy Spirit that can make that revolution."[90] Alan Walker, founder of the famous Life Line Centre in Sydney, Australia, sees no hope except in the same revolutionary Power. So, preaching "The Spirit and World Revolution," he discloses his faith in the divine dynamic which is able to give energy and endurance for wrestling with the explosive problems of our century.

Racialism, poverty, war—these are the fronts on which the world revolution is forming. Here the Holy Spirit summons all who would be obedient to Him to action stations. No longer can response to the Spirit be understood merely in terms of personal forgiveness and salvation. No longer can the doctrine of the Holy Spirit be confined to a man's relationship with his Maker. No longer can an experience of the Holy Spirit be enjoyed only as a private possession and a personal extravagance. The wind of the Spirit is blowing in our faces from out of the heart of the world. We must respond and live.[91]

The Spirit's power—bestowed by God, as Christians who have been jolted wide-awake by sin and need in the shape of hunger and poverty and injustice and despair are driven to pray—can set its recipients free. The Spirit is able to liberate them from inhibiting fear—the fear of conflict, the fear of loneliness, the fear of suffering, the fear of failure, the fear of the future, the fear of life, and the fear of death.

Very commonly no doubt it is assumed that a prayerful relationship to the Holy Spirit robs a man of autonomy, reducing him from innovative revolutionary to passive puppet. But Emil Brunner exposes the mistakenness of this assumption.

What happens is not something that short-circuits man as a free subject, that estranges him from himself, but something on the contrary that

90 Ellul, "Between Chaos and Paralysis," p. 750.
91 Alan Walker, *Breakthrough: Rediscovery of the Holy Spirit* (Nashville, Tenn.: Abingdon Press, 1969), p. 76.

alone makes him really free and really active. The reason for this is that it frees him from a life in contradiction to a life in the truth, and heals and integrates his will and makes it genuinely his own, a will which when sinful was never truly *his* will but lay under the domination of an alien power. To be led by the Spirit of God is not to be possessed. On the contrary, it is to be liberated from possession, from the alien domination of evil.[92]

With the experience of freedom there can come a courage which is defiant when defiance is called for and which nerves a person for persecution if New Testament radicalism brings hardship and suffering into his life. Alan Paton, battling against racism in South Africa and facing possible imprisonment, was supported staunchly by his wife, Dorrie. In the touching memoir written after her death, *For You Departed*, he asks:

Where did your courage come from? It was from your religion, of course, that strange Christianity of yours that took seriously the story of the Cross, that understood with perfect clarity that one might have to suffer for doing what one thought was right, that rejected absolutely that kind of crossless geniality that calls itself Christian.[93]

It is this quiet courage, Spirit-created in response to prayer, which alone can give the lie to the blistering remark a militant Communist once flung at Emilio Castro: "You Christians will never make a revolution, because you do not dare to accept the consequences of one."[94]

It is this quiet courage which can transmute love from attitude into action, even if the action is misunderstood, unpopular, costly, illegal, and hazardous. It is this quiet courage which can prompt a contemporary Christian not only to avow with Simon Peter, "We ought to obey God rather than man," but also to engage in a specific implementation of that text. For instance, Arthur Gish, a Church of the Brethren revolutionary, advocates civil disobedience as

a witness against evil itself, and also against the immorality of silence

92 Quoted by Arthur G. Gish, *The New Left and Christian Radicalism* (Grand Rapids, Mich.: William B. Eerdmans Publishing Co., 1970), p. 127.

93 Alan Paton, *For You Departed* (New York: Charles Scribner's Sons, 1969), p. 135.

94 Castro, *op. cit.*, p. 104.

and passive cooperation with evil. To cooperate with evil is to condone it. It is to live beside a napalm factory and do nothing to shut it down. We must never tolerate what is radically evil. All too often tolerance serves the cause of oppression, for the tyrant goes on his way while others remain silent and still. We must refuse cooperation with evil and actively witness against it.[95]

Gish's advocacy of civil disobedience brings to the fore another aspect of the radical freedom which the Holy Spirit can bestow, a willingness to recognize a fellow Christian's right and duty to obey God responsibly in loyalty to his understanding of the New Testament, although his understanding may be radically unconventional. His mode of obedience may be antipodal to that of the Christian majority, but unless it is biblically proscribed, its authentically Christian character must not be impugned. This makes for experimentation, open-endedness, and a proper humility. It prevents any one policy from being absolutized and thus guards against an idolatrous rigidity within the Church. It makes, Ellul says, for a creative obedience which is the opposite of stultifying liberalism.

From the fact of the action of the Holy Spirit, each one's work is thoroughly personalized, as well as his life. He is no longer just any man, this person laid hold of by grace. He is no longer one of the mass of mankind. He is a person. . . . This personalization causes each life to become singular. There is not one Christian life. There are as many Christian lives as there are Christians. There are not Christian works, except insofar as the Holy Spirit pushes a man to make decisions and to fulfill holiness. Thus one lives in the world endlessly deployed along paths which open up step by step as one follows them, without their in any sense being mapped in advance. One lives in ever-surprising novelty.[96]

The power of the Holy Spirit, obtained through importunate prayer, does something more. It stimulates and sustains that discipline which is essential for living as a radical Christian. Love, if it is merely human, may speedily wither as it meets the blighting intransigence of an unromantic and unloving world. The radical Christian therefore needs dogged steadfastness, especially in view of frustration and disappointment. He needs an endur-

[95] Gish, *op. cit.*, p. 137.
[96] Ellul, *To Will and To Do*, p. 219.

ance which of himself he does not possess.

Moreover, the Spirit's power which can provide steadfastness can provide likewise the strength to carry on the struggle which radical Christianity entails. Here as elsewhere Ellul cuts to the heart of the matter.

We cannot give everything into the hands of God (believing that God will open the eyes, ears, and hearts of men), until we have wrestled with God, till the break of day, like Jacob ... until we have struggled to the utmost limits of our strength, and have known the despair of defeat. If we do not do this, our so-called "confidence in God, and our orthodoxy" are nothing less than hypocrisy, cowardice, and laziness. ... When we have really understood the actual plight of our contemporaries, when we have heard their cry of anguish, and when we have understood why they won't have anything to do with our "disembodied" Gospel, when we have shared their sufferings, both physical and spiritual, in their despair and their desolation, when we have become one with the people of our own nation and of the universal Church, as Moses and Jeremiah were one with their own people, as Jesus identified Himself with the wandering crowds, "sheep without a shepherd," *then* we shall be able to proclaim the Word of God—but not till then! [97]

Paradoxically, the Spirit's enablement, appropriated in faith, produces greater faith when it is appropriated. Faith, a stubborn faith which trusts God to do the humanly impossible, is precisely what the radical Christian needs in his struggle which seems to leave the world unchanged. And the Gospel furnishes ground for faith that the humanly impossible can nevertheless take place. The Gospel reinforces the conviction of the Old Testament prophets, as expounded by Martin Buber, that man, because of his God-relationship, is

a centre of surprising creation. Because and so long as man exists, factual change of direction can take place toward salvation as well as toward disaster, starting from the world in each hour, no matter how late. ... As in the life of a single person, so also in the life of the human race; what is possible in a certain hour and what is impossible cannot be adequately ascertained by foreknowledge. ... In the midst of the faithful execution of a plan we are surprised by secret openings and insertions. Room must be left for such surprises, however; planning as though they were impossible renders them impossible. ... Inner transformation simply means ...

97 Ellul, *The Presence of the Kingdom*, pp. 140, 141.

that the customary soul enlarges and transfigures itself into the surprised soul.[98]

In the midst of those forces which squelch and suppress, suddenly by the grace of God there is a happening in response to some man's faithfulness, a revolutionary surprise. And in order to exercise revolutionary faithfulness a radical Christian must have a Spirit-generated faith. Stanley Jones states this need almost epigrammatically:

The early Christians did not say in dismay, "Look what the world has come to," but in delight, "Look what has come to the world." They saw not merely the ruin, but the resources for the reconstruction of that ruin. They saw not merely that sin did abound, but that grace did much more abound. ... That same sense of confidence must possess you if you are to pass from an anaemic noncreative nay-saying type of person to one who is master of himself and his circumstances and his destiny. But this confidence and faith must not be based on self-hypnosis, a mental and spiritual fool's paradise. ... The whole secret of abundant living can be summed up in this sentence: "Not your ability, but your response to God's ability."[99]

And the secret of abundant living is the secret of revolutionary living too, a confidence in God's ability to do what man in himself is unable to do.

But one further factor in Christian radicalism remains to be highlighted. The evangelical activist, awakened to the anguish and agony of his world—indeed, providentially awakened by the anguish and agony of his world—does not stand alone. He belongs to the Church, a community of believers. Sometimes within that community he discovers to his delight that there are other Christians who have been radicalized by the Spirit of God. Sometimes in a complacent, culture-conforming community which is Christian only in name, he must serve by the power of God's Spirit as a catalyst to radicalize the fellowship. In either case, he is to work prayerfully helping to transform the Church into

---

[98] Quoted by Norman K. Gottwald, "Prophetic Faith and Contemporary International Relations," *Biblical Realism Confronts the Nation*, Paul Peachey, ed. (Scottdale, Pa.: Herald Press, 1963), pp. 84-85.

[99] Quoted by Paul S. Rees, *Don't Sleep Through the Revolution* (Waco, Tex.: Word Books, 1969), p. 21.

an effective agency for the revolution of redemptive love; and, as he does this, he reciprocally is encouraged and energized by the members of the community. Together with his fellow believers, in short, he seeks to create a Church which is genuinely biblical, a revolutionary Church for which, Jürgen Moltmann assures us, "disillusioned atheists are waiting today."

This will be a church of beggars and rebels, of men who look up and raise their heads because redemption is near. It will only be of this church, which stands solely for Jesus' Testament of God's new creation, that one will be able to say: She is the sacrament of hope for the earth. For in the potsherds of the present church one will be able to recognize the coming kingdom. [100]

Such a radicalized church, taking its discipleship with a joyful seriousness, will be a revolutionary catalyst in society. Imagine the power of a fellowship composed of revolutionaries like those Ernst Käsemann finds in the Revelation of John.

They fight, not to achieve power, but because they have to become like their Lord. Their wish is, not to conquer the world, but to defend their Lord's claim to the earth, and they die in doing so. Their aim is not the overthrow of the existing order, but the testimony that He who makes all things new is on the way. They are nothing else than the Creator's deputies in a world given to apostasy, and so they have to deal with those who have set up in their own name against their Lord, who do not regard power as a mandate from the Creator, and who therefore misuse it. Thus far, Christians who accept the call to resistance are not simply witnesses to God's reign and tokens of its realization. They are at the same time representatives of a misused creation, the spokesmen of all who are oppressed, the people of the desert who remind everyone that Egypt must be finally abandoned, and that salvation is to be found only in the exodus. [101]

The possible influence of so revolutionary a church was suggested by the admission of a famous radical fifty years ago: "We socialists would have nothing to do if you Christians had continued the revolution begun by Jesus." [102]

100 Jürgen Moltmann, "The Category of the New in Theology," *The Future as the Presence of Shared Hope,* Maryellen Muckenhirn, ed. (New York: Sheed & Ward, 1968), p. 31.

101 Käsemann, *op. cit.*, p. 140.

102 Häring, *op. cit.*, p. 25.

Bibliography

Adler, Mortimer J., *The Time of Our Lives: The Ethics of Common Sense*. New York: Holt, Rinehart and Winston, 1970.

Aldwinckle, R. F., "Did Jesus Believe in God?" Martin E. Marty and Dean G. Peerman, eds., *New Theology No. 5*. New York: The Macmillan Company, 1968.

Ali, Tarig, ed., *The New Revolutionaries*. New York: William Morrow & Company, Inc., 1969.

Alves, Rubem A., *A Theology of Human Hope*. Washington, D.C.: Corpus Books, 1969.

Arendt, Hannah, *On Revolution*. New York: The Viking Press, 1962.

Austin, Alan D., ed., *The Revolutionary Imperative: Essays Toward a New Humanity*. Nashville, Tenn.: National Methodist Student Movement, 1966.

Bailyn, Bernard, *The Ideological Origins of the American Revolution*. Cambridge, Mass.: Harvard University Press, 1967

Barnhouse, Donald Grey, *God's Discipline: Romans 12:1-14:12, Exposition of Bible Doctrines*, vol. 9. Grand Rapids, Mich.: William B. Eerdmans Publishing Co., 1964.

Beals, Carleton, *The Nature of Revolution*. New York: Thomas Y. Crowell Company, 1970.

Berger, Peter L., and Richard J. Neuhaus, eds., *Movement and Revolution*. Garden City, N. Y.: Doubleday & Company, Inc., 1970.

Braaten, Carl E., *The Future of God: The Revolutionary Dynamics of Hope*. New York: Harper & Row, 1969

————, "Toward a Theology of Hope," Martin E. Marty and Dean G. Peerman, eds., *New Theology No. 5*, New York: The Macmillan Company, 1968.

Brandon, S. G. F., *Jesus and the Zealots: A Study of the Political Factor in Primitive Christianity*. New York: Charles Scribner's Sons, 1967.

Bright, Bill, *Revolution Now*. San Bernardino, Calif.: Campus Crusade for Christ, Inc., 1969.

Brinton, Crane, *The Anatomy of Revolution*. New York: Vintage House, 1965.

Brogan, D. W., *The Price of Revolution*. New York: Harper & Brothers, 1951.

Cain, Arthur H., *Young People and Revolution*. New York: The John Day Company, 1970.

Campsie, John, *Objection to Murder: The Conscience of the Unilateralist*. Toronto: McClelland & Stewart, Ltd., 1967.

Camus, Albert, "Neither Victims Nor Executioners," Paul Goodman, ed., *Seeds of Liberation*. New York: George Braziller, Inc., 1964.

———, *The Rebel*. New York: Alfred A. Knopf, 1954.

Carmichael, Stokely, "Black Power." David Cooper, ed., *To Free a Generation: The Dialectics of Liberation*. London: Collier Books, 1969.

Carothers, J. Edward, *The Churches and Cruelty Systems*. New York: Friendship Press, 1970.

Castro, Emilio, "Conversion and Social Transformation," Harvey Cox, ed., *The Church amid Revolution*. New York: Association Press, 1967.

Celestin, George, "A Christian Looks at Revolution." Martin E. Marty and Dean G. Peerman, eds., *New Theology No. 6*. New York: The Macmillan Company, 1969.

Chaix-Ruy, Jules, *The Superman from Nietzsche to Teilhard de Chardin*. Notre Dame, Ind.: University of Notre Dame Press, 1968.

Cook, Fred J., *What So Proudly We Hail*. Englewood Cliffs, N. J.: Prentice-Hall, Inc., 1968.

Cox, Harvey, "Ernst Bloch and 'The Pull of the Future.' " Martin E. Marty and Dean G. Peerman, eds., *New Theology No. 5*. New York: The Macmillan Company, 1968.

———, *God's Revolution and Man's Responsibility*. Valley Forge, Pa.: Judson Press, 1965.

_____, *On Not Leaving It to the Snake*. New York: The Macmillan Company, 1967.

_____, *The Secular City: Secularization and Urbanization in Theological Perspective*. New York: The Macmillan Company, 1965.

Cullmann, Oscar, *Jesus and the Revolutionaries*. New York: Harper & Row, 1970.

_____, *The State in the New Testament*. New York: Charles Scribner's Sons, 1956.

Dewart, Leslie, *Christianity and Revolution*. New York: Herder & Herder, 1963.

Dickey, Samuel, *The Conservative Revolution of Jesus: A Study of Some of His Social Attitudes*. New York: George H. Doran Company, n.d.

Douglas, James W., *The Non-Violent Cross: A Theology of Revolution and Peace*. New York: The Macmillan Company, 1968.

Douglas, William O., *Points of Rebellion*. New York: Vintage Books, 1970.

_____, *The U.S. and Revolution, an Occasional Paper on the Free Society*. Santa Barbara, Calif.: The Center for the Study of Democratic Institutions, 1961.

Drinan, Robert F., *Vietnam and Armageddon: Peace, War and the Christian Conscience*. New York: Sheed & Ward, 1970.

Eller, Vernard, *The Promise: Ethics in the Kingdom of God*. Garden City, N.Y.: Doubleday & Company, Inc., 1970.

Ellul, Jacques, *The Presence of the Kingdom*. Philadelphia: The Westminster Press, 1951.

_____, *To Will and To Do*. Philadelphia: Pilgrim Press, 1969.

_____, *Violence, Reflections from a Christian Perspective*. New York: The Seabury Press, 1969.

Emorey, N., *A Serious Call to an American (R)Evolution*. New Haven, Conn.: Bulldog Books, 1967.

Fanon, Frantz, *Toward the African Revolution*. New York: Grove Press, Inc., 1967.

_____, *The Wretched of the Earth*. New York: Grove Press, Inc., 1968.

Ford, Leighton, *One Way to Change the World*. New York: Harper & Row, 1970.

Fosdick, Harry Emerson, *The Man from Nazareth: As His Contemporaries Saw Him*. New York: Harper & Brothers, 1949.

Furfey, Paul Henly, *The Respectable Murderers: Social Evil and Christian Conscience*. New York: Herder & Herder, 1966.

Gingerich, Melvin, *The Christian and Revolution*. Scottdale, Pa.: Herald Press, 1968.

Gish, Arthur G., *The New Left and Christian Radicalism*. Grand Rapids, Mich.: William B. Eerdmans Publishing Co., 1970.

Goldston, Robert, *The Negro Revolution*. New York: New American Library, 1968.

Gollwitzer, Helmut, "The Demands of Freedom." Alan D. Austin, ed., *The Revolutionary Imperative*. Nashville, Tenn.: National Methodist Student Movement, 1966.

Gottwald, Norman K., "Prophetic Faith and Contemporary International Relations," Paul Peachey, ed., *Biblical Realism Confronts the Nation*. Scottdale, Pa.: Herald Press, 1963.

Haley, Jay, *The Power Tactics of Jesus Christ*. New York: Grossman Publishers, 1969.

Hamilton, Kenneth, "Reconciliation and New Humanity," Allen O. Miller, ed., *Reconciliation in Today's World*. Grand Rapids, Mich.: William B. Eerdmans Publishing Co., 1969.

Häring, Bernard, *A Theology of Protest*. New York: Farrar, Straus, & Giroux, 1970.

Harrington, Michael, *Toward a Democractic Left*. New York: The Macmillan Company, 1968.

Hill, Christopher, *Puritanism and Revolution*. New York: Schocken Books, 1958.

Hough, Joseph C., Jr., *Black Power and White Protestants: A Christian Response to the New Negro Pluralism*. New York: Oxford University Press, 1968.

Hutchinson, Paul, *World Revolution and Religion*. New York: Abingdon Press, 1931.

IDO-C, *When All Else Fails: Christian Arguments on Violent Revolution.* Philadelphia: Pilgrim Press, 1970.

James, Howard, *Children in Trouble: A National Scandal.* Boston: Christian Science Publishing Society, 1969.

Käsemann, Ernst, *Jesus Means Freedom: A Polemical Survey of the New Testament.* London: SCM Press, Ltd., 1969.

Koestler, Arthur, *Darkness at Noon.* New York: The Modern Library, 1941.

Kateb, George, *Utopia and Its Enemies.* New York: The Free Press of Glencoe, 1963.

Lefever, Ernest W., "Criteria for a Just Revolution," Charles C. West, ed., *Ethics, Violence and Revolution.* New York: The Council on Religion and International Affairs, 1969.

Lehmann, Paul L., *Ethics in a Christian Context.* New York: Harper & Row, 1963.

————, "The Shape of Theology for a World in Revolution," Alan D. Austin, ed., *The Revolutionary Imperative.* Nashville, Tenn.: The Board of Education of The Methodist Church, 1966.

Lochman, J. M., "The Church in a Socialist Society," Harvey Cox, ed., *The Church amid Revolution.* New York: Association Press, 1967.

————, "Ecumenical Theology of Revolution," Martin E. Marty and Dean G. Peerman, eds., *New Theology No. 6.* New York: The Macmillan Company, 1969.

Luttwak, Edward, *Coup d'Etat: A Practical Handbook.* Greenwich, Conn.: Fawcett Publications, Inc., 1969.

Mackay, John A., *Christian Reality and Appearance.* Richmond, Va.: John Knox Press, 1969.

Maier, Hans, *Revolution and Church: The Early History of Christian Democracy, 1789-1901.* Notre Dame, Ind.: University of Notre Dame Press, 1965.

Marcuse, Herbert, "Liberation from the Affluent Society," David Cooper, ed., *To Free A Generation: The Dialectics of Liberation.* London: Collier Books, 1969.

————, "Repressive Toleration," Robert P. Wolff, Barrington Moore, Jr., and Herbert Marcuse, *A Critique of Pure Tolerance.* Boston: Beacon Press, 1965.

Martin, Everett Dean, *Farewell to Revolution*. New York: W. W. Norton & Co., Inc., 1935.

Matthiessen, Peter, *Sal Si Puedes: Cesar Chavez and the New American Revolution*. New York: Random House, 1969.

McCormick, Rory, *Americans Against Man*. New York: Corpus Books, 1970.

McHale, John, *The Future of the Future*. New York: George Braziller, 1968.

Mehl, Roger, "The Basis of Christian Social Ethics," John C. Bennett, ed., *Christian Social Ethics in a Changing World*. New York: Association Press, 1966.

Melady, Thomas, and Margaret, *House Divided: Poverty, Race, Religion and the Family of Man*. New York: Sheed & Ward, 1969.

Merleau-Ponty, Maurice, *Humanism and Terror*. Boston: Beacon Press, 1969.

Merton, Thomas, *Faith and Violence: Christian Teaching and Christian Practice*. Notre Dame, Ind.: University of Notre Dame Press, 1968.

Metz, Johannes B., "Creative Hope." Martin E. Marty and Dean G. Peerman, eds., *New Theology No. 5*. New York: The Macmillan Company, 1968.

Michener, James A., *America vs. America: The Revolution in Middle-Class Values*. New York: New American Library, 1969.

Miller, Donald G., "God Reconciles and Makes Free," Allen O. Miller, ed., *Reconciliation in Today's World*. Grand Rapids, Mich.: William B. Eerdmans Publishing Co., 1969.

Moltmann, Jürgen, "The Category of the New in Theology," Maryellen Muckenhirn, ed., *The Future as the Presence of Shared Hope*. New York: Sheed & Ward, 1968.

_____, *Religion, Revolution and the Future*. New York: Charles Scribner's Sons, 1969.

_____, *Theology of Hope: On the Ground and the implications of the Christian Eschatology*. London: SCM Press, Ltd., 1967.

_____, "Toward a Political Hermeneutics of the Gospel," Martin E. Marty and Dean G. Peerman, eds., *New Theology No. 6*. New York: The Macmillan Company, 1969.

Montefiore, Hugh, *The Question Mark: The End of Homo Sapiens*. London: Collins, 1969.

Morris, Colin, *Unyoung, Uncolored, Unpoor*. Nashville, Tenn.: Abingdon Press, 1969.

Morris, William Dale, *The Christian Origins of Social Revolt*. London: George Allen & Unwin Ltd., 1949.

Neal, Stephen, *A Genuine Human Existence: Towards a Christian Psychology*. Garden City, N. Y.: Doubleday & Company, Inc., 1959.

Nelson, Truman, *The Right of Revolution*. Boston: Beacon Press, 1968.

Neuhaus, Richard J., "The Thorough Revolutionary," Peter L. Berger and Richard J. Neuhaus, eds., *Movement and Revolution*. Garden City, N. Y.: Doubleday & Company, Inc., 1970.

Novak, Michael, *A Theology for Radical Politics*. New York: Herder & Herder, 1969.

O'Brien, William V., *Nuclear War, Deterrence and Morality*. Westminister, Md.: Newman Press, 1967.

———, *War and/or Survival*. Garden City, N. Y.: Doubleday & Company, Inc., 1969.

O'Collins, Gerald, *Man and His New Hopes*. New York: Herder & Herder, 1969.

Oglesby, Carl, "Vietnamese Crucible," Carl Oglesby and Richard Shaull, eds., *Containment and Change: Two Dissenting Views of American Society and Foreign Policy in the New Revolutionary Age*. New York: The Macmillan Company, 1967.

Ogletree, Thomas W., "The Shifting Focus of Theological Reflection," Martin E. Marty and Dean G. Peerman, eds., *New Theology No 6*. New York: The Macmillan Company, 1969.

O'Meara, Thomas F., and Donald M. Weisser, eds., *Projections: Shaping an American Theology for the Future*. Garden City, N. Y.: Doubleday & Company, Inc., 1970.

Oxtoby, Gordon C., *Prediction and Fulfillment in the Bible*. Philadelphia: Westminster Press, 1966.

Paton, Alan, *For You Departed*. New York: Charles Scribner's Sons, 1969.

Peachey, Paul, ed., *Biblical Realism Confronts the Nation.* Scottdale, Pa.: Herald Press, 1963.

Petry, Ray C., *Christian Eschatology and Social Thought.* New York: Abingdon Press, 1956.

Pierard, Richard V., *The Unequal Yoke.* Philadelphia: J. B. Lippincott Company, 1970.

Pollard, William G., *Man on a Spaceship.* Claremont, Calif.: Claremont College, 1967.

Potter, Ralph B., *War and Moral Discourse.* Richmond, Va.: John Knox Press, 1969.

Ramsey, Paul, *The Just War.* New York: Charles Scribner's Sons, 1968.

——, *War and the Christian Conscience.* Durham, N.C.: Duke University Press, 1961.

Rees, Paul S., *Don't Sleep Through the Revolution.* Waco, Tex.: Word Books, 1969.

Robinson, John A. T., *Christian Freedom in a Permissive Society.* London: SCM Press Ltd., 1970.

Scarlett, William, *The Christian Demand for Social Justice.* New York: New American Library, 1949.

Schlink, Basilea, *World in Revolt.* Minneapolis, Minn.: Bethany Fellowship, Inc., 1969.

Scott, R. B. Y., *The Relevance of the Prophets.* New York: The Macmillan Company, 1953.

Shaull, Richard, "Christian Faith as Scandal in a Technocratic World." Martin E. Marty and Dean G. Peerman, eds., *New Theology No. 6.* New York: The Macmillan Company, 1969.

——, "The Christian in the Vortex of Revolution," Thomas F. O'Meara and Donald M. Weisser, eds., *Projections: Shaping an American Theology for the Future.* Garden City, N. Y.: Doubleday & Company, Inc., 1970.

——, "God and the Human Revolution," Donald E. Hartsock, ed., *Contemporary Religious Issues.* Belmont, Calif.: Wadsworth Publishing Co., Inc., 1968.

———, "Revolutionary Change in Theological Perspective," Harvey Cox, ed., *The Church amid Revolution*. New York: Association Press, 1967.

———, "Revolution. Heritage and Contemporary Option," Carl Oglesby and Richard Shaull, eds., *Containment and Change: Two Dissenting Views of American Society and Foreign Policy in the New Revolutionary Age*. New York: The Macmillan Company, 1967.

Shklar, Judith N., *After Utopia: The Decline of Political Faith*. Princeton, N. J.: Princeton University Press, 1957.

Sibley, Mulford O., *The Obligation to Disobey: Conscience & the Law*. New York: The Council on Religion and International Affairs, 1970.

Skinner, Tom, *Words of Revolution*. Grand Rapids, Mich.: Zondervan Publishing House, 1970.

Smart, James D., *The Quiet Revolution: The Radical Impact of Jesus on Men of His Time*. Philadelphia: The Westminster Press, 1969.

Smith, Rolland F., "A Theology of Rebellion," Martin E. Marty and Dean G. Peerman, eds., *New Theology No. 6*. New York: The Macmillan Company, 1969.

Stevick, Daniel B., *Civil Disobedience and the Christian*. New York: The Seabury Press, 1969.

Streeter, B. H., ed., *The Spirit*. New York: The Macmillan Company, 1921.

Thielicke, Helmut, *Theological Ethics*, vol. 2., *Politics*. Philadelphia: Fortress Press, 1969.

Thompson, J. M., *Robespierre and the French Revolution*. New York: Collier Books, 1967.

Thrupp, Sylvia L., ed., *Millennial Dreams in Action*. New York: Schocken Books, 1970.

Toynbee, Arnold J., *America and the World Revolution*. New York: Oxford University Press, 1962.

VandenBerg, Frank, *Abraham Kuyper*. Grand Rapids, Mich.: William B. Eerdmans Publishing Co., 1960.

Waelder, Robert, *Progress and Revolution: A Study of the Issues of Our Age*. New York: International Universities Press, Inc., 1967.

Walker, Alan, *Breakthrough: Rediscovery of the Holy Spirit*. Nashville, Tenn.: Abingdon Press, 1969.

Walzer, Michael, *The Revolution of the Saints: A Study in the Origins of Radical Politics*. Cambridge, Mass.: Harvard University Press, 1965.

Weinberg, Arthur and Lila, *Instead of Violence*. Boston: Beacon Press, 1963.

Weismann, Steve, "New Left Man Meets the Dead God," Martin E. Marty and Dean G. Peerman, eds., *New Theology No. 5*. New York: The Macmillan Company, 1968.

Willis, David, "Reconciliation and Stewardship," Allen O. Miller, ed., *Reconciliation in Today's World*. Grand Rapids, Mich.: William B. Eerdmans Publishing Co., 1969.

Yoder, John H., *Karl Barth and the Problem of War*. Nashville, Tenn.: Abingdon Press, 1970.

DATE DUE
